HOW
MONEY
WORKS

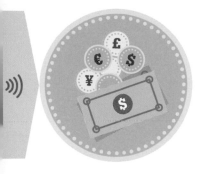

HOW MONEY WORKS

THE FACTS VISUALLY EXPLAINED

Senior editor	Kathryn Hennessy	**Publisher**	Liz Wheeler
Project editor	Sam Kennedy	**Publishing director**	Jonathan Metcalf
Senior art editor	Gadi Farfour	**Art director**	Karen Self
Project art editor	Saffron Stocker	**Senior jacket designer**	Mark Cavanagh
UK Editors	Alison Sturgeon, Allie Collins, Diane Pengelley, Georgina Palffy, Jemima Dunne, Tash Khan	**Jacket editor**	Clare Gell
US Editors	Christy Lusiak, Margaret Parrish	**Jacket design development manager**	Sophia MTT
Designers	Clare Joyce, Vanessa Hamilton, Renata Latipova	**Pre-production producer**	Gillian Reid
Managing editor	Gareth Jones	**Senior producer**	Mandy Inness
Senior managing art editor	Lee Griffiths	**Special sales & custom publishing manager**	Michelle Baxter

Contents

This Paperback Edition, 2021
First American Edition, 2017
Published in the United States by DK Publishing
1450 Broadway, Suite 801, New York, NY 10018

Copyright © 2017 Dorling Kindersley Limited
DK, a Division of Penguin Random House LLC
22 10 9 8 7 6 5 4 3 2
002–326197–June/2021

Published in Great Britain by Dorling Kindersley Limited.
A catalog record for this book is available from the Library
of Congress.
ISBN: 978-0-7440-4983-1

Printed in China

Penguin
Random
House

For the curious
www.dk.com

MIX
Paper from
responsible sources
FSC™ C018179

This book was made with Forest Stewardship
Council™ certified paper—one small step in
DK's commitment to a sustainable future.
For more information go to
www.dk.com/our-green-pledge

GOVERNMENT FINANCE AND PUBLIC MONEY 84

Contributors

Beverly Harzog (consultant and writer) is a consumer credit expert and best-selling author. Her articles have appeared in *The Wall Street Journal*, *New York Daily News*, ABCNews.com, ClarkHoward.com, CNNMoney.com, and MSNMoney.com. Her expert advice has been featured in numerous media outlets, including television, radio, print, and websites.

Marianne Curphey is an award-winning financial writer, blogger, and columnist. She has worked as a writer and editor at *The Guardian*, *The Times*, and *The Telegraph*, and a wide range of financial websites and magazines.

Emma Lunn is an award–winning personal finance journalist whose work regularly appears in high profile newspapers such as *The Guardian*, *The Independent*, and *The Telegraph*, as well as a number of specialty publications and websites.

PERSONAL FINANCE 148

James Meadway is an economist and policy advisor who has worked at the New Economics Foundation—an independent British think tank—the UK Treasury, the Royal Society, and for the Shadow Chancellor of the Exchequer.

Philip Parker is a historian and former British diplomat and publisher, who studied at the Johns Hopkins School of Advanced International Studies. A critically acclaimed author, he has written books that focus on the history of world trade.

Alexandra Black studied business communications before writing for financial newspaper group Nikkei Inc. in Japan and working as an editor at investment bank JP Morgan. She has written numerous books and articles on subjects as diverse as finance, business, technology, and fashion.

Introduction

Money is the oil that keeps the machinery of our world turning. By giving goods and services an easily measured value, money facilitates the billions of transactions that take place every day. Without it, the industry and trade that form the basis of modern economies would grind to a halt and the flow of wealth around the world would cease.

Money has fulfilled this vital role for thousands of years. Before its invention, people bartered, swapping goods they produced themselves for things they needed from others. Barter is sufficient for simple transactions, but not when the things traded are of differing values, or not available at the same time. Money, by contrast, has a recognized uniform value and is widely accepted. At heart a simple concept, over many thousands of years it has become very complex indeed.

At the start of the modern age, individuals and governments began to establish banks, and other financial institutions were formed. Eventually, ordinary people could deposit their money in a bank account and earn interest, borrow money and buy property, invest their wages in businesses, or start companies themselves. Banks could also insure against the sorts of calamities that might devastate families or traders, encouraging risk in the pursuit of profit.

Today it is a nation's government and central bank that control a country's economy. The Federal Reserve (known as "The Fed") is the central bank in the US. The Fed issues currency, determines how much of it is in circulation, and decides how much interest it will charge banks to borrow its money. While governments still print and guarantee money, in today's world it no longer needs to exist as physical coins or notes, but can be found solely in digital form.

This book examines every aspect of how money works, including its history, financial markets and institutions, government finance, profit-making, personal finance, wealth, shares, pensions, Social Security benefits, and national and local taxes. Through visual explanations and practical examples that make even the most complex concept immediately accessible, *How Money Works* offers a clear understanding of what money is all about, and how it shapes modern society.

MONEY
BASICS

> The evolution of money

The evolution of money

People originally traded surplus commodities with each other in a process known as bartering. The value of each good traded could be debated, however, and money evolved as a practical solution to the complexities of bartering hundreds of different things. Over the centuries, money has appeared in many forms, but, whatever shape it takes, whether as a coin, a note, or stored on a digital server, money always provides a fixed value against which any item can be compared.

The ascent of money

Money has become increasingly complex over time. What began as a means of recording trade exchanges, then appeared in the form of coins and notes, is now primarily digital.

Barter
(10,000–3000BCE)
In early forms of trading, specific items were exchanged for others agreed by the negotiating parties to be of similar value. *See pp.14–15*

Evidence of trade records
(7000BCE)
Pictures of items were used to record trade exchanges, becoming more complex as values were established and documented. *See pp.16–17*

Coinage
(600BCE–1100CE)
Defined weights of precious metals used by some merchants were later formalized as coins that were usually issued by states. *See pp.16–17*

SUPPLY AND DEMAND

The economic law of supply and demand states that when the price of a commodity (such as oil) falls, consumers tend to use, or demand, more of it, and when its price rises, the demand decreases. One of the key factors affecting price is the amount of a commodity available—its supply. Low supply will push prices up, as consumers are willing to pay more for something that is difficult to obtain, and high supply will push prices down as consumers will not pay a premium for something that is plentiful.

$80.9 trillion
estimated amount of money in existence today

Bank notes
(1100–2000)
States began to use bank notes, issuing paper IOUs that were traded as currency, and could be exchanged for coins at any time. *See pp.18–19*

Digital money
(2000 onward)
Money can now exist "virtually," on computers, and large transactions can take place without any physical cash changing hands. *See pp.222–223*

Macro versus Microeconomics

Macroeconomics studies the impact of changes in the economy as a whole. Microeconomics examines the behavior of smaller groups.

Macroeconomics
This measures changes in indicators that affect the whole economy.

❭ **Money supply** The amount of money circulating in an economy.

❭ **Unemployment** The number of people who cannot find work.

❭ **Inflation** The amount by which prices rise each year.

Microeconomics
This examines the effects that decisions of firms and individuals have on the economy.

❭ **Industrial organization** The impact of monopolies and cartels on the economy.

❭ **Wages** The impact that salary levels, which are affected by labor and production costs, have on consumer spending.

Barter, IOUs, and money

Barter—the direct exchange of goods—formed the basis of trade for thousands of years. Adam Smith, 18th-century author of *The Wealth of Nations*, was one of the first to identify it as a precursor to money.

Barter in practice

Essentially, barter involves the exchange of an item (such as a cow) for one or more of a perceived equal "value" (for example a load of wheat). For the most part the two parties bring the goods with them and hand them over at the time of a transaction. Sometimes, one of the parties will accept an "I owe you," or IOU, or even a token, that it is agreed can be exchanged for the same goods or something else at a later date.

PROS AND CONS OF BARTER

Pros

> **Trading relationships** Fosters strong links between partners.

> **Physical goods are exchanged** Barter does not rely on trust that money will retain its value.

Cons

> **Market needed** Both parties must want what the other offers.

> **Hard to establish a set value on items** Two goats may have a certain value to one party one day, but less a week later.

> **Goods may not be easily divisible** For example, a living animal cannot be divided.

> **Large-scale transactions can be difficult** Transporting one goat is easy, moving 1,000 is not.

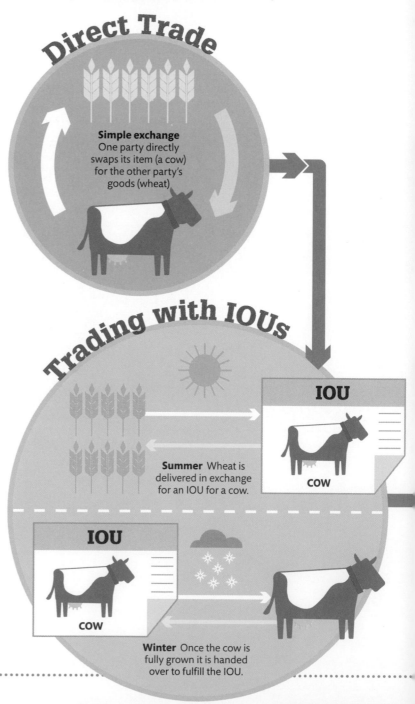

Direct Trade

Simple exchange One party directly swaps its item (a cow) for the other party's goods (wheat)

Trading with IOUs

IOU — COW

Summer Wheat is delivered in exchange for an IOU for a cow.

IOU — COW

Winter Once the cow is fully grown it is handed over to fulfill the IOU.

How it works

In its simplest form, two parties to a barter transaction agree on a price (such as a cow for wheat) and physically hand over the goods at the agreed time. However, this may not always be possible—for example, the wheat might not be ready to harvest, so one party may accept an IOU to be exchanged later for the physical goods. Eventually these IOUs acquire their own value and the IOU holder could exchange them for something else of the same value as the original commodity (perhaps apples instead of wheat). The IOUs are now performing the same function as actual money.

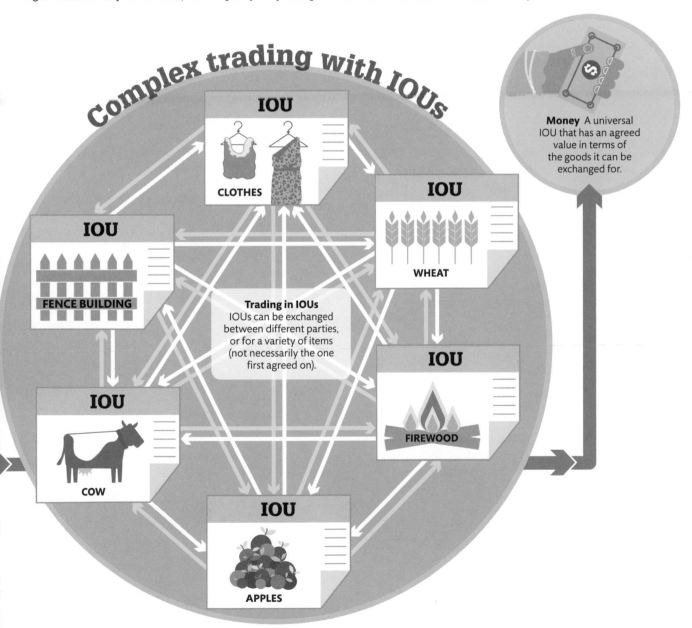

Complex trading with IOUs

IOU CLOTHES

IOU WHEAT

IOU FENCE BUILDING

Trading in IOUs
IOUs can be exchanged between different parties, or for a variety of items (not necessarily the one first agreed on).

IOU FIREWOOD

IOU COW

IOU APPLES

Money A universal IOU that has an agreed value in terms of the goods it can be exchanged for.

Artifacts of money

Since the early attempts at setting values for bartered goods, "money" has come in many forms, from IOUs to tokens. Cows, shells, and precious metals have all been used.

Characteristics of money

Money is not money unless it has all of the following defining characteristics: Money must have value, be durable, portable, uniform, divisible, in limited supply, and be usable as a means of exchange. Underlying all of these characteristics is trust—people must be confident that if they accept money, they can use it to pay for goods.

How it works

Bartering was a very immediate form of transaction. Once writing was invented, records could be kept detailing the "value" of goods traded as well as of the "IOUs." Eventually tokens such as beads, colored cowrie shells, or lumps of gold were assigned a specific value, which meant that they could be exchanged directly for goods. It was a small step from this to making tokens explicitly to represent value in the form of metal discs—the first coins—in Lydia, Asia Minor, from around 650 BCE. For more than 2,000 years, coins made from precious metals such as gold, silver, and (for small transactions) copper formed the main medium of monetary exchange.

Item of worth
Most money originally had an intrinsic value, such as that of the precious metal that was used to make the coin. This in itself acted as some guarantee the coin would be accepted.

Timeline of artifacts

Sumerian cuneiform tablets
Scribes recorded transactions on clay tablets, which could also act as receipts.

Lydian gold coins
In Lydia, a mixture of gold and silver was formed into disks, or coins, stamped with inscriptions.

• 5,000 BCE •   • 4,000 BCE •   • 1,000 BCE •   • 600 BCE •   • 600 BCE •

Barter
Early trade involved directly exchanged items—often perishable ones such as a cow.

Cowrie shells
Used as currency across India and the South Pacific, they appeared in many colors and sizes.

Athenian drachma
The Athenians used silver from Laurion to mint a currency used right across the Greek world.

Store of value

Money acts as a means by which people can store their wealth for future use. It must not, therefore, be perishable, and it helps if it is of a practical size that can be stored and transported easily.

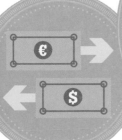

GEORG SIMMEL AND *THE PHILOSOPHY OF MONEY*

Published in 1900, German sociologist Georg Simmel's book *The Philosophy of Money* looked at the meaning of value in relation to money. Simmel observed that in premodern societies, people made objects, but the value they attached to each of them was difficult to fix as it was assessed by incompatible systems (based on honor, time, and labor). Money made it easier to assign consistent values to objects, which Simmel believed made interactions between people more rational, as it freed them from personal ties, and provided greater freedom of choice.

Means of exchange

It must be possible to exchange money freely and widely for goods, and its value should be as stable as possible. It helps if that value is easily divisible and if there are sufficient denominations so change can be given.

Unit of account

Money can be used to record wealth possessed, traded, or spent—personally and nationally. It helps if only one recognized authority issues money—if anybody could issue it, then trust in its value would disappear.

Han dynasty coin
Often made of bronze or copper, early Chinese coins had holes punched in their center.

Byzantine coin
Early Byzantine coins were pure gold; later ones also contained metals such as copper.

Arabic dirham
Many silver coins from the Islamic empire were carried to Scandinavia by Vikings.

• 200BCE • 27BCE • 700CE • 900CE • 900CE •

Roman coin
Bearing the head of the emperor, these coins circulated throughout the Roman Empire.

Anglo-Saxon coin
This 10th century silver penny has an inscription stating that Offa is King ("rex") of Mercia.

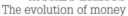

The economics of money

From the 16th century, understanding of the nature of money became more sophisticated. Economics as a discipline emerged, in part to help explain the inflation caused in Europe by the large-scale importation of silver from the newly discovered Americas. National banks were established in the late 17th century, with the duty of regulating the countries' money supplies.

By the early 20th century, money became separated from its direct relationship to precious metal. The Gold Standard collapsed altogether in the 1930s. By the mid-20th century, new ways of trading with money appeared such as credit cards, digital transactions, and even forms of money such as cryptocurrencies and financial derivatives. As a result, the amount of money in existence and in circulation increased enormously.

GOLD AND SILVER FROM THE NEW WORLD

1540–1640
Potosi inflation
The Spanish discovered silver in Potosi, Bolivia, and caused a century of inflation by shipping 350 tons of the metal back to Europe annually.

COPPER

1542–1551
The great debasement
England's Henry VIII debased the silver penny, making it three-quarters copper. Inflation increased as trust dropped.

1970
Great inflation
In the US, inflation accelerated quickly. The stock market plummeted 40% in an 18-month period.

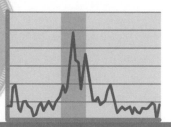

FROM 1844
Gold Standard
The British pound was tied to a defined equivalent amount of gold. Other countries adopted a similar Gold Standard.

1970s
Credit cards
The creation of credit cards enabled consumers to access short-term credit to make smaller purchases. This resulted in the growth of personal debt.

1990s
Digital money
The easy transfer of funds and convenience of electronic payments became increasingly popular as internet use increased.

GRESHAM'S LAW

The monetary principle "bad money drives out good" was formulated by British financier Sir Thomas Gresham (1519-71). He observed that if a country debases its currency—reducing the precious metal in its coins—the coins would be worth less than the metal they contained. As a result, people spend the "bad" coins and hoard the "good" undebased ones.

16 billion
the number of bitcoins in circulation in 2016—worth $9 billion

JOINT-STOCK COMPANY

1553
Early joint-stock companies

Merchants in England began to form companies in which investors bought shares (stock) and shared its rewards.

1694
Bank of England

The Bank of England was created as a body that could raise funds at a low interest rate and manage national debt.

1775
US dollar

The Continental Congress authorized the issue of United States dollars in 1775, but the first national currency was not minted by the US Treasury until 1794.

1696
The Royal Mint

Isaac Newton became Warden and argued that debasing undermined confidence. All coins were recalled and new silver ones were minted.

1999
Euro

Twelve EU countries joined together and replaced their national currencies with the Euro. Bank notes and coins were issued three years later.

2008
Bitcoin

Bitcoin—a form of electronic money that exists solely as encrypted data on servers—is announced. The first transaction took place in January 2009.

Emergence of modern economics

By the 18th century, people began to study the economy more closely, as thinkers tried to understand how the trade and investment decisions of individuals could have an effect on prices and wages throughout a country.

How it works

With the massive expansion of trade that accompanied the discovery of the Americas and the growth of nation states in Europe in the 16th and 17th centuries, individuals began to think in more detail about the idea of economics. They variously suggested that controlling the level of imports (mercantilism), trading only in the goods a country made best (comparative advantage), or choosing not to intervene in the markets (laissez-faire) might improve their people's economic well-being. In the 18th century, economist Adam Smith proposed that government intervention—controlling wages and prices—was unnecessary because the self-interested decisions of individuals, who all want to be better off, cumulatively ensure the prosperity of their society as a whole. In addition, he believed that in a freely competitive market, the impetus to make profit ensures that goods are valued at a fair price.

Adam Smith's "invisible hand"

In his book *The Wealth of Nations* (1776), the Scottish economist Adam Smith suggested that the sum of the decisions made by individuals, each of whom wanting to be better off, results in a country becoming more prosperous without those individuals ever having consciously desired that end. According to Adam Smith, where there is demand for goods, sellers will enter the market. In the pursuit of profit they will increase the production of these goods, supporting industry.

Furthermore in a competitive market, a seller's self-interest limits the price rises they can demand in that if they charge too much, buyers will stop purchasing their goods or lose sales to competitors willing to charge less. This can have a deflationary effect on prices and ensures that the economy remains in balance. Smith referred to this market mechanism, which turns individual self-interest into wider economic prosperity, as an "invisible hand" guiding the economy.

SELLER A

$4

Seller A is charging too much for his goods but still makes sales because he is the only seller and enjoys an effective monopoly.

BUYER

Buyers reduce their purchases as prices are prohibitively high.

NEW!

SELLER B

$2

Seller B sees an opportunity to enter the market and sets up her own stall, selling at a lower price in order to undercut A.

As Seller B's price is lower, buyers begin to buy from her instead of Seller A.

PROTECTIONISM AND MERCANTILISM

Adam Smith's encouragement of free trade and competition was at odds with the dominant economic theories of his time. Most thinkers supported some form of protectionism—an economic policy in which a government imposes high trade tariffs in order to protect its industry from competition. In Europe at the time this took the form of mercantilism, which held that to be strong, a country must increase its exports and do everything possible to decrease its imports, as exports brought money into a country, while imports enriched foreign merchants. This theory led to strict governmental trade controls—the Navigation Acts forbade trade between Britain and its colonies in anything other than British ships.

Mercantilism began to go out of fashion in the late 18th century under the pressure of new ideas about economic specialization put forward by Adam Smith and David Ricardo.

> "By pursuing his own interests, he frequently promotes that of the society more effectually than when he really intends to promote it"
>
> Adam Smith, *The Wealth of Nations* (1776)

SELLER A — $3

Seller A drops his price slightly in order to regain customers and compete with Seller B.

SELLER B — $3

Seller B sees she can raise her price slightly and her goods will still be in demand.

The goods have found a price at which buyers are happy to continue to purchase. The "invisible hand" has worked and the market is now in equilibrium.

✓ NEED TO KNOW

> **Market equilbrium** When the amount of certain goods demanded by buyers matches the amount supplied by sellers—the point at which all parties are satisfied with a good's price.

> **Laissez-faire** An economic theory that holds that the market will produce the best solutions in the absence of government interference. Trade, prices, and wages do not need to be regulated, as the market itself will correct imbalances in them.

> **Comparative advantage** The idea that countries should specialize in those goods they can produce at the lowest cost. By avoiding producing goods in which they do not have a comparative advantage, countries will become more efficient and therefore better off.

Economic theories and money

Since the birth of modern economic thought, economists have tried to work out how the quantity of money in an economy affects prices and the behavior of consumers and businesses.

Keynes' general theory of money

In his 1935 book *General Theory*, John Maynard Keynes argued that government spending and taxation levels affect prices more than the quantity of money in the economy. He proposed that in times of recession a government should increase spending to encourage employment, and reduce taxes to stimulate the economy.

GOVERNMENT
When output is shrinking and unemployment rising, a government must decide how to react.

INVESTMENT AND SPENDING
As demand falls, firms reduce production, which raises unemployment and lowers demand.

STIMULATING DEMAND
The government increases its spending, for example on infrastructure. This reduces unemployment.

Fisher's quantity theory of money

The most common version of this theory was articulated by Irving Fisher, who argued that there is a direct link between the amount of money in the economy and price level, with more money in circulation increasing prices.

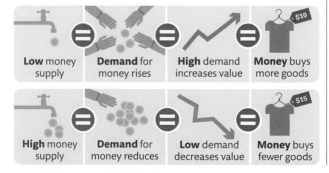

Low money supply | **Demand** for money rises | **High** demand increases value | **Money** buys more goods

High money supply | **Demand** for money reduces | **Low** demand decreases value | **Money** buys fewer goods

Marx's labor theory of value

The German economist Karl Marx argued that the real price (or economic value) of goods should be determined not by the demand for those goods, but by the value of the labor that went into producing it.

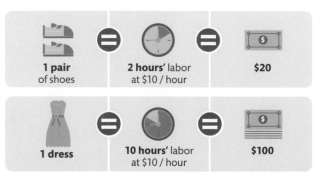

1 pair of shoes | **2 hours'** labor at $10 / hour | $20

1 dress | **10 hours'** labor at $10 / hour | $100

How it works

Scholars in the early 16th century were the first to note that the abundance of silver coming into Spain from the New World led to increased prices. Economists of the 18th-century Classical School believed that the market would correct for such imbalances, reaching an equilibrium price by itself. By the early 20th century, some economists believed that intervention by the government was necessary to maintain a balanced economy, arguing that government spending could boost employment by increasing overall demand.

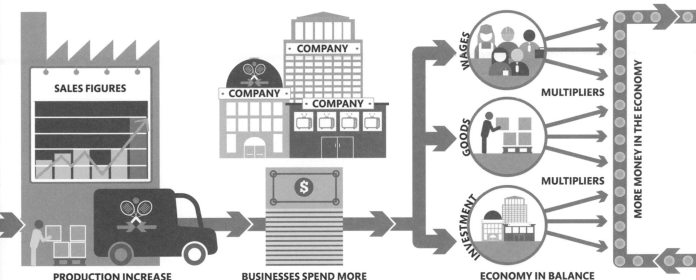

PRODUCTION INCREASE
With more people in employment, consumer spending rises. Increased demand leads to increased production.

BUSINESSES SPEND MORE
With demand rising, firms invest more, opening more factories and providing more employment.

ECONOMY IN BALANCE
With levels of investment and production high, and employment and wages rising, the stimulation of extra government spending is no longer needed.

Hayek's business cycle

Austrian economist Friedrich Hayek noted a cycle in the economy, in which interest rates fall during a recession. This leads to an overexpansion of credit, necessitating a rise in interest rates to counter excess demand.

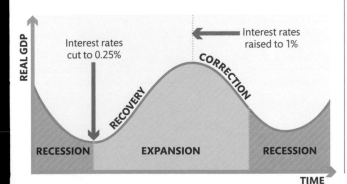

Friedman's monetarism

Milton Friedman argued that governments could raise or lower interest rates to affect the money supply. Cuts would stimulate consumer spending; rises would restrict it and reduce the amount of money in the supply.

PROFIT-MAKING AND FINANCIAL INSTITUTIONS

> Corporate accounting > Financial instruments
> Financial markets > Financial institutions

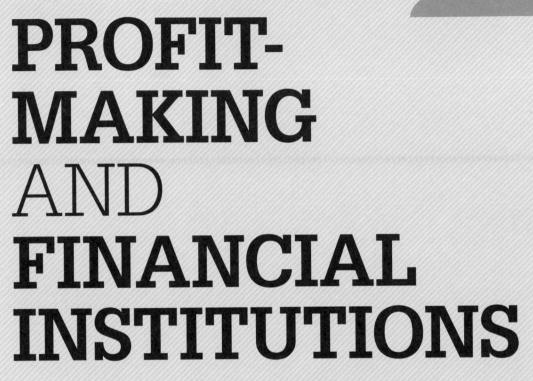

Corporate accounting

Companies use money in different ways—some borrow to pay for investment to grow bigger, while others prefer to hold a lot of cash and to rely on income generation rather than borrowing in order to expand. Much depends on the type of business and the management style. Start-ups and smaller companies tend to need a lot of cash in the early days, while larger, more established companies are better at growing their income internally and may hoard cash.

Cashflow

This indicates how much income a business is generating, and how this compares to its costs and the expenses that it has to pay out. A company is said to have a positive cashflow if its income exceeds its expenses. *See pp.36–39*

Smoothing earnings

This business practice, aimed at reducing volatility in income and reported profit, uses accounting techniques to limit fluctuations in company earnings. *See pp.34–35*

Net income

This is the income that a company reports at the end of the financial year after costs and expenses have been deducted. It is calculated by starting with the revenue earned and then taking away the cost of tax, expenses, banking and interest charges, depreciation of assets, staff costs, and any other expenses involved in operating the business. *See pp.28–29*

Income = $10,000

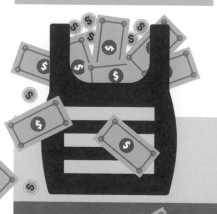

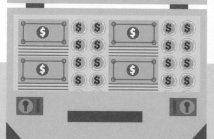

$216 billion

cash reserves **held by** Apple **in April 2016,
out of $1.7 trillion held by** US nonfinancial
companies **at that time**

Expenses

These are the costs a business incurs on a regular basis. They might include staff wages, insurance premiums, utility bills, and other expenses involved in the running of the company.

Assets

These are the items that a company owns, some of which generate income, and many of which may appreciate in value. Businesses often choose between buying assets that will fall in value or leasing equipment.

Gearing ratio

Capital gearing is the balance between a company's capital (its available money or assets) and its funding by short- or long-term loans, expressed as a percentage. A company with relatively low gearing is regarded as being less risky and in a better position to cope with an economic downturn. *See pp.40–41*

Debt = $2,000

Expensing vs Capitalizing

When a business incurs a cost or an expense it needs to record it in the company accounts, either by showing the full amount at the time it happens, or by spreading the cost over a number of years. *See pp.30–31*

Depreciation

This is a measure of how much the value of an asset falls over time, often due to use or "wear and tear." Companies can record the reduction in the value of assets such as vehicles, machinery, or other equipment as depreciation in their accounts. This will then reduce the company's tax liability and reduce their taxable profit. *See pp.32–33*

THE ACCOUNTANT

Net income

When a business reports how it has fared financially over the year, it provides investors with a figure for its net income. This is a good way to understand how much real profit a business is making.

How it works

If businesses were simply to report the money they had earned, this would give an unrealistic picture of the underlying health of the business. For example, a business could be earning plenty of revenue, but also incurring a lot of expenses via investment in new markets, premises, or machinery at the same time.

In order for investors to work out whether a company is financially healthy, therefore, they need to be able to see how it is managing costs, and whether it is spending money in the right way.

Net income is a good way to understand how much real profit a business is making, and whether that profit is likely to be sustained in the future. It is also a way of calculating earnings per share (see "Need to know"), which investors use to weigh up the value of a company and its shares.

Analyzing the balance of revenue earned against the cost of tax, investment, and other expenses is one of a number of ways to assess how a company is faring compared with its competitors, and if it has a sound financial basis going forward.

Calculating net income

For investors trying to decide whether a particular company represents a good investment opportunity, net income helps them to understand the way the business is run and is a guide to the real profit the company is making, rather than just the revenues it is generating. Revenue earned is the starting point, and the cost of tax, banking and interest charges, depreciation of assets, staff costs, and any other expenses involved in operating the business are deducted from this figure.

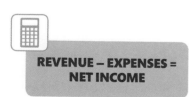

REVENUE – EXPENSES = NET INCOME

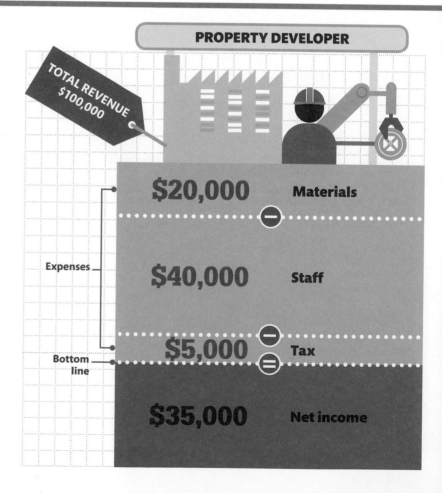

PROPERTY DEVELOPER

TOTAL REVENUE $100,000

$20,000 Materials

Expenses

$40,000 Staff

$5,000 Tax

Bottom line

$35,000 Net income

INFLATING EARNINGS

Some companies omit certain expenses from their calculations to make net income appear higher, while others inflate earnings to make profits appear higher, for example by including projected future earnings. This is at best unethical, and potentially illegal. In 2014, British grocery chain Tesco launched an investigation after discovering its first-half earnings estimate had been inflated by around $407 million due to alleged accounting errors. So, while net income is an important indicator of a company's financial health, it should not be used as the only means of assessment.

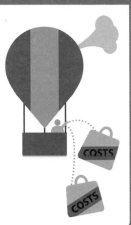

$18.4 billion

Apple's first quarter net income in 2016 – the highest quarterly profits in history

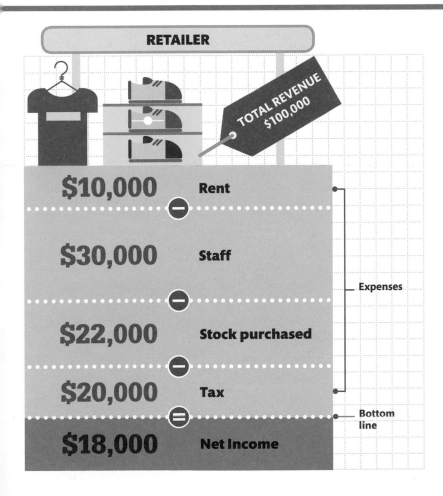

RETAILER

TOTAL REVENUE $100,000

$10,000	⊖	Rent
$30,000	⊖	Staff
$22,000	⊖	Stock purchased
$20,000	⊖	Tax
$18,000	⊜	Net Income

Expenses

Bottom line

✔ NEED TO KNOW

❯ **Bottom line** Refers to the bottom of the income statement, and is another expression for net income.

❯ **Earnings per share** Net income divided by the number of shares in issue; it is seen as an indicator of a company's profitability.

❯ **Expenses** The costs incurred in running a business that have to be settled immediately, rather than paid off gradually over a number of years.

❯ **Depreciation of assets** The decline in value of assets that the company has bought; this may be a plant for manufacturing processes, or specialty machinery.

❯ **Banking and interest charges** The cost of finance, including loans, debts, mortgages, and other amounts owing.

Expensing vs capitalizing

When a business incurs a cost it needs to record it in its company accounts. The company can do this for the full amount at the time it happens, or spread the cost over several years.

Capitalizing and expensing in practice

All companies have costs and expenses. Some such as electricity and other utilities, insurance, staff wages, and food need to be paid for upfront, so these are expensed. To qualify as capital expenditure, an asset must be useful for more than one year. Businesses have to decide which option best fits their business model. A ski resort buys a new ski lift, snowplow, and bus, as well as some furniture, and capitalizes the cost.

Assets

SKI LIFT
The significant cost of building the lift is spread over a number of years.

SNOWPLOW
The snowplow is paid off over several years, as deductions from annual income.

FURNITURE
Furniture appears on the balance sheet as a cost spread over three years.

PASSENGER BUS
The passenger bus is recorded as a depreciating asset as its value will fall

Capitalizing

A business may decide to capitalize a cost, and then spread it over a number of years. Capitalizing means recording an expense as an asset, and then allowing for its depreciation, or fall in value, over time. Accounting this way may be the difference between reporting a profit or a loss if the cost or expense is particularly large.

THE BALANCE SHEET

When to capitalize

For businesses wanting to have a smoother flow of reported income and for start-up businesses, it can be attractive to capitalize purchases because by keeping costs down, a business can report a higher income in its early years. However, there are tax implications if it is making a larger profit as a result.

When to expense

If a firm expenses some of its costs, its profitability may be lower. This may be useful in order to reduce tax; lower profits mean lower taxation. A company may also choose to expense a cost if it has had a good year and wants to show high profitability in later years. Some costs, such as staff payments, must be expensed.

How it works

Business owners and managers have a choice. They can record an expense as it occurs or at the time of payment and reduce the annual profit accordingly. This practice, known as expensing, will show up immediately in the account. If the expense will provide value for more than one year, it can be recorded as an asset once depreciation is accounted for. Known as capitalizing, this practice has the advantage of taking costs out of the business gradually, rather than in one lump sum. The profit-and-loss account is not as dramatically affected in this case.

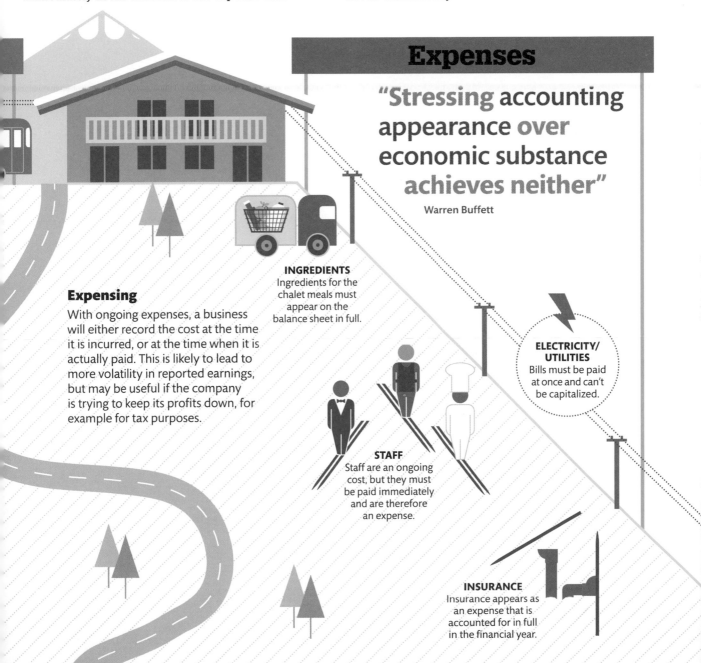

Expenses

"Stressing accounting appearance over economic substance achieves neither"

Warren Buffett

INGREDIENTS
Ingredients for the chalet meals must appear on the balance sheet in full.

ELECTRICITY/ UTILITIES
Bills must be paid at once and can't be capitalized.

Expensing

With ongoing expenses, a business will either record the cost at the time it is incurred, or at the time when it is actually paid. This is likely to lead to more volatility in reported earnings, but may be useful if the company is trying to keep its profits down, for example for tax purposes.

STAFF
Staff are an ongoing cost, but they must be paid immediately and are therefore an expense.

INSURANCE
Insurance appears as an expense that is accounted for in full in the financial year.

Depreciation, amortization, depletion

The cost of a company's assets and its use of natural resources can be deducted from its income for accounting and tax purposes. Depreciation, amortization, and depletion allow the company to spread this cost.

Calculating depreciation

A delivery company buys a van for $25,000. Over time, the vehicle will need to be replaced. The company can record the reduction in the value of the vehicle in its accounts as depreciation.

PURCHASE VALUE − SCRAP VALUE / USEFUL ECONOMIC LIFE (YEARS)	=	ANNUAL DEPRECIATION ($)
$25,000 − $5,000 / 5	=	$4,000

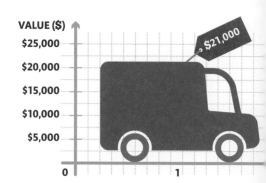

Calculating amortization

A company buys the patent for a computer design. The initial cost of this intangible asset can be gradually written off over several years and can be used to reduce the company's taxable profit.

INITIAL COST / USEFUL LIFE	=	ANNUAL AMORTIZATION ($)
$21,000 / 7	=	$3,000

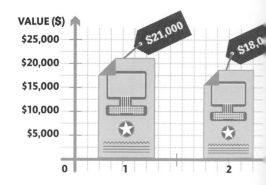

Calculating depletion

A forestry company knows that it has a finite number of trees. Depletion records the fall in value of the forest with its remaining reserves, as the product—wood pulp—is extracted over time.

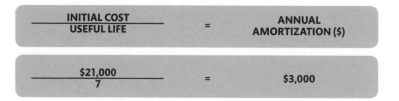

COST − SALVAGE VALUE / TOTAL UNITS	X	UNITS EXTRACTED	=	DEPLETION EXPENSE ($)
$10,000,000 − $1,000,000 / 60,000	X	6,000	=	$900,000

How it works

Depreciation is used to calculate the declining value of tangible assets (such as a machine or vehicle). It is a measure of how much the value of an asset falls over time, particularly due to use, or wear and tear. Amortization is a term used in accounting to describe how the initial cost of an intangible asset (one without a physical presence, such as a patent) can be gradually written off over a number of years. Depletion is the reduction in value of an asset that is a natural resource. Unlike amortization, which deals with nonphysical assets, depletion records the fall in value of actual reserves. It could be applied to coal or diamond mines, oil and gas, or forests, for example.

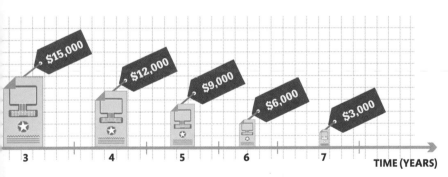

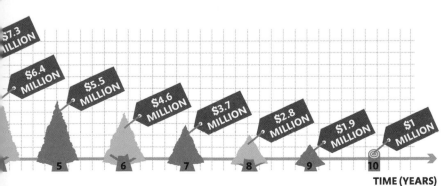

! WARNING

> **Country differences** There are different ways of allowing for depreciation, and accounting methods vary from one country to another. When working out how much a company is allowing for the cost of depreciation, it is important to know which method is being used in its accounts.

> **Purchasing vs leasing assets** Business owners have to make a choice between buying assets that they own but that will fall in value over time, or leasing equipment on which they will pay rent. As they do not own leased equipment, they cannot record its depreciation in value over time and there is no depreciation charge to be used to reduce the company's taxable profit.

60%
the value the average car loses after 3 years on the road

Smoothing earnings

This is a business practice aimed at reducing volatility in company income and reported profit. Smoothing involves the use of accounting techniques to limit fluctuations in a company's earnings.

How it works

Investors like to see companies demonstrate a steady increase in income and profits over time, rather than large fluctuations between income in good and bad years.

It is possible for companies to smooth their earnings to avoid these sorts of large fluctuations. For example, managers can manipulate figures by choosing when to make provision (set aside money) for large expenses. Rather than making large investments, paying back loans, or making provision for big costs in a year in which income has been low, they can instead make provision for those costs in a subsequent year, when the company's income has increased.

Smoothing earnings is generally a legal and legitimate practice and is a way of spreading profits over a number of years. By using this accounting practice, the financial statements of a company will show regular and steady growth, which encourages people to invest in it. However, it can also be used illegally, to disguise or hide losses and encourage investors to buy into a company that is insolvent.

Volatile earnings

Company A does not keep money in reserve to pay for large expenses or to cover its running costs in case of a downturn in profits. It is therefore more vulnerable to fluctuations in its income.

Good times: company spends
Profits are higher than anticipated, so the company spends money on new equipment, staff bonuses, and advertising. It does not keep any money in reserve.

Slump: company has no reserves
The company suffers an unexpected downturn in profits, but has no money set aside. It may struggle to meet its running costs and will be less attractive to investors.

SPEND

EMPTY

FAMOUS ACCOUNTING SCANDALS

Even large, well-known companies can be guilty of manipulating their profit-and-loss accounts. The biggest scandals of recent years included that of Enron, at the time one of the top seven US companies.

ENRON (2001)
Shareholders in this large US company lost a combined $74 billion. When the company collapsed, accountants found that the balance sheet had huge hidden debts that had not been declared.

WORLDCOM (2006)
This communications company appeared to have far more assets than it actually owned, thanks to false entries detailing sales that never existed. It may have inflated its assets by as much as $11 billion.

BERNIE MADOFF (2008)
Investors were paid returns out of their own money, and the business was only sustained by new investors being recruited. Investors in the scheme lost around $65 billion.

LEHMAN BROTHERS (2008)
This investment bank, founded in 1850, had $50 billion of losses in the form of worthless assets on its balance sheet. It went bankrupt, a major factor in the global financial crisis.

Smoother earnings

Company B smooths its earnings by setting money aside during profitable years to use at a later date, for example to repay a loan or cover any unexpected large expenses.

Figures are managed

Income is higher than usual, so the extra revenue is stockpiled and then pushed on to the following year. Profits therefore appear to be steadily increasing.

⚠ WARNING

Reading a company's financial statement does not always give the full picture. Some of the world's biggest corporate finance scandals have involved hidden losses, loans made to look like income, and misstated profits to make the company in question appear solvent when it is not.

"We're not managing profits, we're managing businesses."

Jack Welch

Cash flow

The money coming into and going out of a business is called cash flow. Inflows arise from financing, operations, and investment, while outflows include expenses, costs of raw materials, and capital costs.

Capital
Investment and lump sums

....

❯ Main source of cash inflow for start-ups

❯ Additional cash injection after the initial start-up

❯ Revenue from flotation (going public) of private companies, and from shares issued by public companies

❯ Also known as cash flow from investing activities

Sales revenue
Cash for goods and services sold

....

❯ Revenue generated by core operations

❯ Profit that does not have to be repaid, unlike loans or capital

❯ Payment received for goods and services provided

❯ Also known as cash flow from operating activities

CASH IN

CASH IN

Cash in hand

CASH OUT

CASH OUT

CASH OUT

Salaries and wages
Payments to employees

....

❯ Money paid to employees who are directly involved in the creation of goods or the provision of services

❯ Salaries paid to staff as a fixed monthly or weekly amount (based on an annual rate)

❯ Wages paid to contractors for hours, days, or weeks worked

Overheads
Payment of bills

....

❯ Rental cost of commercial property; utility bills (water, electricity, gas, telephone, and internet); office supplies and stationery

❯ Salaries and wages of employees not directly involved in creating goods and services (known as indirect labor)

Loan repayments
Debt servicing and shareholder profit

....

❯ Interest on long-term loans for asset purchases and on short-term loans for working capital

❯ Repayments on loans

❯ Commission paid to factoring (payment-collecting) companies

❯ Share repurchases and dividend payments to shareholders

How it works

Cash flow is the movement of cash into and out of a business over a set period of time. Cash flows in from the sale of goods and services, from loans, capital investment, and other sources. It flows out to pay rent, utilities, employees, suppliers, and interest on loans. Timing income to correspond with outgoings is key.

Loans
Bank loans and overdrafts

❯ Working-capital loans to meet shortfalls, using anticipated income as collateral

❯ Advances on sales invoices from factoring (payment-collecting) companies

❯ Short-term overdrafts

❯ Also known as cash flow from financing activities

Other revenue
Grants, donations, and windfalls

❯ Grants from government or other institutions – usually for research and development

❯ Donations and gifts (not-for-profit organizations)

❯ Sales of assets and investments

❯ Repayment received for loans made to other organizations

❯ Tax refunds

CASH IN

CASH IN

or stock

CASH OUT

CASH OUT

CASH OUT

Suppliers
Payments for materials and services

❯ Cost of raw materials needed to manufacture goods for sale

❯ Cost of stock—local or imported

❯ Fees for services (consulting or advertising) to generate revenue

❯ Payments to contractors involved in providing goods and services

Tax
Payments to tax authorities

❯ Corporation tax based on profits shown in annual financial statements

❯ Payroll tax paid by employers on behalf of employees

❯ Sales tax and/or VAT on goods or services

❯ The type and rate of taxes vary depending on national tax laws

Equipment
Purchase of fixed assets

❯ Cost of building and equipment, such as computers and phones, office furniture, vehicles, plant, and machinery

❯ Offset by depreciation. *See pp.32–33.*

Cash flow management

The survival of a business depends on how it handles its cash flow. A company's ability to convert its earnings into cash—its liquidity—is equally important. No matter how profitable a business is, it may become insolvent if it cannot pay its bills on time. A new business may even become a victim of its own success and fail through "insolvency by overtrading" if, for example, it spends too much on expansion before payments come in, and then runs out of cash to pay debts and liabilities.

In order to manage cash flow, it is essential for companies to forecast cash inflows and outflows. Sales predictions and cash conversion rates are important. A schedule of when payments are due from customers, and of when a business has to pay its own wages, bills, suppliers, debts, and other costs, can help to predict shortfalls. If cash flow is mismanaged, a business may have to hand out money before it receives payment, leading to cash shortages. Smart businesses, such as supermarkets, receive stock on credit, but are paid in cash—generating a cash surplus.

⚠ WARNING

Top five cash flow problems

> **The slow** payment of invoices.

> **A gap** between credit terms—for example, outgoings set at 30 days and invoices set at 60–120 days.

> **A decline** in sales due to the economic climate, competition, or the product becoming outmoded.

> **Underpriced products**, usually in start-ups that are competing.

> **Excessive outlay** on payroll and overheads, for example when buying rather than hiring assets.

Positive and negative cash flow

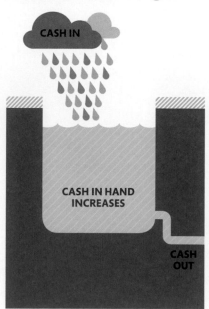

Positive cash flow

Cash flowing into the business is greater than cash flowing out. The stock, or reserve of cash, increases. A business in this position is thriving.

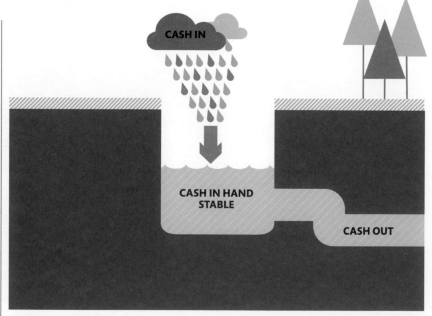

Stable cash flow

Cash flows into the business at the same rate at which it flows out. A business doing well may decide that it can afford to increase its investments or pay higher dividends. Despite these extra expenses, the fact that its cash stock remains stable is a sign that a business is healthy.

✓ NEED TO KNOW

❯ **Factor** A third party which, for a commission, collects payment from a business's customers.

❯ **Accounts payable** Payments a business has to make to others.

❯ **Accounts receivable** Payments a business is due to receive.

❯ **Aging schedule** A table charting accounts payable and accounts receivable according to their dates.

❯ **Cash flow gap** The interval between when payments are made and when they are received.

❯ **Cash conversion** Successful businesses convert their product or service into cash inflows before their bills are due.

❯ **Operating cash flow** Inflows and outflows relating to a company's day-to-day activity.

❯ **Investing cash flow** Movement of money into and out of a company from investments in bonds, businesses, or stock markets.

❯ **Financing cash flow** Payments due to or from debitors and creditors.

80%
of small business start-ups fail due to poor cash flow management

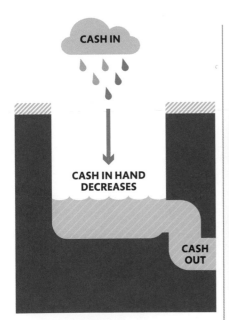

CASH IN

CASH IN HAND DECREASES

CASH OUT

Negative cash flow
Less cash is flowing into the business than is flowing out. Over time, the stock of cash will decrease and the business will face difficulties.

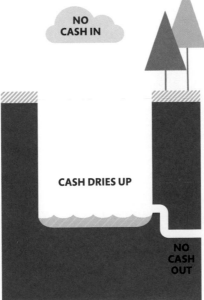

NO CASH IN

CASH DRIES UP

NO CASH OUT

Bankruptcy
If cash flowing out continues to exceed cash flowing in, cash levels will drop so low that the business will become insolvent, having no cash to pay its bills.

HANDLING THE FLOW

A business with a cash surplus might:

❯ Invest or move excess cash into an account where it will earn interest.

❯ Upgrade equipment to improve production efficiency.

❯ Take on new staff, develop products, or buy other companies to expand the business.

❯ Pay creditors early or pay down debt before it is due to improve credit credentials.

A business with a cash shortage might:

❯ Lower prices to increase sales, or raise them to increase profit.

❯ Invoice promptly and chase outstanding payments.

❯ Ask suppliers to extend credit.

❯ Offer discounts in return for quicker payment.

❯ Use an overdraft or short-term loan to pay off pressing expenses.

❯ Continue to forecast cash flow and plan to avert future problems.

Gearing ratio and risk

COMPANY HAS MORE DEBT
A high proportion of debt to equity is also described as a high degree of financial leverage. Typical examples of debt are loans and bonds.

Capital gearing is the balance between the capital a company owns and the funding it gets from short- or long-term loans. Investors and lenders use it to assess risk.

How it works

Most businesses operate on some form of gearing (also called financial leverage), funding their operations in part by borrowing money via loans and bonds. If the level of gearing is high (that is, the business has taken on large debt in relation to its equity), investors will be concerned about the ability of the business to repay the debt. However, if the company's profit is sufficient to cover interest payments, high gearing can provide better shareholder returns. The optimum gearing level depends on how risky a company's business sector is, the gearing levels of its competitors, and the company's maturity. Gearing ratios vary from country to country. Firms in Germany and France often have higher ratios than those in the US and UK.

Equity finance (shares)

Pros

> Low gearing is seen as a measure of financial strength
> Low risk attracts more investors and boosts credit rating
> Finance from shares does not have to be repaid
> Shareholders absorb losses
> Angel investors share expertise
> Good for start-ups, which may take a while to become profitable

Cons

> Shared ownership, so company founders and directors have limited control of decisions
> Profit is shared in return for investors risking their funds
> There is a legal obligation to act in the interests of shareholders
> Complex to set up

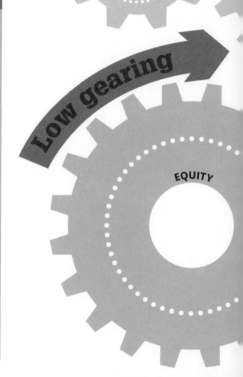

EQUITY

Low gearing

EQUITY

Gearing ratio calculation

Analysts and potential investors assess the financial risk of a company with this calculation, presented as a percentage.

$$\frac{\text{LONG-TERM DEBT}}{\left(\begin{array}{c}\text{SHARE CAPITAL} + \\ \text{RESERVES} + \\ \text{LONG-TERM DEBT}\end{array}\right)} \times 100$$

Low gearing

A software company is going public. Its ratio of 21.2 percent tells investors that it has relatively low gearing and is well positioned to weather economic downturns.

$$\frac{\$1.2\ \text{MILLION}}{\left(\begin{array}{c}\$2\ \text{MILLION} + \$2.455\ \text{MILLION} + \\ \$1.2\ \text{MILLION}\end{array}\right)} \times 100 = 21.2\%$$

High gearing

DEBT

DEBT

COMPANY HAS LESS DEBT
A low proportion of debt to equity is also described as a low degree of financial leverage. Equity typically comes from reserves and share capitals.

Debt finance (loans)

Pros

〉 Debt payments do not change with profitability

〉 Interest payments are tax deductible

〉 Debt does not dilute ownership

〉 Company retains control of decision-making

〉 Repayment is a known amount that can be planned for

〉 Quicker and simpler to set up

〉 Small business loans at favorable rates may be available to start-ups

Cons

〉 High gearing is considered a measure of financial vulnerability, as debt payments must be made even if profits are low

〉 High risk may put off investors and adversely affect credit rating

〉 Loans and interest must be paid, even if operating profit shrinks

〉 Debt may be secured on fixed assets of a company. Unpaid lenders can seize assets and force bankruptcy

〉 Tax authorities and lenders are to be paid first in the event of insolvency

✓ NEED TO KNOW

〉 **Interest cover ratio** An alternative method of calculating gearing: operating profit divided by interest payable.

〉 **Overleveraged** A situation in which a business has too much debt to meet interest payments on its borrowing.

〉 **Deleverage** The immediate payment of any existing debt in order to reduce gearing.

〉 **Creditors** Those to whom a debt is due or a payment needs to be made (shareholders are always behind loan-holders in the order of repayment).

〉 **Dilution** Angel investors—people who provide finance and invest in the future of a start-up company—will usually receive shares in return. This is known as diluting ownership, as the angel investors will own part of the company and may hold sufficient shares to have a controlling stake.

High gearing

A water company is the only water provider in the area, with several million customers. Although high, the ratio of 64 percent is acceptable for a utility company with a regional monopoly and a good reputation.

$$\left(\frac{\$360 \text{ MILLION}}{\$82 \text{ MILLION} + \$120 \text{ MILLION} + \$360 \text{ MILLION}}\right) \times 100 = 64\%$$

25%
the ratio at or below which a company is traditionally said to have low gearing

How companies use debt

When a company wants to expand, it has two main funding options—
to borrow money or to issue shares to investors. Borrowing money at a
fixed price enables it to budget for costs and calculate potential profits.

How it works

By taking on debt—in other words, borrowing money—a firm receives a lump sum of cash, paying back the full amount with interest in regular payments over a fixed term to its creditors. It also retains control over its business strategy, unlike when shares are sold.

By issuing shares, a company is selling ownership (equity) stakes in the business. A firm that raises money via issuing shares may have to allow larger shareholders a say in how the business is run. If the company then makes a profit, it may have to pay dividends to shareholders. Unlike loans, shares do not get "paid off"; dividends are paid as long as shares exist.

Firms may use both methods to fund investment, and each approach has different pros and cons, but without the facility to borrow, a company would be unable to take on large projects and make long-term commitments.

If a lender is concerned about how a company is being run, or its future ability to pay its debt, it may have the option to withdraw the loan or ask the company to reschedule its debt, thereby paying a higher rate of interest to compensate the lender for the increased potential risk.

Business expansion

Some companies, for example those in air travel, car manufacturing, or house building, tend to have higher levels of debt because they have to purchase stock, raw materials, or land well before they sell their products or services.

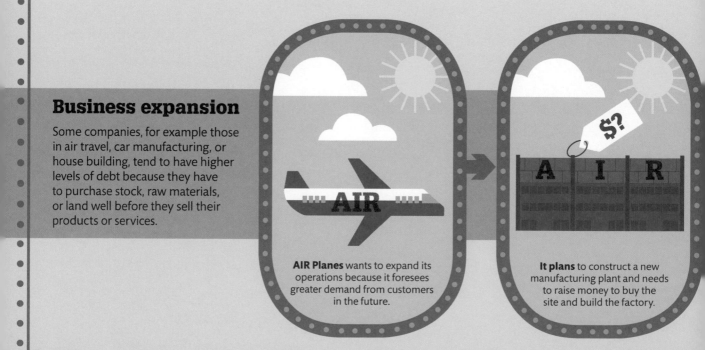

AIR Planes wants to expand its operations because it foresees greater demand from customers in the future.

It plans to construct a new manufacturing plant and needs to raise money to buy the site and build the factory.

✓ NEED TO KNOW

> **Creditors** Banks, loan companies, and individuals to whom a firm owes money.

> **Dividends** Profits paid to a company's shareholders.

> **Interest payment** The amount of interest charged on a loan. This is usually fixed and has to be paid on time in installments—even if the company is struggling and losing money.

> **Lifecycle** The "debt phase" a company is in. Start-ups tend to be funded by small bank loans and seed capital, turning to venture capital when they expand, which may involve issuing shares.

GETTING THE BALANCE RIGHT

A company that borrows money as opposed to issuing shares has fixed liabilities and a time table for repayment. It retains more independence as the creditors don't have a share of the profits or a say in how the company is run. There are also tax advantages—it is cheaper for a firm to bear the cost of debt than equity.

Too much debt, and it won't attract any lenders, as it is seen as too risky. But using debt, it is able to retain more of its profits.

Too little debt, and it may be forced to give away too much control and profits to new shareholders.

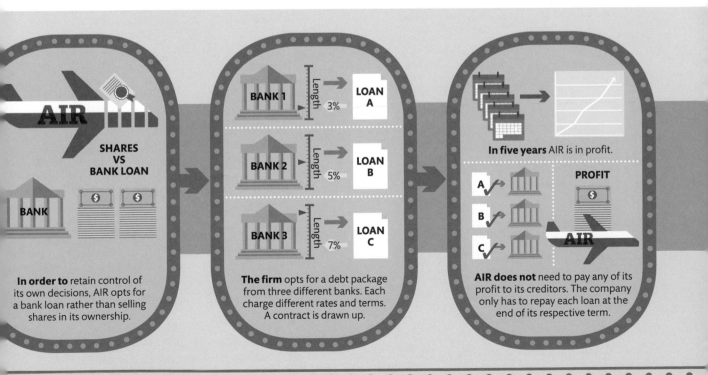

In order to retain control of its own decisions, AIR opts for a bank loan rather than selling shares in its ownership.

The firm opts for a debt package from three different banks. Each charge different rates and terms. A contract is drawn up.

AIR does not need to pay any of its profit to its creditors. The company only has to repay each loan at the end of its respective term.

Financial reporting

Financial reporting is when a company publishes statements showing its assets (what it owns), its liabilities (what it owes), and its financial status. This information is used by investors to keep track of the company's progress.

How it works

There are legal requirements around financial reporting to ensure that a company gives a full and fair statement of its financial affairs. The company must show its performance over the year or half year, any significant changes to its financial position, and whether it has made money or incurred liabilities or losses during the year.

Two financial reports are usually issued per year—the half-year report, and the annual report. For firms that are publicly owned—i.e. their shares are traded on the stock market—the annual report must be made public and freely available for investors to read.

Companies usually publish a number of documents: an annual report showing the firm's activities during the year; a balance sheet showing its current assets and liabilities, and the working capital (difference between the two); a statement of cash flows and statement of stockholder's equity; and financial details on its website for investors. This information is used by investors to keep track of the company's progress.

 WARNING

A balance sheet is a snapshot of a company's financial position on one particular day. Although it is a good guide to the financial health of a company, doctored reports can, and in the past have been used to, hide large debts or liabilities, and not reveal them to the auditors who are checking the annual report or balance sheet. Auditors may be alerted to fraud by a number of "red flags" or warning signs—these could be anything from negative cash flows that miraculously become positive the following year, to sales registered before they have been made, to an unusual rise in gross margin.

Case study: **balance sheet**

This example, from a water company, shows how a balance sheet works.

ASSETS, LIABILITIES, AND CAPITAL

Fixed assets

Intangible assets

Tangible assets

Investments

Current assets

Stock and work in progress

Debtors

Cash at the bank and in hand

Total current assets

Creditors—amounts coming due within one year

Net current assets

Total assets less current liabilities

Creditors—amounts coming due after more than one year

Provisions for liabilities and charges

Retirement benefit obligations

Deferred income

Net assets

Stockholders' equity

Issued share cap

Retained profit (or earnings)

Shareholders' funds

SYMBOLS FOR DEBITS AND CREDITS

Accountants use a number of different terms and symbols to indicate debits and credits. Some use "Dr" for debits and "Cr" for credits, others use "+" for debits and "–" for credits. On this balance sheet, brackets are used to show credits (negative numbers).

	Year 2013 $m	Year 2012 $m
	0	0
	2,167.1	2,069.2
	–	–
	7.0	6.3
	162.6	153.9
	181.0	211.0
	350.6	371.2
	(198.8)	(171.7)
	151.8	**199.5**
	2,318.9	**2,268.7**
	(1,891.5)	(1,811.9)
	(114.9)	(115.3)
	(93.1)	(83.0)
	(17.2)	(17.9)
	202.2	**240.6**
	81.3	81.3
	120.9	159.3
	202.2	**240.6**

Fixed assets (or non-current assets) cannot easily be converted into cash and are usually bought for long-term use. They are either tangible, such as land, or intangible, such as brand logos.

Intangible assets are assets that are not physical—for example intellectual property (IP) or trademarks. They have a value but are distinct from tangible assets such as stock, property, and premises.

Current assets include all assets that could be converted into cash—cash reserves within the business and petty cash; stock; insurance claims; office equipment; accounts receivable.

Debtors are individuals or companies that owe the firm money. Debtors will usually have an agreement with their creditors about terms of payment.

Creditors are the individuals or organizations to which the company owes money. Here, the money must be repaid in the current financial year.

Net current assets are current assets after money due to creditors has been deducted.

Total assets less current liabilities are all the assets that the company owns that are not likely to be exchanged for cash, as well as cash, and other liquid assets, minus liabilities.

Liabilities due are loans, mortgages, or outstanding debt that the company owes, and on which it is likely to have to pay interest.

Net assets are the company's total assets minus the total liabilities it has. It is the amount of value left and is sometimes called shareholders' equity.

Issued share cap is the total number of shares held by the company's shareholders.

Retained profit is profit that has not been paid out as dividends to shareholders and may be reinvested or used to pay debt in the long term.

Shareholders' funds, or owner's equity, is the company's remaining net capital; this can be reinvested or paid out annually as a dividend.

Financial instruments

A financial instrument is something that has value and can be traded. This might be cash or currency, shares, assets, or debts and loans. It can include evidence of an ownership of interest in a company or other entity. Many records of financial instruments are now held electronically.

How they work

Financial instruments are legal agreements that require one party to pay (or promise to pay) money—or something else that has a value—to another person or organization. There are usually conditions attached to an agreement. These conditions might cover the amount and timing of payments of interest, cash, capital gains, premiums, or provision of insurance cover as part of the agreement. As proof that you own a financial instrument, you might hold an actual document, such as a share certificate, an insurance policy, or a contract for a debt or a loan, but shares can also be held in an online account.

WHY HOLD FINANCIAL INSTRUMENTS?

Growth and dividends

Investors buy and trade financial instruments in order to receive a straightforward capital gain, or to receive interest from a bond or from dividends of shares.

Risk control

Buying assets that perform independently of each other (shares from one country, and government bonds from another, for example) can help reduce risk in a portfolio.

Preparing for the unexpected

An investor wishing to hedge their portfolio might buy insurance against that portfolio falling in value. Holding an insurance certificate gives protection against losses that have been set out and agreed in the policy.

Shares

Companies issue shares to investors in return for money. A legal agreement between a company and a shareholder might include the payment of dividends (when and if the company can afford to do so) or perks for as long as the investor holds the shares.
See pp.48–49

Currency

Different currencies can be held and traded by investors to exploit movements in exchange rates for profit.
See pp.58–59

16%
rise in the value
of Google shares
in a single day
on Friday, July
17th, 2015

Derivatives–
options and futures

The value of derivatives
depends on the performance
of an underlying asset. They
are traded to provide capital
growth, or to limit risk within
a business or a portfolio.
Professional investors may use
them to hedge their portfolios.
See pp.52–53

Bonds and
loans

These are IOUs between
a company and an investor.
The investor effectively loans
a company or government
money and, in return, the
borrower pays interest to the
investor over a set period, at
a set rate, with a specified date
for the return of the capital.
See pp.50–51

✓ NEED TO KNOW

❯ **Capital gain** Profit from the sale
of assets such as shares.

❯ **Risk** The chance that an
investment's return may be lower
or different than expected.

❯ **Portfolio** A range of investments
held either by an individual or by
an organization.

Insurance

An insurance policy involves a
company or individual paying
a premium to an insurance
company, entering into a
contract that promises monetary
compensation in the event
of them suffering a pre-agreed
loss scenario. *See pp.78–79*

Funds

An investment fund (such
as an ETF fund) is a supply of
capital belonging to a group of
investors. This money is invested
by the fund in the hope that the
fund's share price will increase,
netting the investors a capital
gain. It may also pay interest.
See pp.80–81

Shares

Shares are units of ownership interest in a corporation that are available for investors to buy or sell. Companies create shares in order to raise capital, which they can invest to grow their business.

How it works

Shareholders are investors who buy the shares a company creates, and who therefore own a part of the company. When shareholders buy a share, it is usually an "ordinary share" or "common share," which means that they can vote in the election of the company's executive team, approve or vote against new share issues and other money-raising activities, and in some cases receive payouts known as dividends. Shareholders are entered on the company's shareholder register, which is a list of all the investors who hold a stake in it. Investors buy shares for capital growth (hoping the underlying value or price of the shares will rise) and for income if the shares pay dividends. Share prices rise and fall based on a company's financial performance, general economic news, and market sentiment—how investors feel about a company or the wider economy. If a share price fluctuates in a short space of time it is said to be volatile. If one company's share price is volatile it can indicate investor worries about that company; if volatility affects all share prices it can indicate instability in entire markets.

Issuing shares

Companies issue shares when they need money to invest or pay off costs. When an investor buys a share, they become a shareholder and own a small part of the company.

A company needs shares to expand its operation. It decides to offer shares to the public via flotation on the stock market.

The company issues shares at $10 per share. The shares are made available via an Initial Public Offering (IPO) at an agreed price.

Individual investors receive their shares at the issue price, in this case $10. The shares can then be bought and sold on the stock exchange.

UNDERSTANDING SHARES

 Once shares have been issued they can then be traded on the stock market.

 Shareholders buy part of a company. If share values fall, there is no guarantee that they will get their money back.

 The price of a share favored by investors tends to rise; if investors lose confidence, the price tends to fall.

 If a company goes bust, shareholders will probably lose most or all of their initial capital.

 If a company does well, shareholders share in the returns. This is what makes buying shares so exciting to investors.

 If a company fails, shareholders lose their investment but they are not responsible for a company's debts.

$169 billion
average daily trading value of the New York Stock Exchange, the largest in the world

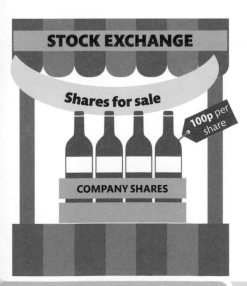

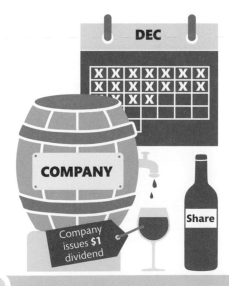

After the IPO allocations, the company makes the shares available on the stock exchange where prices are affected by market performance.

After six months the shares gain 10% in value. Shareholders who sell shares they bought at $10 have now made a profit of $1 per share.

After another six months the company pays a dividend of $1 per share. Investors still holding their shares gain this $1 profit.

Bonds

Companies and governments sell bonds to raise money without issuing shares. They are effectively fixed-term loans bought by investors who receive interest until the end of that term.

How it works

Bonds are securities for long-term debt, although they are not always held until the end of their term. The price of a bond rises and falls depending on current interest rates, and on how likely investors feel the bond issuer is to repay the initial sum invested. There are different kinds of bonds such as savings bonds, company bonds, and government bonds (also known as US treasury securities), and some can be traded between investors. In savings bonds, investors deposit a lump sum with a retail savings institution (such as a bank), receive regular interest, and are repaid the original sum in full. In other types of bonds, repayment of the original sum is not guaranteed, since the issuer could go bust. Because the risk of government default is so small, gilts are seen as the least risky bond type.

Investing in bonds

When choosing a bond, investors must balance the total sum received in interest against the likelihood of the capital sum (initial cash investment) actually being repaid at the end of the term. They must also decide whether a bond offers good value by analyzing its current yield. This compares the interest paid by the bond with its current value on the secondhand market. Although bondholders have a slightly higher chance of being paid than shareholders if a company collapses, there is no guarantee of payment.

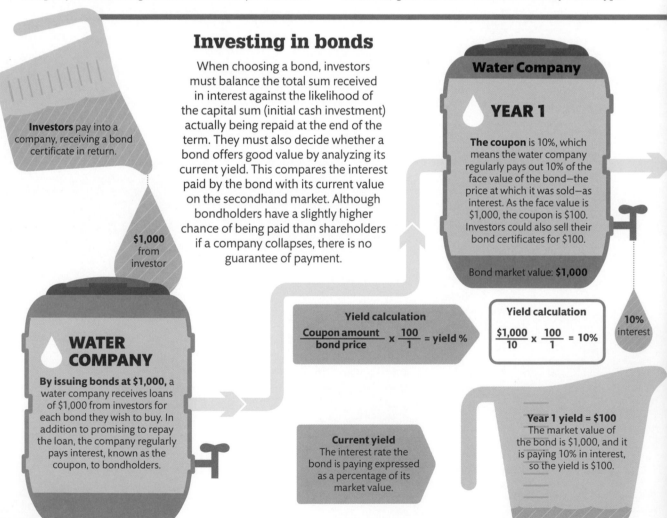

Investors pay into a company, receiving a bond certificate in return.

$1,000 from investor

WATER COMPANY

By issuing bonds at $1,000, a water company receives loans of $1,000 from investors for each bond they wish to buy. In addition to promising to repay the loan, the company regularly pays interest, known as the coupon, to bondholders.

Water Company

YEAR 1

The coupon is 10%, which means the water company regularly pays out 10% of the face value of the bond—the price at which it was sold—as interest. As the face value is $1,000, the coupon is $100. Investors could also sell their bond certificates for $100.

Bond market value: **$1,000**

Yield calculation

$$\frac{\text{Coupon amount}}{\text{bond price}} \times \frac{100}{1} = \text{yield \%}$$

Yield calculation

$$\frac{\$1,000}{10} \times \frac{100}{1} = 10\%$$

10% interest

Current yield
The interest rate the bond is paying expressed as a percentage of its market value.

Year 1 yield = $100
The market value of the bond is $1,000, and it is paying 10% in interest, so the yield is $100.

✓ NEED TO KNOW

> **Face value** The initial price at which the bond was issued.

> **Market or par value** The price at which a bond is traded.

> **Coupon** The amount of interest paid to bond investors.

> **Yield** A general term that relates to the return on the capital invested in a bond.

> **Savings bonds** Cash deposits on which a regular interest rate is paid.

> **Securities** Financial instruments, such as bonds, that can be traded.

> **Junk bonds** Bonds of highly risky companies.

> **Default** When a company fails to honor a repayment on a bond that it has sold to an investor.

16.5%
highest ever bond rate offered by US banks due to high interest rates in the 1980s

---

Water Company

 YEAR 2

The company does well and is seen as a safe investment so the bond's market value—the price other investors will pay for it—increases. Some investors may choose to sell their bond certificates for a 20% profit, but others will keep them for the regular interest.

Bond market value: **$1,200**

Yield calculation

$$\frac{100}{\$1,200} \times \frac{100}{1} = 8.33\%$$

$100 interest

Year 2 yield = 8.33%
At $1,200, the interest remains the same but the bond yield falls to 8.33% as the bond provides 10% of $1,000 on a $1,200 investment.

Water Company

 YEAR 3

After a difficult year the company looks less reliable, so the market value of its bonds decreases. The bond still provides regular interest. Any new investors would receive the same interest payment—a higher rate of regular interest for a lower initial investment.

Bond market value: **$800**

Yield calculation

$$\frac{\$100}{\$800} \times \frac{100}{1} = 12.5\%$$

$100 interest

Year 3 yield = 12.5%
The interest the bond pays remains at $100, but the bond can now be bought for $800. The yield therefore rises to 12.5%.

Water Company

YEAR 4

At the end of the bond's term, the company repays the original capital sum, plus any interest that has accrued, on a specified date known as the maturity date. The bondholder receives no further interest once the bonds have matured.

Bond market value: **Maturity**

Repayment **$1,000**

Return on bond = $300
The bondholder receives the full redemption of $1,000, plus the total interest of $300 that has been accrued over the three years.

Derivatives

A type of financial instrument, the value of derivatives is based on the price of an underlying asset or index. They are commonly used by investors to spread risk, and/or to speculate.

How it works

Investors may buy derivatives in order to reduce the amount of volatility in their portfolios, since they can agree on a price for a deal in the present that will, in effect, happen in the future, or to try to increase their gains through speculation. Derivatives can enable an investor to gain exposure to a market via a smaller outlay than if they bought the actual underlying asset. The most common are futures and options—leveraged products in which the investor puts down a small proportion of the value of the underlying asset and hopes to gain by a future rise in the value of that asset.

Derivatives for hedging

Companies use derivatives to protect against cost fluctuations by fixing a price for a future deal in advance. By settling costs in this way, buyers gain protection—known as a hedge—against unexpected rises or falls in, for example, the foreign exchange market, interest rates, or the value of the commodity or product they are buying.

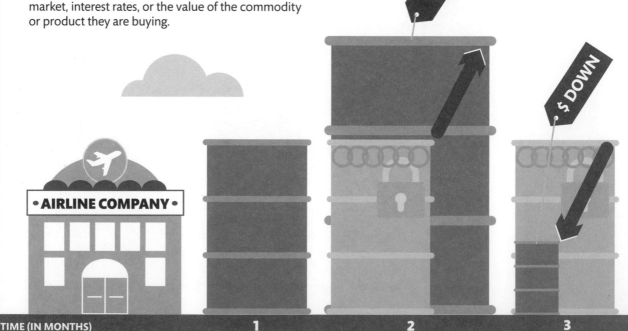

PRICE

TIME (IN MONTHS)   1   2   3

$ UP

$ DOWN

AIRLINE COMPANY

A US-based airline company reviews its stock levels and decides that it will need to buy jet fuel for its fleet of planes in three months' time.

To protect itself from potential future price increases, it can buy fuel at today's prices for delivery and payment at a future date, known as a forward transaction. If the price of fuel then falls instead of rising, however, the company will be locked in to paying a higher price.

WARNING

Referred to as financial weapons of mass destruction, derivatives can be volatile. Relying on debt leverage, they use complex mathematical models and not all traders clearly understand the risks they are taking. They can suffer large and catastrophic losses as a result.

$6.2 billion
was lost on derivative trading by JP Morgan Chase & Co.

Derivatives for speculation

Investors may buy or sell an asset in the hope of generating a profit from the asset's price fluctuations. Usually this is done on a short-term basis in assets that are liquid (easily traded).

AIRLINE COMPANY
Options to buy

$.50

Available for limited time period: $.50 option on $5 share price.

$10

$5

$
PROFIT

AIRLINE COMPANY
Options to buy
Expired

$5

$1

SMALL LOSS
$

An investor notices a company's share price going up and buys an option on the shares—a right to buy shares at a future date.

If share prices do rise, the investor can profit by buying at the fixed option price and selling at the current higher price.

If share prices fall, the investor can sell the option or let it lapse, losing a fraction of the value of the asset itself.

Financial markets

The flow of money around the world is essential for businesses to operate and grow. Stock markets are places where individual investors and corporations can trade currencies, invest in companies, and arrange loans. Without the global financial markets, governments would not be able to borrow money, companies would not have access to the capital they need to expand, and investors and individuals would be unable to buy and sell foreign currencies.

Financial markets in action

Thanks to the global financial markets, money flows around the world between investors, businesses, customers, and stock markets. Investors are not restricted to placing their money with companies in the country where they live, and big businesses now have international offices, so money needs to move efficiently between countries and continents. It is also important for the growth of the global economy that people are able to invest money outside of their domestic markets.

Inside the stock exchange

Buying and selling occurs in real time, and prices change by the second.

Brokers trade shares (also known as stocks), bonds, commodities (raw materials), and specialty financial products such as futures and options.

Buyers specify which share or asset to buy, at what price, and in what volume.

Investors buy via brokers, who set prices and make commission on sales.

When shares are easy to buy and sell, the market is said to be liquid. When there are fewer buyers and sellers, the market is said to be illiquid.

A stock is known by its "ticker"— usually a shortened version of its trading name.

Buying shares or options

Investors study data to decide whether to buy or sell financial assets. Data is updated regularly to reflect changes in supply and demand. *See pp.62–63*

FINANCIAL MARKETS AROUND THE WORLD

New York, US

The New York Stock Exchange (NYSE) is the largest in the world (market capitalization—the market value of its outstanding shares: $14.14 trillion), followed by the NASDAQ, which is also based in New York, ($5.63 trillion).

Toronto, Canada

The Toronto Stock Exchange (TSE) in Canada is run by the TMX Group ($1.45 trillion).

Tokyo, Japan

The Japan Exchange Group (JPX), based in Tokyo, is the largest exchange in Asia ($3.73 trillion).

China

China has three stock exchanges: the Shanghai Stock Exchange (SSE), ($2.9 trillion); Shenzhen Stock Exchange (SZSE) ($2.36 trillion); and the Stock Exchange of Hong Kong (SEHK) ($2.32 trillion).

London, UK

The London Stock Exchange (LSE) is Europe's largest ($2.68 trillion).

European Union

Euronext has headquarters in Amsterdam, Brussels, Lisbon, London, and Paris ($2.56 trillion).

Frankfurt, Germany

Deutsche Börse is based in Frankfurt (FWB) ($1.24 trillion).

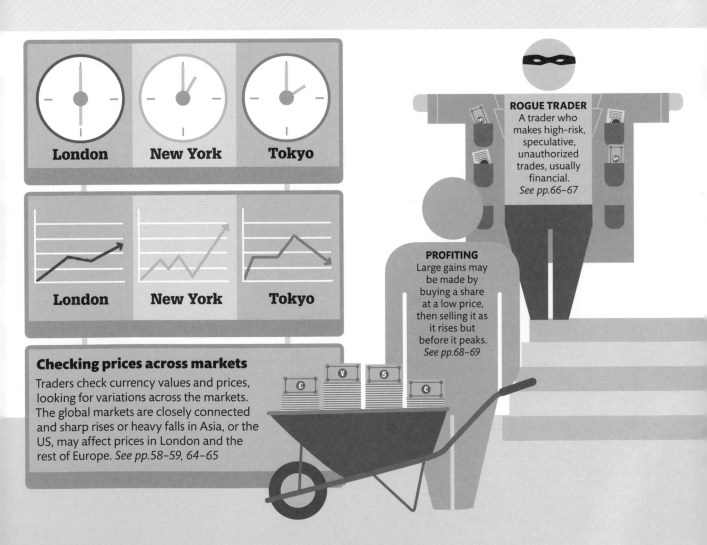

London **New York** **Tokyo**

London **New York** **Tokyo**

Checking prices across markets

Traders check currency values and prices, looking for variations across the markets. The global markets are closely connected and sharp rises or heavy falls in Asia, or the US, may affect prices in London and the rest of Europe. See pp.58–59, 64–65

ROGUE TRADER
A trader who makes high-risk, speculative, unauthorized trades, usually financial.
See pp.66–67

PROFITING
Large gains may be made by buying a share at a low price, then selling it as it rises but before it peaks.
See pp.68–69

The money market

Banks and companies use the money market to buy and sell financial assets that have short maturity dates, and that are easy and quick to exchange.

How it works

The money market exists to provide the loans that financial institutions and governments need to carry out their day-to-day operations. For instance, banks may sometimes need to borrow in the short term to fulfill their obligations to their customers, and they use the money market to do so.

For example, most deposit accounts have a relatively short notice period and allow customers access to their money either immediately, or within a few days or weeks. Because of this short notice period, banks cannot make long-term commitments with all of the money they hold on deposit. They need to ensure that a proportion of it is liquid (easily accessible) in market terms. Otherwise, if a large number of customers wish to withdraw their money at the same time, there may be a shortfall between the money the bank has lent and the cash deposits it needs to return to savers.

Banks may also find that they have greater demand for mortgages or loans than they do for savings accounts at certain times. This creates a mismatch between the money they have available and the money they have loaned out, so the bank will need to borrow in order to be able to fulfill the demand for loans.

Who uses the money market

The primary function of the money market is for banks and other investors with liquid assets to gain a return on their cash or loans. They provide borrowers such as other banks, brokerages, and hedge funds with quick access to short-term funding. The money market is dominated by professional investors, although retail investors with more than $50,000 can also invest. Smaller deposits can be invested via money market funds. Banks and companies use the financial instruments traded on the money market for different reasons, and they carry different risks.

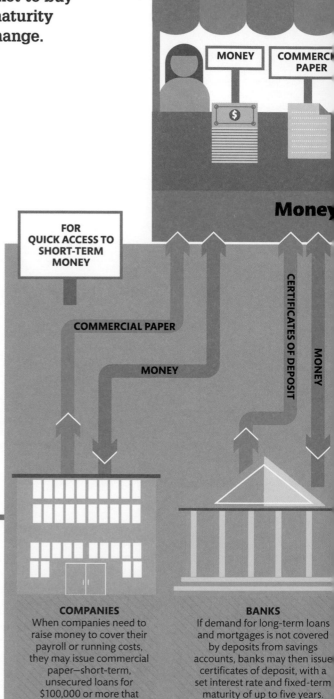

MONEY

COMMERCIAL PAPER

Money

FOR QUICK ACCESS TO SHORT-TERM MONEY

COMMERCIAL PAPER

MONEY

CERTIFICATES OF DEPOSIT

MONEY

COMPANIES
When companies need to raise money to cover their payroll or running costs, they may issue commercial paper—short-term, unsecured loans for $100,000 or more that mature within 1–9 months.

BANKS
If demand for long-term loans and mortgages is not covered by deposits from savings accounts, banks may then issue certificates of deposit, with a set interest rate and fixed-term maturity of up to five years.

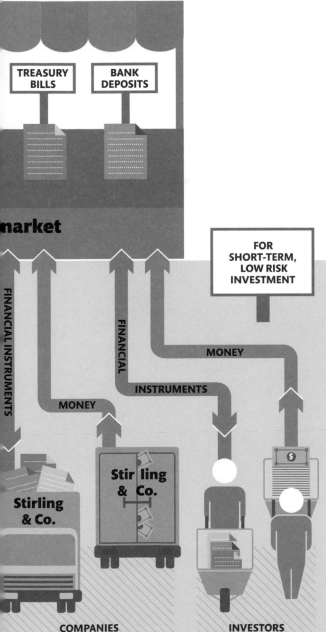

TREASURY
BILLS

BANK
DEPOSITS

market

FINANCIAL INSTRUMENTS

FINANCIAL

FOR
SHORT-TERM,
LOW RISK
INVESTMENT

MONEY

INSTRUMENTS

MONEY

Stir ling
& Co.

Stirling
& Co.

COMPANIES
A company that has a cash
surplus may "park" money for a
time in short-term, debt-based
financial instruments such as
treasury bills and commercial
paper, certificates of deposit,
or bank deposits.

INVESTORS
Individuals seeking to
invest large sums of
money at relatively low
risk may invest in
financial instruments.
Sums of less than
$50,000 can be invested
in money market funds.

WHAT IS TRADED ON THE MONEY MARKET?

LEAST
RISK

❭ **Treasury bills** Short-term government securities that mature within three months to one year of issue, also known as T-bills. They are acquired at a discount on their face or "par" value, which is then paid in full on maturity. T-bills are considered effectively risk-free.

MEDIUM
RISK

❭ **Certificates of deposit** Fixed term savings certificates issued with a set interest rate by banks. Rates depend on length of maturity, with longer terms getting better rates. The main risks are being locked in to low interest rates if rates rise, and early withdrawal penalties.

❭ **Bank deposits** Money deposited in banks, often for a fixed term. Interest rates vary, based on the amount deposited and on deposit liquidity. Risk depends on bank creditworthiness, and whether it is insured by the FDIC.

HIGH
RISK

❭ **Commercial paper** Short-term, unsecured debt issued by a company. Only companies with good credit ratings issue commercial paper because investors are reluctant to buy the debt of financially compromised companies. They tend to be issued by highly rated banks and are traded in a similar way to securities. Asset values are in the thousands or millions of dollars.

✓ NEED TO KNOW

❭ **Money market funds** Collectives that offer "baskets" of financial instruments to individual investors, allowing them to invest in the money market with a sum of less than $50,000.

❭ **Federal funds rate** The rate at which financial institutions borrow and lend to each other overnight. It is a very influential interest rate in the US economy—if the rate goes up, so does the cost of borrowing.

Foreign exchange and trading

Known as forex, foreign exchange and trading refers to the buying and selling of currencies. This trading of currencies can occur between banks, financial institutions, governments, and individuals.

Forex profit and loss

A trader wants to sell some UK pound sterling (GBP) and buy euros (EUR) because they think that the value of the pound is going to fall against the euro. If their prediction is right, they can sell the euros for a profit, but if their prediction is wrong, they will take a loss when they sell. Investors who wish to speculate on the forex market may use a forex broker and give them a deposit, or borrow money (known as margin) from them to buy currency.

! WARNING

Forex markets usually trade on small differences—for example the US dollar–euro rate changing by a few cents—so sudden shocks can catch investors unprepared.On January 15, 2015, the Swiss National Bank (SNB) unexpectedly announced that it would no longer hold the Swiss franc at a fixed exchange rate with the euro. This caused panic in the forex markets. At one point on that day the Swiss franc rose by 30 percent against the euro and 25 percent against the US dollar.

①

Investor A looks at the price of the two currencies on the forex market. The EUR/GBP is trading at £0.79 to buy and £0.77 to sell.

②

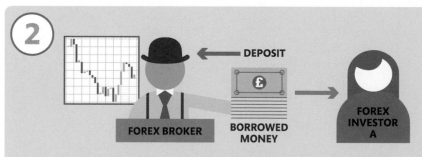

DEPOSIT

FOREX BROKER   BORROWED MONEY   FOREX INVESTOR A

Investor A thinks that this is a good price and decides to trade, borrowing £79,000 to do so.

③

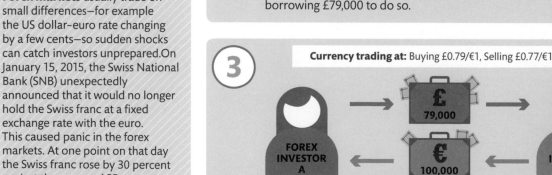

Currency trading at: Buying £0.79/€1, Selling £0.77/€1

FOREX INVESTOR A   £ 79,000   FOREX INVESTOR B

€ 100,000

Investor A buys €100,000 for £79,000 from Investor B. They do this via a currency brokerage, which charges them both a commission.

How it works

The forex market provides a service to individuals, businesses, and governments who need to buy or sell currencies other than that used in their country.

This might be in order to travel abroad, to make investments in another country, or to pay for import products or convert export earnings.

It is also a marketplace in which currencies are bought and sold purely to make profit via speculation. When trading very large volumes of currency, even small fluctuations in price can provide profits or losses.

The forex market is open 24 hours, 5 days a week, which makes it unusual, as equity markets have set daily trading hours and are closed overnight.

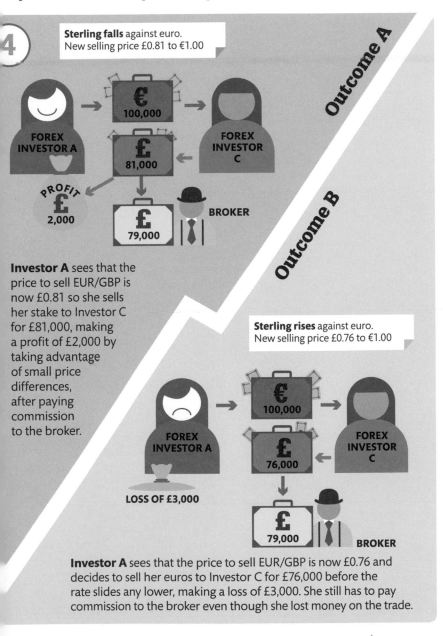

Sterling falls against euro.
New selling price £0.81 to €1.00

Outcome A

Investor A sees that the price to sell EUR/GBP is now £0.81 so she sells her stake to Investor C for £81,000, making a profit of £2,000 by taking advantage of small price differences, after paying commission to the broker.

Sterling rises against euro.
New selling price £0.76 to €1.00

Outcome B

Investor A sees that the price to sell EUR/GBP is now £0.76 and decides to sell her euros to Investor C for £76,000 before the rate slides any lower, making a loss of £3,000. She still has to pay commission to the broker even though she lost money on the trade.

10%
drop in value of UK£ against US$ the morning after Brexit vote

✓ NEED TO KNOW

❯ **Currency pair** Two currencies that are being traded—for example US dollar and the euro.

❯ **Spread** The difference between the price at which one of a currency pair is sold, and the price at which it can be bought; spreads change depending on the liquidity of the markets and the demand for the currencies being traded.

❯ **Leverage** The option for individuals to trade higher values of currency than the cash in their forex account would cover.

❯ **Stop loss** An order placed with a broker to sell currency once it reaches a certain price, to limit the losses investors experience when the market moves against them.

❯ **Margin call** A request from a forex broker for an investor to increase their deposit, as the value of their investment has fallen below a certain point.

Primary and secondary markets

In order for shares to be bought and sold, there needs to be a market where they can be traded. There are different types of markets, depending on the type of share and the size of the trade.

Primary market

A private company may decide to issue shares because it needs money to expand and grow, and it wants access to a wide pool of potential investors. The company sells (or "floats") these new shares in the primary market in an Initial Public Offering (IPO). A company that is preparing to float will use the services of several investment banks to gauge and gather support for the sale of its shares from institutional and private investors before setting a price. The shares are then sold to the public and institutional investors by the company using the services of a specialty broker.

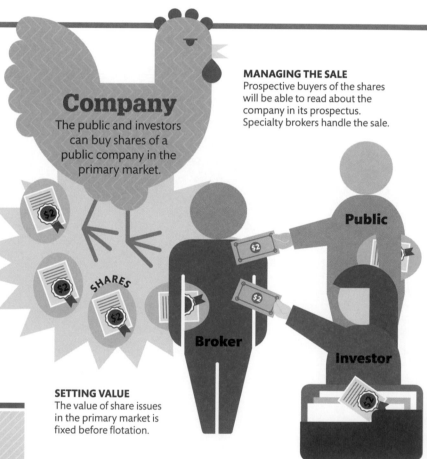

Company
The public and investors can buy shares of a public company in the primary market.

SHARES

Broker

MANAGING THE SALE
Prospective buyers of the shares will be able to read about the company in its prospectus. Specialty brokers handle the sale.

Public

Investor

SETTING VALUE
The value of share issues in the primary market is fixed before flotation.

⚠ WARNING

There must be a secondary market for selling on shares bought in the primary market. If no one is interested in buying them, or there is no place to trade them, the market for them becomes illiquid. Investment scams often involve investors being sold securities that cannot be sold on in a secondary market because they are not listed on the exchanges or have no intrinsic value or potential. A share is only tradeable when other investors want to buy or sell it.

802 billion
The number of shares traded on the NYSE in 2008

How it works

The primary market is where new shares are created and first issued, whereas the secondary market is where shares that have already been issued are traded between investors. When a company is preparing to float on the primary market, investment banks will set a price at which the new shares will be offered. They may also underwrite the Initial Public Offering (IPO) and guarantee to take on unsold shares. The issue price is fixed, but shares may be resold at a different price on the stock exchange (in the secondary market) from the first day of issue.

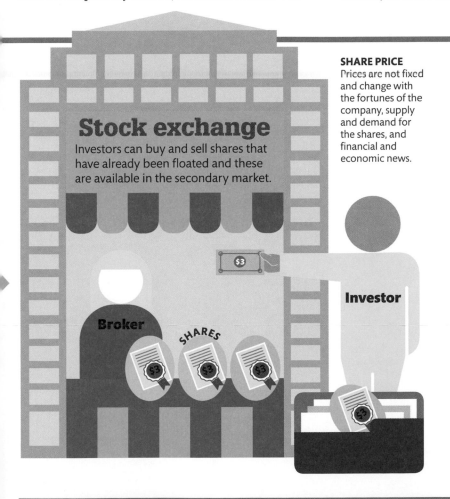

Stock exchange
Investors can buy and sell shares that have already been floated and these are available in the secondary market.

Broker

SHARES

$3

Investor

SHARE PRICE
Prices are not fixed and change with the fortunes of the company, supply and demand for the shares, and financial and economic news.

Secondary market

When investors talk about shares being bought and sold, they are usually talking about transactions taking place in the secondary market. This is where shares are traded between investors. Trading is facilitated by brokers or dealers who take commission on trades. Dealers also earn profit on the spread, or difference, between the price at which they buy and sell shares. These dealers are known as market makers and maintain liquidity by offering a buy and sell price at which they will accept trades. The secondary market includes the London Stock Exchange, New York Stock Exchange, the Nasdaq, and other stock exchanges in countries around the world.

THIRD AND FOURTH MARKETS

Institutional investors such as pension funds or hedge funds tend to trade stocks and shares in significant volumes. The third and fourth markets cater to these higher-volume trades. The third market operates between large investors and broker-dealers. The fourth market caters to large investors who buy and sell shares to each other. The cost of trades tends to be lower than in primary and secondary markets because there are no brokers' commissions. Although the stock may be listed on the main stock exchanges, the trades that take place are not put through them, and large trades can be made anonymously.

Predicting market changes

Being able to predict what might happen in the stock market is extremely useful to investors looking to profit from buying financial assets.

How it works

Investors use analysis to try to understand where a company, share, or stock market might be heading. They want to determine whether it is likely to increase in value or whether there are factors that signal an impending fall in price or downward cycle. Investors also need to know how markets and economies are behaving, and how that behavior is likely to affect the performance of other sectors or companies, before deciding to buy shares of companies that they think will do well in the hope of achieving capital growth.

However, prediction techniques are far from foolproof and there is no statistically significant evidence to show that correct predictions are based on anything other than luck.

Predicting the stock market

Accurate market analysis and forecasting can help investors buy or sell shares at the right time, invest in the right sectors or geographical regions, and limit their shares' downside while maximizing their potential profit.

Professional traders have developed ways to evaluate the future direction of a company, share, or index. Two approaches are often used: technical analysis and fundamental analysis.

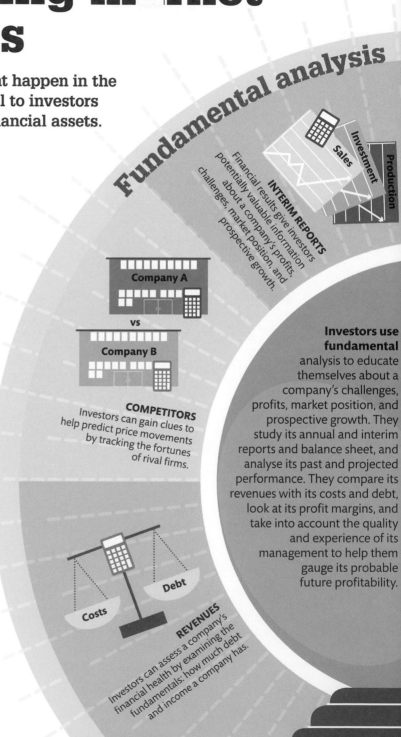

Fundamental analysis

INTERIM REPORTS
Financial results give investors potentially valuable information about a company's profits, challenges, market position, and prospective growth.

Company A

vs

Company B

COMPETITORS
Investors can gain clues to help predict price movements by tracking the fortunes of rival firms.

REVENUES
Investors can assess a company's financial health by examining the fundamentals: how much debt and income a company has.

Debt

Costs

Investors use fundamental analysis to educate themselves about a company's challenges, profits, market position, and prospective growth. They study its annual and interim reports and balance sheet, and analyse its past and projected performance. They compare its revenues with its costs and debt, look at its profit margins, and take into account the quality and experience of its management to help them gauge its probable future profitability.

Investment

Sales

Production

Technical analysis

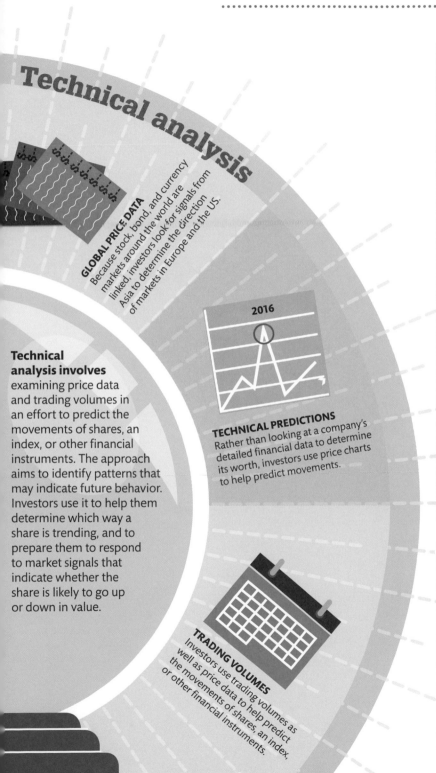

GLOBAL PRICE DATA
Because stock, bond, and currency markets around the world are linked, investors look for signals from Asia to determine the direction of markets in Europe and the US.

Technical analysis involves examining price data and trading volumes in an effort to predict the movements of shares, an index, or other financial instruments. The approach aims to identify patterns that may indicate future behavior. Investors use it to help them determine which way a share is trending, and to prepare them to respond to market signals that indicate whether the share is likely to go up or down in value.

2016

TECHNICAL PREDICTIONS
Rather than looking at a company's detailed financial data to determine its worth, investors use price charts to help predict movements.

TRADING VOLUMES
Investors use trading volumes as well as price data to help predict the movements of shares, an index, or other financial instruments.

GLOBAL DATA ANALYSIS

Asian markets open up to 8 hours ahead of European and US markets due to the time difference. Because stock, bond, and currency markets around the world are intimately linked, what happens on the Asian markets can affect markets in the Eurozone, UK, or US, and have a bearing on opening prices when these markets begin trading later in the day. For this reason, investors often look for signals from Asia to determine the likely direction of other markets.

✓ NEED TO KNOW

❱ **Hedging** A strategy that involves investors buying shares they think are likely to rise in price while also selling shares they think will fall, in order to maintain a market-neutral position.

❱ **Technical analysis** Research aimed at identifying patterns that indicate if a share is trending up or down.

❱ **Fundamental analysis** An assessment of revenues, costs, debt, profit margins, and management.

 Arbitrage

When there are price differences between two similar assets being traded on different exchanges across the world, traders may seek to take advantage of the discrepancy in order to make a profit. This practice is known as arbitrage.

Transatlantic trades

When a company is listed on both the UK and US exchanges, arbitrage may be possible. For example, if a trader can buy shares in Company A on the US exchange for $2.99 each and sell them on the UK exchange for £2.30 each, which was equal to $3.01, the trader will make a profit of $0.02 per share. In practice, arbitrage works by exploiting small price differences such as these at high volumes, using computer programs to trade almost instantaneously. These trades take place so quickly that the biggest profits are made by the organizations with the fastest computers.

HIGH-FREQUENCY TRADERS (HFT)

Computing power enables HFT to search the markets for tiny anomalies to exploit. A computer program automatically evaluates and carries out a large number of trades at high speeds—faster than any person could do. It is possible to make a lot of money from very small price differences in this way.

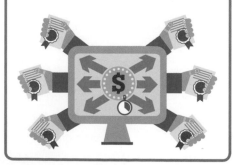

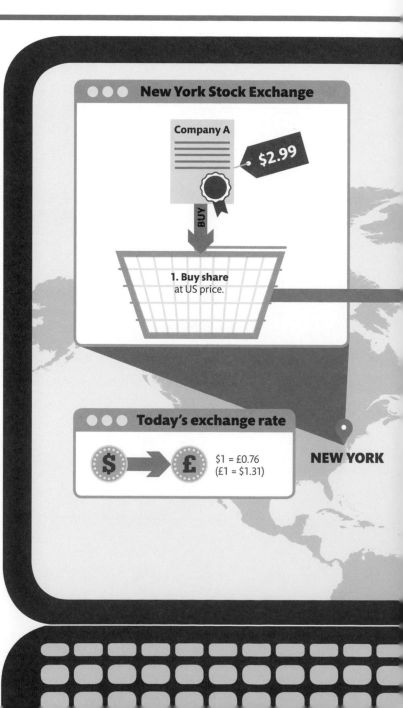

New York Stock Exchange

Company A
$2.99
BUY

1. Buy share at US price.

Today's exchange rate

$1 = £0.76
(£1 = $1.31)

NEW YORK

How it works

Arbitrage is the practice of buying a tradeable asset in one market and almost simultaneously selling it at a higher price in a different market. Conversely, it is also the practice of selling an asset in one market and buying it for a cheaper price in another. Arbitrage, as currently practiced in stock and bond markets, is only possible due to the computing power now available, so large volumes of transactions can exploit small differences in prices within milliseconds.

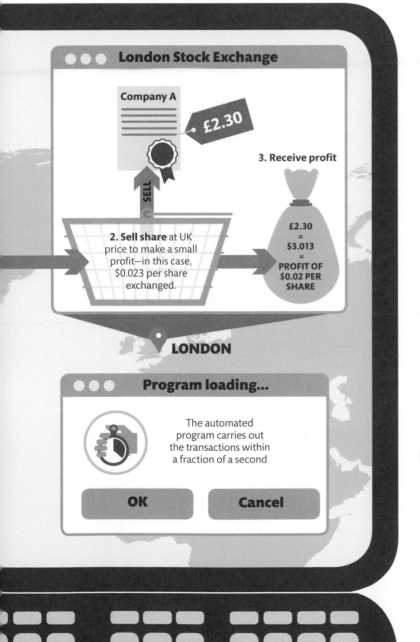

London Stock Exchange

Company A

£2.30

SELL

3. Receive profit

2. Sell share at UK price to make a small profit—in this case, $0.023 per share exchanged.

£2.30
=
$3.013
=
PROFIT OF
$0.02 PER
SHARE

LONDON

Program loading...

The automated program carries out the transactions within a fraction of a second

OK   Cancel

WHEN ARBITRAGE GOES WRONG

In 1998, hedge fund Long-Term Capital Management (LTCM) lost $4.6 billion as a result of arbitrage trades in bonds that went wrong.

The price difference between the bonds being traded was relatively small, so in order to make a profit LTCM had to carry out large volumes of trades. These trades were also highly leveraged using billions of dollars borrowed from other financial companies.

This high leverage and the 1998 Russian financial crisis prompted investors to move their capital to less risky investments. LTCM sustained huge losses and was in danger of defaulting on its loans. The US government had to intervene in order to prevent a collapse of the debt markets and damage to the global economy.

60%
of US equity trading was estimated to be High-Frequency Trading at its height in 2009

Manipulating the stock market

Stock market manipulation can take many forms—such as artificially fixing prices higher or lower—with the aim of interfering with the market for personal gain.

How it works

A trader can manipulate the market by processing a lot of small sell orders in an attempt to drive down the price of a share. This can cause other shareholders to panic and sell their shares, sending the price down even further.

Conversely, a lot of small buy orders may push up a share price to convince other investors that good news is about to be announced. Market manipulation is highly unethical but not always illegal.

Pushing share prices down

- **Large volumes** If a large investor sells off its stock, prices may fall because of an increase in supply. That same investor can then buy the stock back later at a lower price, having locked in profits at the higher price.

- **Short selling** Rogue traders borrow shares that are sold at a high price, then manipulate the price down so that they can buy the shares back at a lower price to return to the original owner.

- **Bad news** If a company issues a profits warning, or a negative report, shares may fall in price.

TRADER

PUSHING SHARE PRICES DOWN

SELL!

SELL NOW

THE MARKET

WARNING

Posting negative or positive information
Investors often like to discuss shares they own
or are thinking of buying with other like-minded
individuals on bulletin boards and investment
forums. These can be a good source of
investment ideas but they can also be used by
unscrupulous traders who post negative or
positive information to inflate or deflate prices.

PUSHING SHARE PRICES UP

BUY!

GO FOR GOLD

THE LIBOR SCANDAL

Manipulation can affect other
areas of the market as well. A
recent example is the Libor rigging
scandal. Libor is a benchmark rate
that banks charge each other for
short-term loans and is regarded
as an important measure of trust
between major global banks.
The scandal involved traders at
10 firms, which the UK's Serious
Fraud Office alleged had conspired
to manipulate the Libor benchmark
between 2006 and 2010 in order
to keep it artificially low.

Pushing share prices up

> **Stock liquidity** In less liquid
  stocks, a relatively small number
  of buy orders can move the price
  up. This makes it easier to
  exaggerate price movements
  through manipulative trades such
  as "pump and dump," where a
  rogue trader encourages investors
  to buy shares, pushing the price
  up so they can then sell their own
  shares at a high price.

> **Good news** Posting positive
  information about a company
  or stock on a bulletin board or
  in an investor chat room can
  encourage other investors to buy.

Day trading

Day trading is the buying and selling of shares, currency, or other financial instruments in a single day. The intention is to profit from small price fluctuations—sometimes traders hold shares for only a few minutes.

How it works

Investors typically buy or sell a share based on their analysis of economic or market trends, research into specific companies, or as part of a strategy to benefit from the regular dividends that companies issue. Unlike such investors, day traders look for small movements in prices that they can exploit to make a quick profit. They may hold shares only momentarily, buying at one price and selling when the price rises by a few cents, perhaps only minutes later. Day traders make profits by trading large volumes of shares in one transaction, or by making multiple trades during the course of the day. They buy (or sell) shares and then sell (or buy) them again before payment becomes due, and usually "close out" all trades (selling the shares they have bought, and vice versa) at the end of the day to protect themselves from off-hours movements in the market. This is different from long-term investing, in which assets are held for longer periods in order to generate capital growth or income.

Liquid shares

Day traders favor shares that are liquid—those that are easy to buy and sell in the secondary market.

At market opening, a day trader looks at the price of BigBank shares, knowing that the bank has just reported increased profits.

BigBank

PROFITS UP

The trader buys 10,000 shares at $490, expecting that the price will continue to rise.

$490
$490
$490
$490

Quantity
10,000

! WARNING

> **High risk** Day traders typically suffer severe losses in their first months of trading, and many never graduate to profit-making status.

> **Stress** Day traders must watch the market nonstop during the day, concentrating on dozens of fluctuating indicators in the hope of spotting market trends.

> **Expense** Day traders pay large sums in commissions, for training, and for computers.

✓ NEED TO KNOW

> **Scalping** A strategy in which traders hold their share or financial asset (known as their "position") for just a few minutes or even seconds.

> **Margin trading** A method of buying shares that involves the day trader borrowing a part of the sum needed from the broker who is executing the transaction.

> **Bid–offer spread** The difference between a price at which a share is sold, and that at which it is bought.

> **Market data** The current trading information for each day-trading market. Rather than using market data that is available free of charge but can be up to an hour old, day traders pay a premium for access to real-time data. Day traders must be able to trade on news or announcements quickly, so they need to watch the market and stay close to their trading screens at all times.

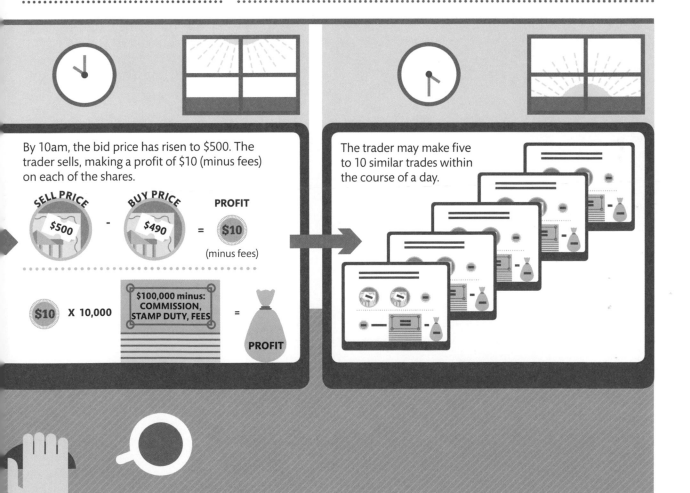

By 10am, the bid price has risen to $500. The trader sells, making a profit of $10 (minus fees) on each of the shares.

SELL PRICE **$500** - BUY PRICE **$490** = PROFIT **$10** (minus fees)

$10 X 10,000 $100,000 minus: COMMISSION, STAMP DUTY, FEES = PROFIT

The trader may make five to 10 similar trades within the course of a day.

Financial institutions

Around the globe, money moves between banks, businesses, governments, organizations, and individuals, crossing time zones, continents, and cultures. At the heart of the global financial systems are the banks, hedge funds, pension funds, and insurance companies that hold and invest the world's money. Without the liquidity that banks provide, organizations and individuals would find it hard to borrow or save money, invest in existing businesses, or start up new businesses.

Services and fees

Financial institutions make money primarily by lending out cash at a higher interest rate than the one they are paying to their depositors. They also make money by investing the cash entrusted to them by customers, and by buying and selling assets for clients and charging a fee for this service. They lose money when debts are not repaid, or only partially repaid, or in the event that they make the wrong investment decision.

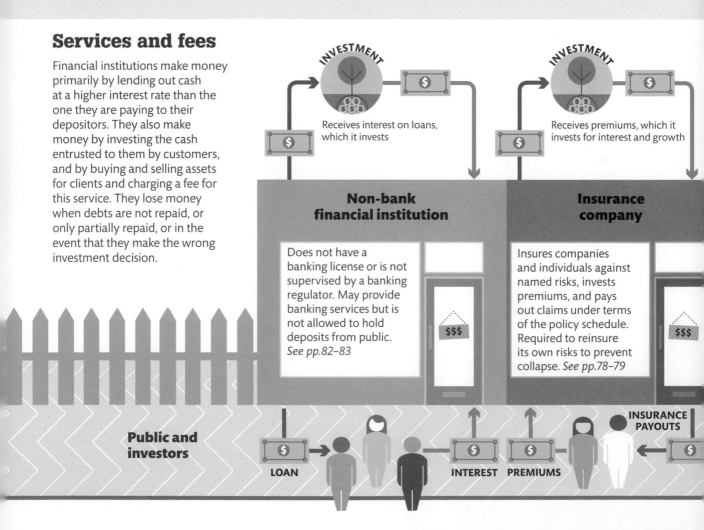

INVESTMENT

Receives interest on loans, which it invests

INVESTMENT

Receives premiums, which it invests for interest and growth

Non-bank financial institution

Does not have a banking license or is not supervised by a banking regulator. May provide banking services but is not allowed to hold deposits from public. *See pp.82–83*

$$$

Insurance company

Insures companies and individuals against named risks, invests premiums, and pays out claims under terms of the policy schedule. Required to reinsure its own risks to prevent collapse. *See pp.78–79*

$$$

Public and investors

LOAN

INTEREST   PREMIUMS

INSURANCE PAYOUTS

INTERRELATED INSTITUTIONS

The worldwide markets are all interconnected and rely on each other. A shock in one market can have an adverse effect in another.

❯ **When Greece was renegotiating** its debt write-off the European stock markets were negatively affected, especially when it seemed as if Greece might leave the euro.

❯ **Fears that the Chinese economy** was slowing down fed into fears about global market growth.

❯ **The result of the Brexit** vote in 2016 led to a sharp drop in the value of the pound.

$639 billion
value of Lehman Brothers investment bank when it filed for bankruptcy in 2008

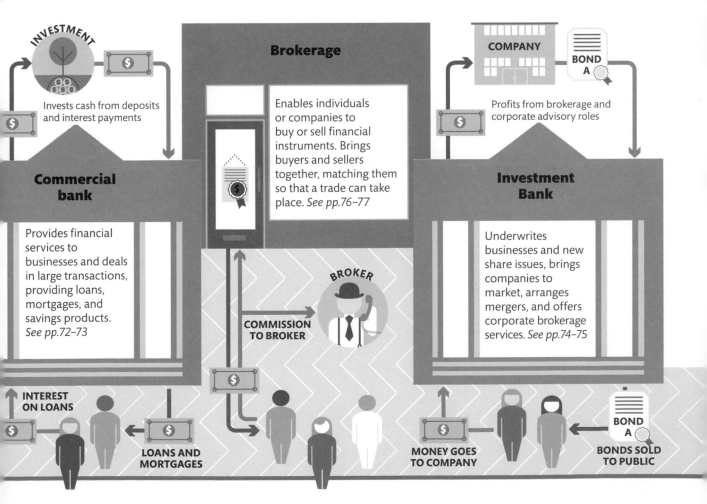

INVESTMENT

Invests cash from deposits and interest payments

Commercial bank

Provides financial services to businesses and deals in large transactions, providing loans, mortgages, and savings products. *See pp.72–73*

Brokerage

Enables individuals or companies to buy or sell financial instruments. Brings buyers and sellers together, matching them so that a trade can take place. *See pp.76–77*

BROKER

COMMISSION TO BROKER

COMPANY

BOND A

Profits from brokerage and corporate advisory roles

Investment Bank

Underwrites businesses and new share issues, brings companies to market, arranges mergers, and offers corporate brokerage services. *See pp.74–75*

INTEREST ON LOANS

LOANS AND MORTGAGES

MONEY GOES TO COMPANY

BOND A

BONDS SOLD TO PUBLIC

Commercial and mortgage banks

Banks make money by lending out money and charging interest on it. They also pay interest—at a lower rate—on deposits that they hold from savers. To remain solvent, banks must maintain a balance between the two.

How it works

Banks need to continually make money in order to pay costs and expenses, make profits, maintain or increase their market share, and make regular dividend payments to shareholders.

Commercial banks provide loans to individuals and sell products to customers including loans, savings accounts, credit cards, overdrafts, and mortgages for prospective home buyers.

Commercial banks advise and lend to businesses, to retail or small-business customers, to business start-ups that need capital to grow, and to large businesses that need multimillion dollar funding for major projects.

Banks can vary the rates they offer to customers in order to boost demand for their products. They do this either because central bank interest rates have been raised or lowered, or because they want to undercut competitors and increase their market share. For example, in order to attract customers, one bank might offer a mortgage loan at a rate lower than that offered by its competitors.

A fine balance

The banking business is constantly in flux, but banks must protect themselves against a sudden significant outflow of savers' money. If this happened it could lead to a run on the bank, which might in turn cause the bank to collapse. In order to guard against this, banks keep capital reserves and offer competitive savings rates in notice accounts. Notice, usually of between 30 and 180 days, has to be given before money can be withdrawn from such accounts.

PROFITABLE INTEREST RATES

Banks constantly adjust the interest rates they charge on debt and the interest they pay on savings and current account balances, depending on market factors and their business objectives. To make a profit, a bank needs to lend money at a higher rate than it pays on the savings and deposit accounts it offers. In the example on the right, the bank pays savers and deposit holders 2% on the money they hold with it. At the same time the bank charges mortgage borrowers 5%, enabling it to achieve an overall profit margin of 3%.

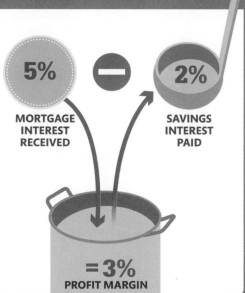

5% MORTGAGE INTEREST RECEIVED − 2% SAVINGS INTEREST PAID

= 3% PROFIT MARGIN

10% capital reserve requirement of largest US banks

INTEREST PAID ON MORTGAGES

Making money

Banks make money from loans by charging interest, from current accounts by charging fees and overdraft penalties, and from business accounts through transaction charges.

Attracting new customers

It is cheaper and easier for banks to sell products to existing customers—a practice known as cross-selling—since they know more about those customers' individual financial circumstances.

INTEREST PAID ON LOANS

INTEREST RATES ON SAVINGS ACCOUNTS

DIVIDENDS TO SHAREHOLDERS

OVERDRAFT CHARGES

MONTHLY OR ANNUAL FEES ON SAVINGS ACCOUNTS

Paying money

Banks pay interest on savings accounts, and usually on credit balances in current accounts. They also pay dividends to shareholders out of their profits.

CHARGES FOR TRANSACTIONS ON BUSINESS ACCOUNTS

Capital reserve

A sum of money that a bank is not permitted to lend or invest. Banks keep capital reserves to protect themselves from mass withdrawals by customers or heavy losses from bad loans. The reserves are typically a fraction of deposits.

ANNUAL FEES AND MONTHLY CHARGES ON CREDIT CARDS

Bank

Investment banks

An investment bank offers distinct financial services, dealing with larger and more complicated financial deals than retail banks.

How it works

Investment banks work with large companies, other financial institutions such as investment houses, insurance companies, pension funds, hedge funds, governments, and individuals who are very wealthy and have private funds to invest.

Investment banks have two distinct roles. The first is corporate advising, meaning that they help companies take part in mergers and acquisitions, create financial products to sell, and bring new companies to market. The second is the brokerage division where trading and market-making—in which the investment bank provides mediation between those who want to buy shares and those who want to sell—take place. The two are supposed to be separate and distinct, so within an investment bank there is a so-called "wall" between these divisions to prevent conflict of interest.

Areas of business

While the brokerage and corporate advising divisions of an investment bank are theoretically distinct, there is inevitably overlap between the two areas of, for example, market-making and underwriting new share issues, or mergers and acquisitions advising and research.

> ## ❗ WARNING
>
> > **Although investment banks** help to keep money moving around the world, if they run into difficulties it can affect cash flow across geographical boundaries.
>
> > **Investment banks** are exposed both to the inherent risks in the assets that they hold, and also the risk that other financial companies with which they are connected might fail. This is called counterparty risk.

Brokerage

Proprietary trading

Investment banks have their own funds, and they can both invest and trade their own money, subject to certain conditions.

Acting as a broker

Banks can match investors who want to buy shares with companies wanting to sell them, in order to create a market for those shares (known as market-making).

Research

Analysts look at economic and market trends, make buy or sell recommendations, issue research notes, and provide advice on investment to high net-worth and corporate clients.

Corporate advising

Bringing companies to market

Investment banks can raise funds for new issues, underwriting Initial Public Offerings (IPOs) in exchange for a cut of the funds they raised.

Bringing companies together

Banks facilitate mergers and acquisitions (M&A) by advising on the value of companies, the best way to proceed, and how to raise capital.

Structuring products

Clients who want to sell a financial product to the public may bring in an investment bank to design it and target the retail or commercial banking market.

✓ NEED TO KNOW

❯ **Initial Public Offering (IPO)** When a private company first issues shares to investors and becomes a public limited company.

❯ **Underwriting** The covering of a potential risk—in return for a fee or percentage.

❯ **Guarantees** The commitment that, in a new share issue, shares will be sold for a minimum price. If the new issue is not popular, the bank may be left holding the shares on its books and may have to sell them at a loss in the future; if the new shares are in demand and the open market price rises above the issue price, the bank will make a profit.

HOW BANKS MAKE AND LOSE MONEY

Making money

❯ Banks receive fees in return for providing advice, underwriting services, loans and guarantees, brokerage services, and research and analysis.

❯ They also receive dividends from investments they hold, interest from loans, and charge a margin on financial transactions they facilitate.

Losing money

❯ The advising division may end up holding unwanted shares if the take-up of an IPO is lower than expected.

❯ The trading division of a bank may make the wrong decisions and end up losing the bank money.

❯ In a year of little corporate activity, banks may have to rely on trading profits to bolster their returns.

❯ Banks may create financial products which they fail to sell on to other investors, leaving them holding loss-making securities or loans—as in the run-up to the 2007–2008 financial crisis.

Brokerages

A broker is the middleman who brings buyers and sellers of stocks and other securities together, and acts as an intermediary for trades.

How it works

A brokerage firm enables individuals or companies to buy or sell financial instruments. Traditionally, brokerages research markets, make recommendations to buy or sell securities, and facilitate those transactions for clients. A stockbroker then makes the trade in the market on behalf of the client, for a commission. Larger institutional trades are still often done in this way, with a broker being instructed to buy or sell a large amount of stock on behalf of a client.

With the advent of the internet, discount and online brokers have automated this process for the wider retail market (private investors), dispensing with the need for stockbrokers to place trades by phone or in person. Online brokers enable retail clients to trade financial securities instantly via an online trading platform, but these brokerage companies may not give advice or provide research. This allows them to offer a much cheaper execution-only service.

Brokerages may also make money by charging fees for managing clients' portfolios and executing trades for them. This is known as a discretionary service, and may involve transaction fees and a management fee taken as a percentage of the value of the client's portfolio.

The broker's role

When an investor wishes to sell some of their shares, they first contact their broker and ask them to quote a price. The broker checks the market and tells them the bid price at which the share is trading—that is, the price at which the broker is willing to buy from a client. It is generally lower than the offer price at which the broker is willing to sell to a client. The difference in price is known as the bid–offer spread, and it is how brokers make money on their deals. Prices can change within seconds on busy trading days for certain assets. The seller then specifies whether they want to go ahead at that price, wait, or sell "at best," which is whatever price the broker can secure for them in the market at the current time. The broker then proceeds to carry out the trade on the investor's behalf.

WHY THE BID–OFFER SPREAD MATTERS

It is important to be aware of the bid–offer spread when trading securities or other financial products. This is the difference between the buying and selling price of a security. For example, one investor wants to buy shares and is given a price—the offer price—of $210. Another investor wants to sell and is quoted a sell, or bid price, of $208. The $2 difference is the bid–offer spread. Securities that are frequently traded, for example those listed on the S&P 500 index of leading shares, tend to have smaller spreads and are called "liquid" because it is easy to find a buyer or seller for them. Those traded less frequently—for example the shares of smaller companies—may have a bigger spread and are therefore less liquid. Liquidity is generally defined by "normal market size," which is the number of shares for which a retail investor should be able to receive an immediate quote.

1994 year the first online broker launched

Sells for $400

x100

$

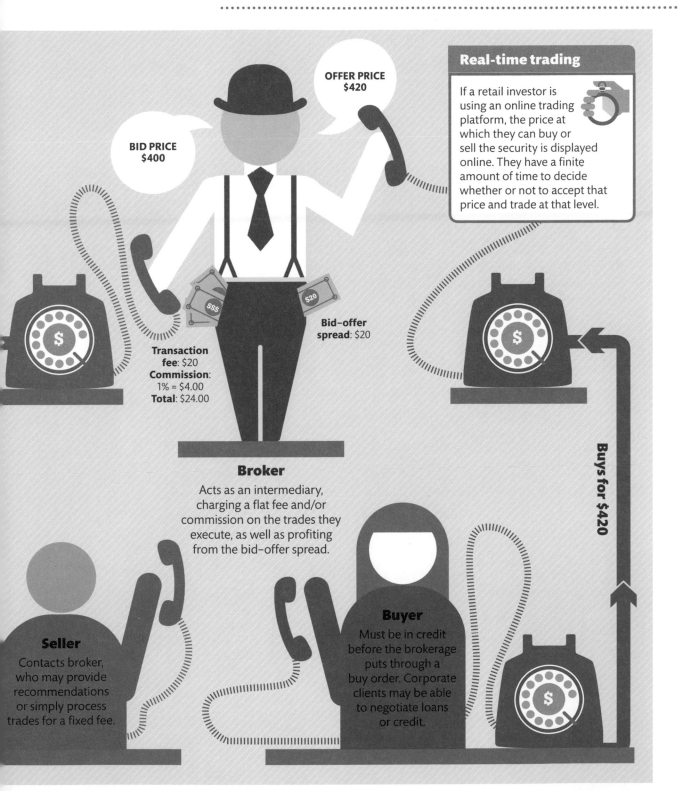

OFFER PRICE
$420

BID PRICE
$400

Real-time trading

If a retail investor is using an online trading platform, the price at which they can buy or sell the security is displayed online. They have a finite amount of time to decide whether or not to accept that price and trade at that level.

Bid–offer spread: $20

Transaction fee: $20
Commission: 1% = $4.00
Total: $24.00

Broker

Acts as an intermediary, charging a flat fee and/or commission on the trades they execute, as well as profiting from the bid–offer spread.

Buys for $420

Seller

Contacts broker, who may provide recommendations or simply process trades for a fixed fee.

Buyer

Must be in credit before the brokerage puts through a buy order. Corporate clients may be able to negotiate loans or credit.

Insurance risk and regulation

Insurance is in essence a form of risk management, by which individuals and other entities pay a fee to transfer a potential financial loss to an insurer in exchange for compensation if the loss occurs.

How it works

Insurance mitigates risks that can be quantified and anticipated as potentially or possibly likely to happen. All types of insurance—life, home, corporate, business, and motor—work in the same way, by pooling risk.

Without insurance, individuals would be exposed to unexpected events leading to financial hardship, such as premature death, accidents, fire, and theft. Businesses would be vulnerable to closure, governments to bankruptcy, and companies unable to grow and develop.

Insurance companies take on the risks of individuals, companies, and governments in exchange for a fee, or premium, which represents a small proportion of the value of the risk they have agreed to cover.

Premiums are based on the insurer's past experience, known as claims history, with regard to that particular risk, and also an assessment of the client's risk as an individual or business.

Relatively small premiums paid by a large group of people are used to fund the payouts required when a small number of those customers make a claim.

Insuring a business

If a business wants to insure against the risk of adverse events, such as a fire destroying its premises, it pays a premium to an insurance company, which promises to pay out a certain amount of money should an adverse event happen. The circumstances on which the insurance company will pay out are listed in the contract between the business and the insurance company, known as the policy schedule. The premium gives cover for all the risks specified in the policy schedule. Risks that are not covered are classed as "exclusions."

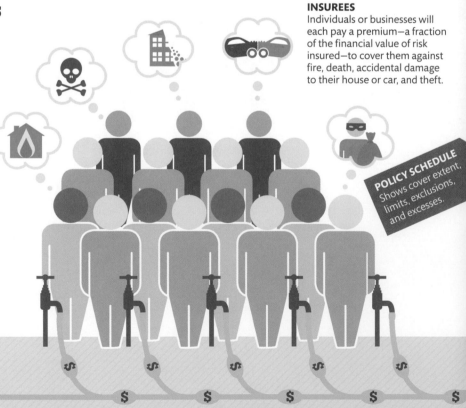

INSUREES
Individuals or businesses will each pay a premium—a fraction of the financial value of risk insured—to cover them against fire, death, accidental damage to their house or car, and theft.

POLICY SCHEDULE
Shows cover extent, limits, exclusions, and excesses.

REGULATION

It is important for the insurance industry to be well regulated in order for it to work properly.

Regulators monitor the insurance industry to make sure that insurers can pay claims made by insurees. They require insurance companies to buy their own insurance—called reinsurance—to ensure they can meet their financial liabilities in full.

This covers the insurance companies' own risks so that if, for example, they have a lot of claims at once, or if one client has a huge and unexpected loss, they can afford to pay without experiencing financial difficulties.

✓ NEED TO KNOW

> **Premium** The amount of money an insurance company charges to provide the cover described in the policy or bond.

> **Excess** The financial contribution the customer must bear on an insurance premium.

> **Surplus** Insurance companies are required to hold a surplus in reserve.

> **Profit** The return received by insurers from the growth and interest on their investments, or by selling insurance to customers at the right price, or by having few claims.

> **Loss** A result of not charging enough in premiums, a fall in the price of investments, or by having large claims to pay out to customers.

> **Investment portfolio** A collection of assets bought with the money insurance companies receive from premiums. Portfolios make money from interest, dividends, and capital gains on trade stocks.

> **Investment income** The income an insurance company receives from the investment of premiums and reserves.

> **Policy** The contract between an insurance company and its customer.

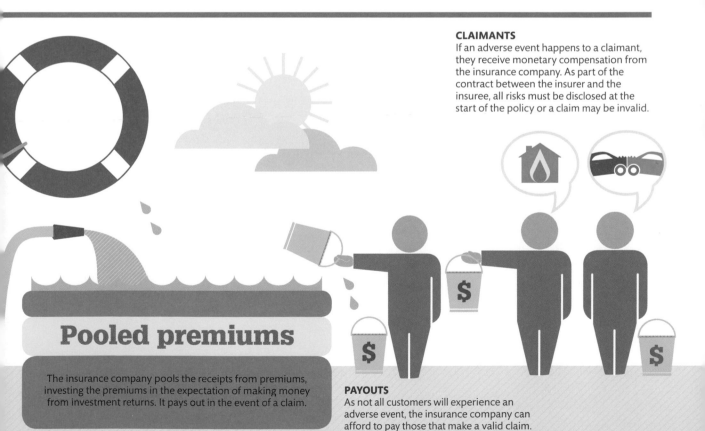

CLAIMANTS
If an adverse event happens to a claimant, they receive monetary compensation from the insurance company. As part of the contract between the insurer and the insuree, all risks must be disclosed at the start of the policy or a claim may be invalid.

Pooled premiums

The insurance company pools the receipts from premiums, investing the premiums in the expectation of making money from investment returns. It pays out in the event of a claim.

PAYOUTS
As not all customers will experience an adverse event, the insurance company can afford to pay those that make a valid claim.

Investment companies

Investment companies buy and sell equities, bonds, and other financial assets on behalf of their clients, and with their clients' cash. Investors buy a stake in a fund and their money is pooled to buy a range of assets.

Investment companies and diversification

Diversified investment companies invest in a wide range of assets and in various securities (cash, bonds, and stocks) within each kind of asset, whereas non-diversified companies invest in a single industry or asset. A diversified portfolio will spread risk, and limit the impact of any market volatility.

INVESTORS' INPUT

FUND MANAGER'S FEE

Investment fund

A fund manager's objective is to create capital growth, or income, or both, for their shareholders and investors. They assess and adjust investments as required.

If the property market is expected to do well, the fund manager might create a portfolio with more exposure to it. Holding an excess amount of a particular security is known as being "overweight."

A fund manager will buy commodities—income-producing assets like gold, natural gas, or beef not usually traded alongside bonds and equities. Investing in them can be a good way of diversifying a portfolio.

Property

Commodities

How it works

Investment companies pool investors' funds to invest in different businesses and assets, potentially giving clients access to markets they could not afford to invest in alone. Fund managers analyze the market, deciding when to buy, sell, or hold. They respond to economic and world news, and try to anticipate movements in global stock markets to make money for clients.

5% the maximum amount of total assets a diversified investment company can hold in a single security according to US law

The fund manager aims to spread risk while creating returns. Fixed income from interest payments is provided by bonds that form part of the investors' portfolio.

Shares are selected by company, country, or sector. The fund may be an income fund that pays out dividends on shares, or a capital growth fund, which aims to grow the original sum invested.

AMOUNT RETURNED TO INVESTORS

Return

The income and growth from a fund is known as the return. This is the net amount after dealing costs, fund management fees, and other costs are deducted. These are charged to the fund, regardless of whether or not the underlying asset value has fallen.

REINVESTED IN FUND

Nonbank financial institutions

A nonbank financial institution (NBFI) is an organization that does not have a banking license, or is not supervised by a banking regulator. It may provide banking services, but cannot hold deposits from the public.

As a consequence of the financial crisis of 2008–2009, regulatory authorities have been reconsidering their approach to financial supervision. In the UK, banks are now required to be more stringent about their lending criteria and to hold higher levels of reserve cash. They are also required to conduct credit checks on their borrowers. In meeting these requirements, traditional banks have tended to reduce the number of customers on their books who are at a medium or high risk of not being able to pay back their loan or mortgage. Increasingly, nonbank lenders have moved into the space that has been vacated by the banks.

Types of NBFI and their business areas

In the last few years, the number of NBFI companies has greatly increased. NBFIs are not subject to the tougher criteria that traditional banks must meet when they lend to individuals or businesses, and may also offer lower interest rates and larger amounts of credit than banks are allowed to provide. There are numerous types of NBFI.

Commercial loan providers

These provide funding to businesses but may not accept deposits from the public, and they are not allowed to provide overdrafts. Their lending criteria may be less stringent than that of a bank. Their services are not aimed at individuals.

Peer-to-peer lenders

These lenders act as middlemen, uniting lenders with borrowers. The idea is that each will receive a better rate—lenders receive more interest than they would on a bank savings account, while borrowers will often pay less interest than they would on a bank loan.

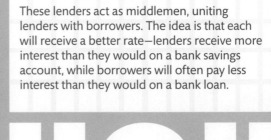

OTHER TYPES OF NBFI

The kinds of NBFI available will vary from country to country.

CREDIT UNIONS
These are member-owned, financial cooperatives that are nonprofit and supported by an affiliated group.

SAVINGS AND LOAN ASSOCIATIONS
Accepts savings deposits and the funds are used to make mortgages and other loans.

SPECIALTY LENDERS
Able to charge high rates of interest, they may target those with poor credit ratings or with court orders against them.

PAWNBROKERS
These offer secured loans to people who put up an asset, such as a car or jewelry, as collateral on the debt.

! WARNING

NBFIs are not accompanied by the same guarantees and protections that are built into products and companies regulated by the government watchdog, the Federal Reserve System, in the US. For the borrower, terms and conditions may be less favorable, while lenders may find it difficult to establish the creditworthiness of those to whom they are lending.

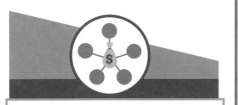

Crowdfunding

This is an emerging means of raising capital in which small projects or businesses can seek investment from individuals, bypassing traditional finance sources. Crowdfunding platforms allow investors to spread risk between projects, though there is a chance the investment will fail.

42% of consumers have used NBFIs in the last 12 months

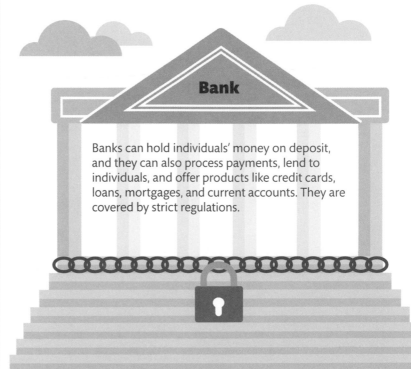

Bank

Banks can hold individuals' money on deposit, and they can also process payments, lend to individuals, and offer products like credit cards, loans, mortgages, and current accounts. They are covered by strict regulations.

GOVERNMENT FINANCE AND PUBLIC MONEY

> The money supply > Managing state finance
> Attempting control > Why governments fail financially

The money supply

The money supply is the total amount of money in the economy at a given time. The government monitors this supply, because of its impact on economic activity and on price levels. It may decide to change financial policy to influence the money supply—for example, by raising or lowering the amount that banks must hold in reserve as actual cash. If the money supply is too low, such as during a recession, or a depression, the government may take steps to try and increase it.

How the money supply is measured

Types of money in an economy are classified in "M" groups. The most liquid, or spendable, form of money is called "narrow" money, and include classes M0 and M1. The definition of "broad money" includes other less liquid, less convertible forms. These are classed as M2, M3, and also M4. How these classes are defined, and what they include or exclude, varies from country to country.

"He who controls the money supply of a nation controls the nation"

James Garfield

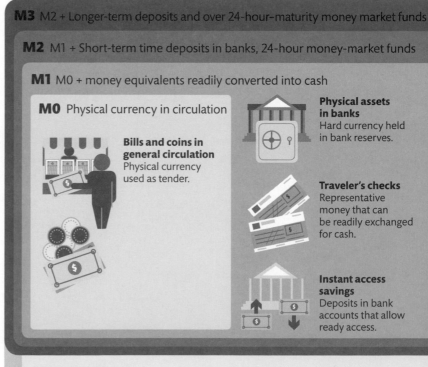

M3 M2 + Longer-term deposits and over 24-hour–maturity money market funds

M2 M1 + Short-term time deposits in banks, 24-hour money-market funds

M1 M0 + money equivalents readily converted into cash

M0 Physical currency in circulation

Bills and coins in general circulation
Physical currency used as tender.

Physical assets in banks
Hard currency held in bank reserves.

Traveler's checks
Representative money that can be readily exchanged for cash.

Instant access savings
Deposits in bank accounts that allow ready access.

Narrow money

M0 and M1 make up the narrow money group. This is money in a form that can be readily used as a medium of exchange, and includes bills, coins, traveler's checks, and some types of bank accounts.

MORE LIQUID

FIAT CURRENCY VS REPRESENTATIVE CURRENCY

Unlike a currency backed by a commodity, such as gold, fiat money does not represent anything, nor can it be redeemed for a set amount of another commodity. The word *fiat* is Latin for "let it be done," and refers to the fact that fiat money is legal tender only because it is backed by a government decree. It has no intrinsic value.

Commodity-backed
Currency used to be backed by gold, which was known as the gold standard.

❯ **Based on a commodity** The value of money is tied to that of a commodity, such as gold.

❯ **Redeemable** Currency is redeemable for an equivalent amount of gold.

❯ **Limited** Money supply is limited by the supply of gold.

Government-backed (fiat)

The state backs paper and digital money—another type of fiat currency (*see pp.88–89*).

❯ **Not based on a commodity** Value is based on faith in the government and economy.

❯ **Not redeemable** Fiat money is not redeemable for anything.

❯ **Unlimited** The government is free to print more if it wishes.

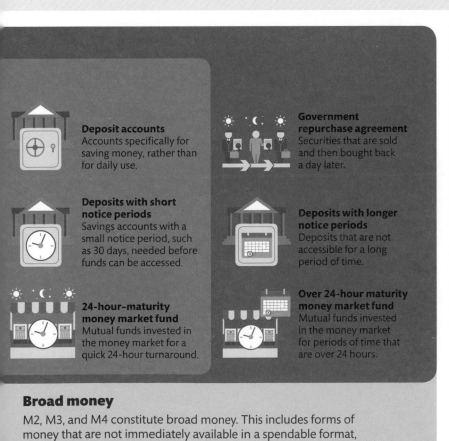

Deposit accounts
Accounts specifically for saving money, rather than for daily use.

Deposits with short notice periods
Savings accounts with a small notice period, such as 30 days, needed before funds can be accessed.

24-hour–maturity money market fund
Mutual funds invested in the money market for a quick 24-hour turnaround.

Government repurchase agreement
Securities that are sold and then bought back a day later.

Deposits with longer notice periods
Deposits that are not accessible for a long period of time.

Over 24-hour maturity money market fund
Mutual funds invested in the money market for periods of time that are over 24 hours.

Broad money

M2, M3, and M4 constitute broad money. This includes forms of money that are not immediately available in a spendable format, and which take time to access.

LESS LIQUID

TAKING THE MEASURE OF THE ECONOMY

The government or the central bank decides which definition of money to use when assessing the money supply. For instance, the US government measures supply by M2, and, since 2006, no longer includes data on M3. Once the data is gathered, the state may decide to make changes to the reserve amount that banks must hold (*see pp.90–91*) or increase the money supply (*see pp.92–95*).

M0

M1

M2

M3

Increasing money circulation

Most of the money in the economy occurs in the form of bank deposits—the appearance of funds in bank accounts. Banks increase money circulation whenever they make loans.

How it works

When a bank decides to give a customer a loan, it will credit their account with the agreed amount. From the moment the loan shows up electronically in that customer's account, they will expect to be able to withdraw it as cash, so the bank must have that cash available in order to be able to hand it over to the customer on demand. Similarly, if the customer wants to use the loan to pay money into a different bank account in a different bank—having for example paid for goods with a debit card—the issuing bank must be able to persuade the second bank to accept the transfer of credit money. Because the issuing bank is liable to meet demands such as these, the deposit money that it has credited to the customer's account is seen as a liability as the bank will have to pay this money out. By contrast, the loan is regarded as an asset for the bank. This is because the bank can expect to recoup the money it has issued as a loan, along with the accrued interest, and it has a legal right to enforce the repayment should the customer refuse to pay. The bank records this transaction using a system of accounting called double entry bookkeeping, which reflects the equal and opposite effects that the issuing of the loan will have on the bank's acconting books (*see right*).

BANK ASSETS AND LIABILITIES

Assets

An asset is something that is owned that can be used to pay debts. Assets usually produce a return over time. A bank's most important asset is its customer loan book, since customers pay interest on loans.

Liabilities

A liability is an obligation that is legally due to be paid. A bank's major liabilities are its customers' bank accounts, since all of its customers expect to be able to withdraw their money at some moment in time.

Balancing the books

Banks increase money circulation when they issue a loan in the form of money deposited in a customer's account. Although the loan and its repayment is an asset, the extra account money is a liability, because if the bank fails to make the money available on demand, it could collapse. To prevent this from occurring, banks maintain tight control of their balance sheets, making sure their liabilities always match their assets. They carefully assess customers who apply for loans to ensure they will be able to make repayments. Central banks (*see pp.100–103*) exist to oversee the whole system and support banks when they face difficulties.

ASSETS

$1.2 trillion
the amount of US currency in circulation

BANK BALANCE SHEET: **LOANS**

Creating credit A balance sheet shows how liabilities are balanced by assets. When a bank makes a loan to a customer, the asset to the bank (the amount of the loan) is balanced exactly by the liability to the bank (the credit deposited in the customer's account).

The balance sheet records assets in one column and liabilities in the other.

Assets	Liabilities
Loan to customer **$1,000**	New money in the customer's account **$1,000**

The value of the loan in the customer's bank account.

The loan to the customer is an asset on which interest will be paid.

The credit in the customer's account is a liability that could be demanded in cash at any time.

The value of credit in the customer's bank account.

Assets	Liabilities
Additional loan to customer **$100** Total loan to customer **$1,100**	Additional new money in the customer's account **$100** Total new money **$1,100**

Further sums borrowed by the customer add to the bank's assets.

The bank is now owed an additional $100 on which interest will be paid.

The bank is now liable to pay an additional $100.

Further sums lent to the customer add to the bank's liabilities.

DOUBLE ENTRY BOOKKEEPING

In accounting, this bookkeeping system requires that every business transaction is entered twice in at least two accounts to demonstrate that each entry has an equal and opposite effect. In practice this means that every debit in an account must be matched and offset by a credit. The sum of all debits must therefore equal the sum of all credits.

LIABILITIES

Banking reserves

Banks are not allowed to loan out all the money they receive as deposits, but instead are required by law to hold a specific percentage of their deposits in reserve as hard currency, that is available to depositors.

How it works

The central bank sets the reserve requirement for commercial banks. This is the minimum percentage of total deposits that banks must hold as actual currency, in case some depositors wish to withdraw deposits as cash. Reserve amounts of hard currency may be stored in bank vaults on site, or held by the central bank in the form of deposits. The reserve amount held by a bank is usually around 10 percent of its total deposits. The remaining 90 percent of deposits, the excess reserve, can be loaned out to other customers. Freeing up capital for loans helps to create wealth in the economy. However, it also means that commercial banks would be unable to honor all withdrawals should all of its depositors try to withdraw their money as cash at the same time. This is a scenario that commercial banks count on as very unlikely; however, in such an event, they can appeal to the central bank for additional reserves. The central bank manipulates the reserve rate to influence how much money commercial banks are able to loan. In theory, a low reserve rate makes it cheaper for banks to lend, and vice versa (*see pp.100–103*). Banks are also paid interest on their reserves at the central bank.

✓ NEED TO KNOW

> **Reserve requirement or reserve ratio** The percentage of total deposits that a bank must keep in reserve as hard currency.

> **Vault cash** Hard currency kept in reserve inside a bank vault.

> **Excess reserves** The amount of a deposit remaining, once the reserve has been set aside, and which may be loaned out to other customers.

> **Deposit liabilities** Money deposited in the bank, which the bank must pay back in the future.

How fractional reserves work

A reserve rate of five percent means that a bank must retain five percent of a $100,000 deposit, that is, hold $5,000 in reserve. The depositor's account will then be credited with the full amount of $100,000 that they deposited. The bank then loans out $95,000 to another customer, crediting their account with $95,000. Now the bank holds $5,000 in cash against claims of $195,000.

CENTRAL BANK SETS RESERVE AT 5%

COMMERCIAL BANK

Total bank reserves **$100,000**

$95,000
Excess reserves are loaned out to other customers, or can be used by the bank to make investments.

$5,000
Required reserves are held in a bank's vault as hard currency (and used for cash withdrawals), or held with the central bank.

THIS IS A SIMPLIFIED EXPLANATION OF THE MULTIPLIER EFFECT

The multiplier effect of the fractional reserve cycle

Wealth is created by loaning out most of a deposit. This original sum is then multiplied many times over as borrowers deposit their loan into other banks, which, in turn, loan money to yet more borrowers.

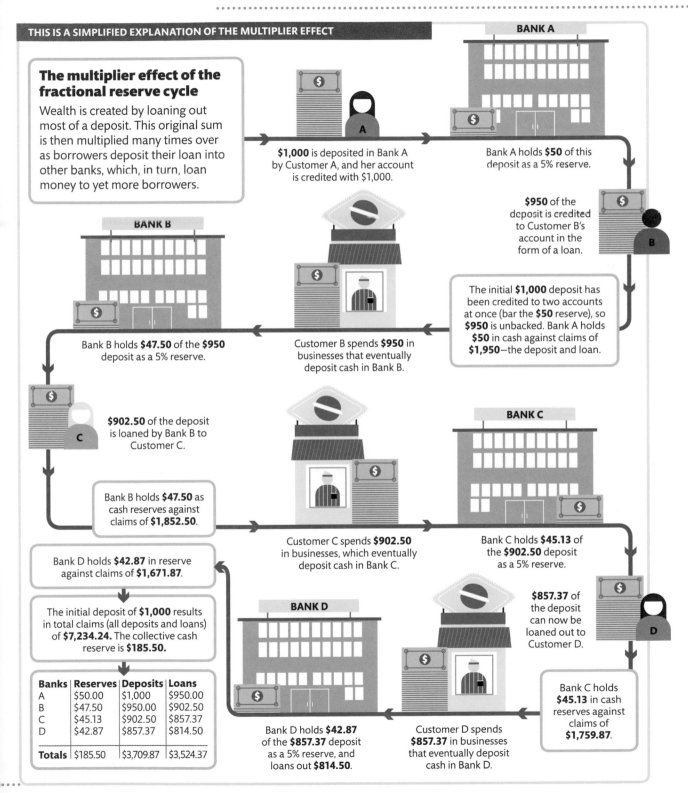

BANK A

$1,000 is deposited in Bank A by Customer A, and her account is credited with $1,000.

Bank A holds **$50** of this deposit as a 5% reserve.

$950 of the deposit is credited to Customer B's account in the form of a loan.

The initial **$1,000** deposit has been credited to two accounts at once (bar the **$50** reserve), so **$950** is unbacked. Bank A holds **$50** in cash against claims of **$1,950**—the deposit and loan.

BANK B

Bank B holds **$47.50** of the **$950** deposit as a 5% reserve.

Customer B spends **$950** in businesses that eventually deposit cash in Bank B.

$902.50 of the deposit is loaned by Bank B to Customer C.

Bank B holds **$47.50** as cash reserves against claims of **$1,852.50**.

BANK C

Customer C spends **$902.50** in businesses, which eventually deposit cash in Bank C.

Bank C holds **$45.13** of the **$902.50** deposit as a 5% reserve.

Bank D holds **$42.87** in reserve against claims of **$1,671.87**.

The initial deposit of **$1,000** results in total claims (all deposits and loans) of **$7,234.24**. The collective cash reserve is **$185.50**.

$857.37 of the deposit can now be loaned out to Customer D.

BANK D

Bank C holds **$45.13** in cash reserves against claims of **$1,759.87**.

Bank D holds **$42.87** of the **$857.37** deposit as a 5% reserve, and loans out **$814.50**.

Customer D spends **$857.37** in businesses that eventually deposit cash in Bank D.

Banks	Reserves	Deposits	Loans
A	$50.00	$1,000	$950.00
B	$47.50	$950.00	$902.50
C	$45.13	$902.50	$857.37
D	$42.87	$857.37	$814.50
Totals	$185.50	$3,709.87	$3,524.37

Recession and the money supply

The way money is used in an economy will change depending on how well or badly that economy is performing. In a recession, the money supply is restricted, which affects the whole economy.

Recessionary cycle

Everything in the economy is linked to everything else through buying and selling, so it is possible for an economic downturn to lead to an ongoing pattern of decline—known as a recessionary cycle. Once a few households or firms (or the government) begin to cut their spending, other firms will start to sell less. In turn, they will want to reduce the amount they are spending on labor, or raw materials, to limit the impact of falling sales. They may also put off making longer-term investment decisions as profits are uncertain, meaning that they contribute even less money to the economy. This can add up to a powerful negative cycle.

If the money supply slows, the wheels of the economy turn more slowly, further restricting the movement of money around the economy, which creates a recessionary cycle.

MONEY SUPPLY

ECONOMY

Consumers have less money to spend. They feel less confident about the future, and so may try to save more and spend less.

In response to decreased demand, producers cut wages and hours, lay off workers, and buy fewer raw materials.

Investors fear that company profits, and the value of stocks, will decrease, and are less willing to invest in new companies.

THE CREDIT CRUNCH

In the early 2000s, banks and other financial institutions began lending money on a very large scale. Regulations were loosened and low interest rates encouraged borrowing. The US and UK were especially affected, with easily available credit encouraging spending by consumers and causing rapid economic growth. However, the very large amount of lending by banks meant that some loans were going to riskier borrowers. In the US, this took the form of "subprime mortgages," where people who were denied a conventional mortgage by banks were loaned money by "subprime lenders." When a number of these borrowers were unable to repay their loans, the whole system was at risk. Financial institutions stopped lending to each other, and consumer lending dried up in the "credit crunch" of 2008. As money was harder to get hold of, spending slowed and the global economy fell into a recession.

How it works

A recession is a period during which the economy, as measured by its GDP, is shrinking, meaning that less is being bought and sold in that economy. This will usually also lead to falling wages or higher unemployment. As more people are out of work, or earning less than they previously were, they have less money to spend. They begin to save their money, fearing for their economic future, which has a further negative effect on the economy as a whole, as it reduces the overall money supply. Demand for goods falls further, companies are forced to cut costs and production, and the recession can worsen. This sets up a vicious circle of decline.

As economic activity decreases, people's expectations about the future worsen. They borrow less money and banks, in turn, may cut lending for fear that anyone borrowing money is less likely to repay it.

Unemployed workers have less money to spend, and by spending less they cause demand for consumer goods to fall still further. Workers on reduced hours and lower wages will also spend less and try to save more.

Companies produce fewer consumer goods, which further reduces their demand for labor and raw materials, slows their growth rate, and causes their profits to fall. Firms begin to fear for their futures and invest even less.

Fewer capital goods, such as machinery and equipment, are sold as companies reduce investment and spending. This hits the profits of the companies producing capital goods and reduces their demand for labor.

✓ NEED TO KNOW

❯ **Expansionary policy** Attempts by a government to make an economy grow faster—for example by cutting taxes, raising government spending, cutting interest rates, or making money easier to borrow.

❯ **Contractionary policy** Attempts by a government to slow an economy down, usually to try to avoid inflation—for example by raising taxes, cutting government spending, or both. It usually involves raising interest rates and making money harder to borrow.

2.4%
the amount by which the US economy grew in 2015

Recession to depression

A sustained period of deep recession is known as a depression. During this time a country's GDP falls for repeated consecutive months by up to 10 percent and unemployment levels soar.

Case study: The Great Depression, 1929–41

The worst economic crisis of the 20th century, economists still debate what caused the Great Depression, how it spread around the world, and why recovery took so long.

1. Prosperity in the US during the "Roaring Twenties" leads to overconfidence and reckless investment. Thousands of ordinary Americans buy stocks and the increasing demand for shares inflates their value.

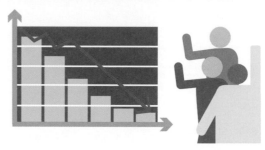

2. By late 1929 there are signs the US economy is in trouble: unemployment is rising, consumer spending is declining, and farms are failing. But still confident of getting rich quick, some people continue to invest.

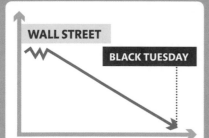

WALL STREET

BLACK TUESDAY

3. Over six days in October 1929, shares on Wall Street's New York Stock Exchange crash. In total $25 billion is lost, and with it people's confidence in the stock market. Many investors go bankrupt, banks lose money, and trade collapses.

4. There are a series of runs on the banks, as shaken customers want to hold on to all their cash (*see right*). Many banks lose their reserves and by 1933 more than half have shut. Banks contract their loans, and the deposits they create, further reducing the US money supply.

CLOSED

5. Loss of confidence, less money, and increased borrowing costs result in reduced spending and demand for goods. Manufacturing slows, workers are laid off, and wages are lowered, further reducing spending power.

CLOSED

How it works

A depression occurs following a protracted period of deep recession, and when an economy is stuck in a perpetual cycle of decline there can be catastrophic results. Banks crash, stock markets plummet, the money supply shrinks, prices fall, investments are rendered almost worthless, there is an increase in defaults and bankruptcies, and unemployment levels rise as individuals and businesses stop spending. Government attempts to stimulate the economy by pumping more money into it no longer work, and low interest rates no longer encourage consumer spending. Instead, government investment to stimulate employment and growth is needed.

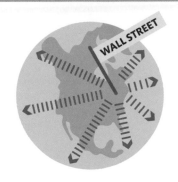

6. The depression spreads around the world as the US, having lent a lot of money to European countries, recalls loans, pulls out of foreign investments, and increases taxes on foreign imports. European banks collapse and unemployment rises.

7. In 1932, US President Franklin D. Roosevelt introduces the New Deal, to fight the depression through economic and social reforms. In Europe, right wing parties emerge, such as Hitler's National Socialist Party, which promises to restore the economy.

40%
the amount the average US income fell between 1929 and 1932

8. Countries that leave the gold standard early, and so can depreciate their currencies to combat deflation, tend to begin recovery sooner. For the US, WWII brings an increase in employment (in industrial production and military service) and government spending, which speeds recovery.

LIQUIDITY TRAP

People tend to hold on to money in economically unstable times because it is a reliable store of wealth that can be exchanged quickly for other assets—a good insurance against an uncertain future. Holding on to money also becomes more profitable when prices are dropping, as a given amount of money will buy ever more goods.

When the desire to save is so great that it overwhelms normal spending activity, the economy can become stuck in a liquidity trap. Any increase in the money supply fails to stimulate economic activity, as people continue to hoard money while they wait for the economy to improve. However, this hoarding slows the economy further and can trap it in a depression.

Managing state finance

In spending money to provide the services that people expect, governments must aim for maximum cost efficiency. They therefore plan to finance the budget from a combination of taxation, borrowing, and (very occasionally) printing new money. Taxation in all its forms is the primary source of funding, with borrowing used as a means to make up the shortfall. Printing money is rare as it risks undermining confidence in the value of the currency itself.

Balancing the books

Government spending today is largely to meet demand, and typically accounts for around one-third of a country's economy. In some countries (such as those in Scandinavia), government spending accounts for a much greater proportion than this. Financing this degree of spending can be a difficult task. While governments aspire to balance their budgets, most borrow a proportion. What matters is that the level of borrowing is controlled so that people have confidence that government debts will always be repaid.

CENTRAL BANK
In the US, the central bank is the Federal Reserve, known as the Fed. A country's central bank manages the currency and money supply, holds central bank reserves, and implements economic targets set by the government.
See pp.100–103

PRINT MONEY
Modern governments very rarely print currency to finance themselves, since doing so carries significant risks.
See pp.124–125

TAXES
Taxation is the safest means of raising money, but is unpopular as it represents a loss of money to the people being taxed.
See pp.106–107

BORROWING
This is a costly option as interest will be charged and money borrowed must be paid back.
See pp.108–109

Government revenue

PRINTING MONEY

Governments can issue their own money, either by printing it or by creating it electronically. However, creating money in this way carries a risk. Since money depends on trust, when a government issues increasing amounts of currency, people may have less confidence in the value of that currency. If their trust collapses completely, hyperinflation may occur (*see pp.132–135*). This is what took place in Germany in the 1920s, for example.

$6.7 trillion
the amount the US government spent in 2016

A BUDGET IN BALANCE
The government budget balance is the overall difference between its revenues and its spending.

CONSUMPTION AND INVESTMENT
Government spending is a mixture of paying for the immediate costs of running services, and investment in things such as roads, hospitals, and universities. Services such as pensions, healthcare, education, welfare, and defense are all major elements of annual spending.
See pp.130–131

DEBT REPAYMENT
Governments must repay their debts. Paying interest on debt can be a significant budget cost.
See pp.110–111

Government spending

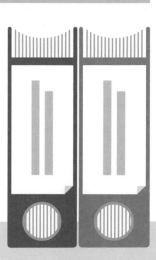

Governments and money

A country's government and central bank play a key role in the circulation of money in the economy. They monitor money supply, send funding to key sectors of society, and ensure that cash flows back to them for state spending.

How it works

A healthy economy requires a good money supply. Although it is difficult to control the supply of money directly, government monetary policy can help to influence it. The most important institution in monetary policy is the central bank (see pp.100–103), which is critical in determining interest rates and can be used to inject more money into the economy via open market operations (see pp.102–103) or through quantitative easing (see pp.124–125). Governments may also control the flow of money via taxes and other capital controls, and by restricting borrowing and lending. However, these mechanisms are imperfect in the modern monetary system, since commercial banks are largely free to decide the terms of their lending. Attempts to directly control money supply tend to fail.

Money supply and a healthy economy

As a healthy body depends on a good blood supply to receive nutrients, so a healthy economy requires a good money supply to keep the cycle of spending going: as one person spends, another earns, then spends, and so on. If this cycle slows, the economy may begin to decline. The government, via the central bank—which is like the beating heart of the economy—helps to keep money flowing. Meanwhile, the government also ensures that funding reaches key areas of society, while collecting revenues for state spending. Economic policies around interest rates, reserve ratios, open market operations, and quantitative easing are all focused on maintaining money supply. A body may have optimal blood supply, but it is down to the cells to effectively utilize the nutrients. In the same way, while a government can improve money supply, economic growth then depends on how effectively individuals and businesses are able to convert this money into useful goods and services to raise living standards.

Money flows out

The central bank uses financial institutions as a conduit to increase the money supply. At the same time, government spending makes up a huge part of the economy.

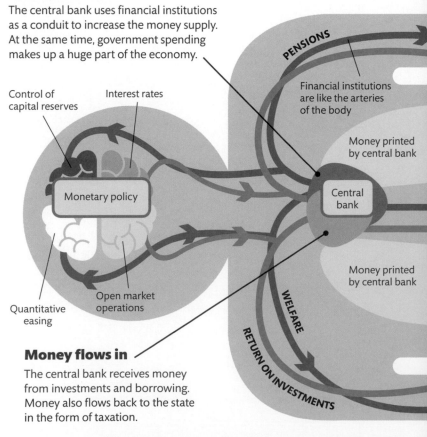

Control of capital reserves

Interest rates

PENSIONS

Financial institutions are like the arteries of the body

Money printed by central bank

Monetary policy

Central bank

Money printed by central bank

Quantitative easing

Open market operations

WELFARE

RETURN ON INVESTMENTS

Money flows in

The central bank receives money from investments and borrowing. Money also flows back to the state in the form of taxation.

✓ NEED TO KNOW

❯ **Money supply** The total amount of money circulating in a country, from currency to less liquid forms.

❯ **Central bank** An institution that provides financial services to the government and commercial banks, implements monetary policies, sets interest rates, and controls money supply.

❯ **Currency in circulation** Money that is physically used to conduct transactions between customers and businesses.

THE CASE FOR INDEPENDENT CENTRAL BANKS

Many central banks were made independent of the government in the early 2000s, although they are still required to be both transparent and accountable. The 2008 crash led some to question whether independent banks are desirable.

Pros

❯ **Monetary policy can be** more impartial as banks have no interest in maintaining electoral popularity.

❯ **As they are unaffected** by the electoral cycle they can plan and implement long-term policies.

❯ **Independent banks** have tended to maintain lower rates of inflation.

Cons

❯ **Unelected banks** cannot be voted out, arguably making them less accountable.

❯ **Central bank** controls may not be enough to avert financial crises without government aid.

❯ **Governments** may blame banks for recessions, so eroding trust.

"Monetary policy **is not a panacea**"

Ben Bernanke

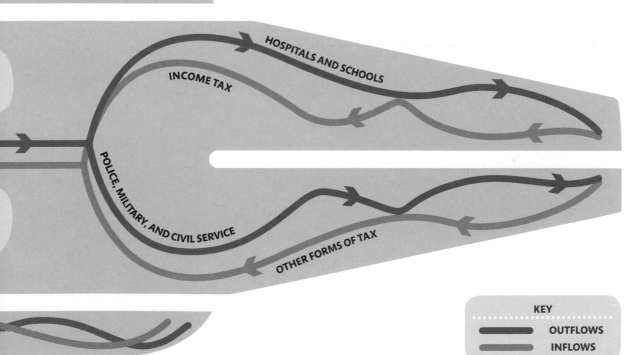

BORROWING

INCOME TAX

HOSPITALS AND SCHOOLS

POLICE, MILITARY, AND CIVIL SERVICE

OTHER FORMS OF TAX

KEY

OUTFLOWS

INFLOWS

The central bank

A central bank is the "bankers' bank," acting as guarantor for the rest of the banking system by supplying extra funding when it's needed. Central banks play a critical role in setting a country's monetary policy.

How it works

A central bank manages a country's currency, money supply, and interest rates, and holds central bank reserves. Commercial banks rely on these central bank reserves to support their day-to-day operations. By altering the amount of the reserves, and the cost of borrowing from them (via the rate of interest, known as the reserve rate or base rate), central banks can assert control over the country's money supply.

The base rate is usually the cheapest rate of interest available for its currency, and because central bank reserves are fundamental to commercial banks' ability to lend, the central bank helps to set interest rates for the entire economy. When the reserve rate rises or falls, interest rates on commercial bank loans do the same. As with the supply and demand of other commodities, when demand for reserve money is high, its price (here the reserve rate or base rate) rises. Conversely, when the demand for reserve money is low, its price falls.

Central banks often focus on regulating other specific economic targets—most typically the rate of inflation. They do this by meeting preset, publicly displayed targets.

LENDER OF LAST RESORT

Because banking contains an element of risk, the stability of the system depends on an institution that can provide protection to banks threatened with failure. Central banks, with their potentially unlimited quantities of central reserves, play the role of "lender of last resort." When a failing bank presents too risky a prospect for lenders, it can still rely on loans from the central bank. This provides a safeguard against financial collapse that could damage the economy.

19 countries
in the **European Union** share a single central bank: the **European Central Bank**

Monetary targets

A central bank's monetary policy objective is usually to deliver price stability (low inflation) and to support the government's economic objectives. Price stability has a role in achieving economic stability more generally, and in providing the right conditions for sustainable growth. Central banks have a range of strategies to achieve this. One is to target the total amount of money in the economy: the money supply. A second strategy is to target a particular exchange rate by altering the amount of currency in circulation to affect the foreign exchange markets, and a third is to target a particular interest rate, as illustrated opposite.

Central bank

The central bank creates and supplies reserve money to commercial banks, giving it huge power over the day-to-day workings of the banking system. Usually, the central bank will try to maintain its target interest rate by pumping reserve money into or out of the banks. This affects demand for reserve money and, therefore, the price the central bank can charge commercial banks to borrow—the reserve rate.

Reserve rate too high

When there is high demand for central bank money, the reserve interest rate rises.

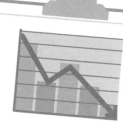

Reserve rate too low

When the demand for central bank money is low, the reserve interest rate falls.

PUSHING RATE DOWN
The central bank buys securities from the commercial banks, so increasing the amount of central bank reserves in the system. As more money is available, the cost of borrowing—the interest rate—decreases.

PUSHING RATE UP
To increase the interest rate, it sells securities to commercial banks, so reducing the quantity of central bank reserves in the system. As a result, demand for money and the cost of borrowing it goes up.

Commercial bank reserves

The central bank pumps more of its money into commercial bank reserves, lowering the interest rate and bringing it back in line with the target interest rate.

The central bank sucks reserve money out of the system, bringing the base rate up and back in line with its target.

TARGET RESERVE INTEREST RATE

Managing the monetary system

By raising or lowering its reserve rate of interest, a central bank can influence the size of commercial banks' reserves, and thus their borrowing and lending rates and the amount of money in circulation. This affects spending, and inflation, because when interest rates are lower, saving is less and borrowing more attractive, and when interest rates are higher, the opposite is true.

✓ NEED TO KNOW

> **Secondary market** The forum in which investors buy and sell bonds issued by the government.

> **Inflation** A general increase in prices and fall in the purchasing value of money.

> **The spread** The difference between the cheapest and the most expensive interest rate.

> **Credit guidance** A form of cheaper lending by the central bank that is designed to meet wider government objectives such as boosting key industries.

> **Reserve ratio** The percentage of depositors' balances that a bank must keep as cash. The reserve ratio is set by the central bank.

Increasing money in circulation

Lowering the reserve (base) rate of interest

The central bank can cut the reserve rate of interest to make it cheaper for commercial banks to borrow from its reserves. The idea is that the commercial banks will then in turn reduce their interest rates to the public.

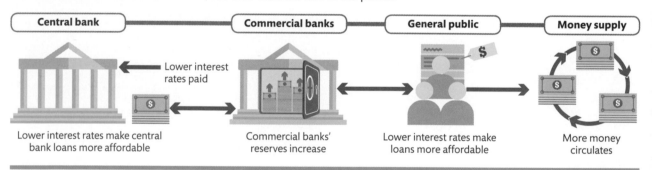

Central bank	Commercial banks	General public	Money supply

Lower interest rates paid

Lower interest rates make central bank loans more affordable

Commercial banks' reserves increase

Lower interest rates make loans more affordable

More money circulates

Open market operations: buying bonds

The central bank buys bonds on the open market using newly created reserves. Investors' deposits from the sale increase the amount of reserve money in the open market, which leads to a lowering of the short-term rate.

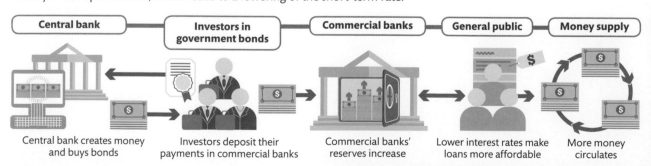

Central bank	Investors in government bonds	Commercial banks	General public	Money supply

Central bank creates money and buys bonds

Investors deposit their payments in commercial banks

Commercial banks' reserves increase

Lower interest rates make loans more affordable

More money circulates

CENTRAL BANK CONTROLS

Credit guidance

The central bank's control of commercial banks' licences helps it to influence how those banks lend. It can, for example, give them incentives to offer very low interest rates to important sectors of the economy.

Open market operations

The central bank buys and sells bonds in the open market to affect the short-term rates of interest.

Credit access

The central bank can restrict commercial banks' access to credit, for example by raising the amount of deposits they must hold as reserves.

1668

the year that the oldest central bank in the world, the Swedish Riksbank, was established

Decreasing money in circulation

Raising the reserve (base) rate of interest

The central bank can curtail commercial banks' lending to the public by raising its reserve rate of interest. This makes it more expensive for commercial banks to borrow from central bank reserves. Commercial banks in turn raise interest rates for borrowers.

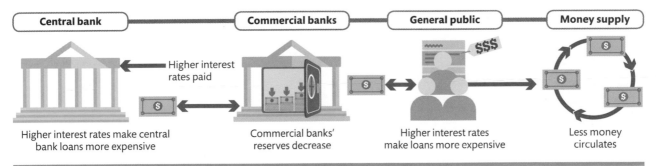

Central bank	Commercial banks	General public	Money supply

Higher interest rates paid

Higher interest rates make central bank loans more expensive

Commercial banks' reserves decrease

Higher interest rates make loans more expensive

Less money circulates

Open market operations: selling bonds

The central bank sells bonds back to the market in exchange for money, causing investors to make withdrawals to buy the bonds, lowering the amount of money in the banking system. Commercial banks respond by raising interest rates.

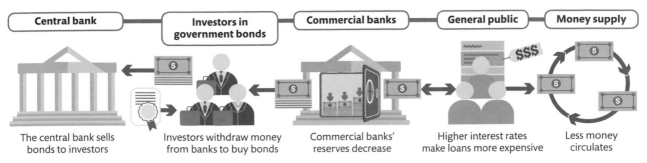

Central bank	Investors in government bonds	Commercial banks	General public	Money supply

The central bank sells bonds to investors

Investors withdraw money from banks to buy bonds

Commercial banks' reserves decrease

Higher interest rates make loans more expensive

Less money circulates

Budget constraint

Governments have financial constraints just as individuals and companies do. When spending exceeds income, the government may need to borrow—or even print—money to cover the shortfall.

How it works

Governments need to pay for the public services they provide and for any other financial commitments they may have. To do this they tax the population, and borrow money if additional funds are needed. In extreme cases it is even possible for governments to print their own cash. Each strategy has its own costs—but printing money is so risky that it is very rarely used directly.

The difference between a government's tax revenues and its spending is known as its budget (or fiscal) deficit. The budget deficit shows how much extra money the government needs to borrow (or print) to finance its spending. It is typical for some governments to run a small budget deficit on an ongoing basis.

Spending and the deficit

Ideally a government's spending commitments (inside the circle) should be covered by tax revenue and other forms of income. However, when a proportion of spending is not covered (budget deficit), the extra funding has to be raised either from borrowing or by printing additional money. Small deficits can usually be dealt with by borrowing alone, but if a deficit grows too large, then the government may find itself in financial difficulties as it may need to borrow increasing amounts simply to keep up with existing payments (*see pp. 146–7*).

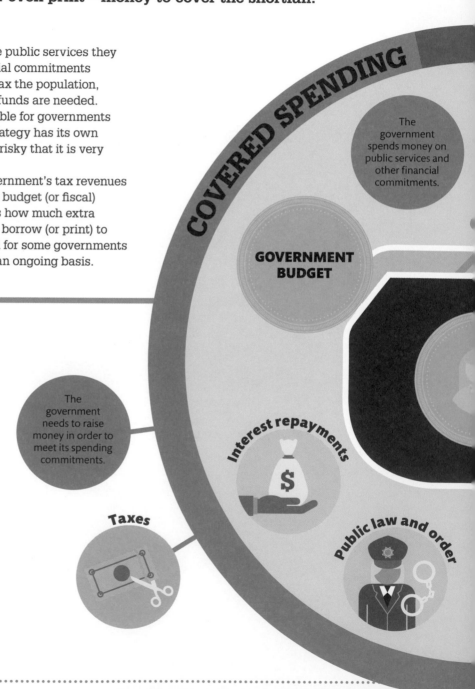

COVERED SPENDING

The government spends money on public services and other financial commitments.

GOVERNMENT BUDGET

The government needs to raise money in order to meet its spending commitments.

Interest repayments

Taxes

Public law and order

When proposed spending is greater than income, the government may need to borrow or even print money.

Borrowing money

Printing money

BUDGET DEFICIT

Welfare

Defense

Housing and the environment

Healthcare

Education

75%
of GDP: Libya's budget deficit— the worst in the world

HOW GOVERNMENTS RAISE MONEY

Governments can raise funds to meet their spending commitments in three different ways. Each strategy has advantages and disadvantages.

❯ **Taxes** Governments can levy taxes on what the population earns and owns, and on foreign trade. Taxes are safe, but unpopular.

SAFE   UNPOPULAR

❯ **Borrowing** Governments can borrow from their own citizens—through pension funds for example—or from abroad. But loans incur interest charges.

LOW POLITICAL RISK   INTEREST PAYMENTS

❯ **Printing money** A government can print its own money. This seemingly simple solution is rare because of the risks it entails (*see pp.144–5*).

LOOKS EASY   HIGH FINANCIAL RISK

How tax works

Taxation is the main way in which governments raise revenue needed to pay for public spending. Governments may tax the public directly (for instance, through income tax) or indirectly (via VAT for example).

How it works

Governments have the unique privilege of being able to demand that anyone in their country pay taxes. These can be divided into "direct" taxes, which are paid from earnings, either by people or institutions, and "indirect" taxes, which are paid for out of consumer spending. Taxes can be levied as a share of spending or income, or as a flat rate. A progressive tax system is one in which richer individuals pay proportionately more tax.

Questions surrounding the level of taxation are hotly debated. As a result, levels of taxation, and laws about who or what pays for which taxes, vary significantly from country to country.

TAXES AND BEHAVIOR

Some taxes are designed to reduce the amount of revenue that goods earn. Because a newly-levied or increased tax on a product puts up its price, that item becomes less attractive to buy. Where a product is harmful, higher taxes—such as on cigarettes—can be a way to reduce public consumption. In cases where consumer behavior does not alter much in response to higher pricing, however, the extra tax is likely to raise much more money. This can make some taxes very appealing for governments looking for revenues.

Direct and indirect taxes

People have to pay taxes on either their income, or on what they spend. Some typical taxes on an individual in the US are shown below.

DIRECT TAXES

FICA tax 15.3%
This tax is a combination of social security tax (12.4%) and Medicare (2.9%), both half paid by the employer and half by the employee.

Income tax
Income tax depends on the filing entity (individual, corporation, etc.) and the amount declared.

Net income
Once taxes on earnings have been paid out, the amount remaining is called "net" income.

NET INCOME

$21 trillion
thought to be hidden
in **tax havens abroad**

INDIRECT TAXES

Other variables
There are a variety of taxes in the US, including capital gains, gifts, imports, and much more.

Excise tax
An indirect tax that applies to specified goods, such as gasoline, or activities, like highway usage by trucks.

Sales tax
This tax is applied at the state level and varies by state. Not all states have sales tax.

TAX EVASION AND AVOIDANCE

Because tax systems vary so widely from country to country, it is possible to exploit the differences in international tax rates in order to reduce the total amount of tax due. This is termed tax "evasion" when it is done illegally, and tax "avoidance" when performed legally, although in practice the boundaries between the two are blurred. Some jurisdictions deliberately set very low tax rates to attract investment; some also provide secrecy around the identity of those investing there. This has led to accusations that such areas are acting as "tax havens." This means that, instead of providing a legitimate location for economic activity, they are allowing major corporations and the very wealthy to avoid paying taxes they should be paying.

Government borrowing

Government borrowing is the main way that governments pay for any spending that is not already covered by taxation. However, excessive borrowing will result in high levels of government debt.

Managing the debt

Governments keep a careful eye on their overall level of debt, since high levels of debt mean greater interest repayments are necessary. Very elevated levels of debt may become impossible to repay if tax revenue proves insufficient to keep pace with interest rates. Furthermore, a heavily indebted country that investors see as a risky prospect may find it difficult to borrow enough to cover day-to-day spending.

Borrowing

Governments typically borrow money by issuing bonds to individuals and financial institutions in exchange for a loan. The government will then pay a fixed rate of interest over a period of time to the investor, paying the bond back in full when it reaches maturity.

Government funds

A typical government receives most of its financing in the form of taxes, but borrowing is also often necessary in order to meet planned expenditures. Any borrowed money will need to be repaid eventually and so a significant portion of the government's budget is reserved for debt payments.

TAX

How it works

Governments will often want to spend more than they earn in taxes. This may happen during a recession, when there is higher unemployment and therefore lower tax revenues. The gap between government tax revenue and what it spends is called the deficit. Governments borrow in order to cover the deficit, maintain spending, and continue to provide services with the aim that debts will eventually be repaid with tax revenue. Most governments run a deficit from time to time, and may run one most of the time. If debts can be repaid, and interest payments are not large, this is not a problem, but there is a risk of default when repayment cannot keep pace with borrowing.

> "A national debt, if it is not excessive, will be to us a national blessing"
>
> Alexander Hamilton, first US Secretary of the Treasury

Repaying the deficit

The higher the deficit, the more money of a government's budget is required in order to pay it off. Governments with a surplus can give more to their debt payments.

Repayment

Any debt that a government takes on must eventually be repaid, along with interest on that debt. A certain level of debt repayment must always be maintained by the government to avoid default or excess interest incurred on that debt.

Government default

If a government fails or refuses to pay back a debt in full it is said to have defaulted. This means that it is unable to keep up repayments on some of the debt it owes.

DANGER OF DEFAULT

Public debt

Public debt is the total amount of money owed by a country's government, and includes historic debt. Nations with big economies and large tax-paying populations can carry more debt than those without.

How it works

The total amount borrowed by a country's government (and by its previous governments) is known as the public or national debt. This is generally calculated as the total debt minus the government's liquid assets. Interest is due on this debt, and it can be substantial. If a government spends more than it collects in taxes in one year, it will be in deficit. Any money it borrows to cover this is then added to the public debt. When the government spends less than it collects in taxes in a year, it has a "surplus," which can be used to pay down the debt. Inflation can also help reduce a debt burden. A state that becomes unable to pay its debt is said to "default," and will find it hard to borrow again.

Carrying debt

Governments usually repay debt using taxes. The more money they raise, the faster they can repay it. The larger a country's economy, the more debt it can safely hold, since a bigger economy can gather more taxes.

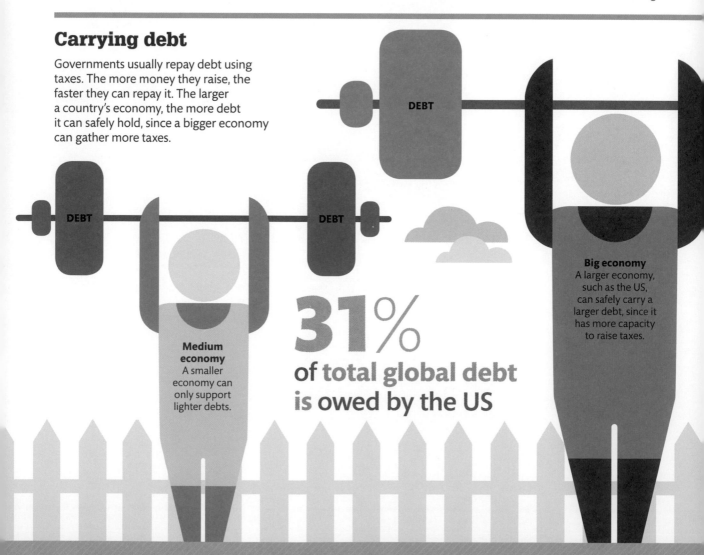

DEBT

DEBT

DEBT

31% of **total global debt is owed by the US**

Medium economy
A smaller economy can only support lighter debts.

Big economy
A larger economy, such as the US, can safely carry a larger debt, since it has more capacity to raise taxes.

GOVERNMENT DEBTS RISE IN WARTIME

War imposes exceptional demands on government spending. Governments typically finance this by borrowing money. The first ever government debts were a direct result of borrowing to fund military campaigns.

GOVERNMENT   DEBT

✓ NEED TO KNOW

❯ **Public/national/sovereign debt** Total debt owed by a government.

❯ **Internal debts** Money that is borrowed from within a government's own country.

❯ **External debts** Money that is borrowed from abroad.

DEBT

INFLATION

DEBT

INFLATION

DEBT

DEBT

DEBT

Weak economy
A struggling economy is liable to default.

Inflation can reduce debt
Rising prices reduce the value of money, lightening the weight of debt repayment.

Accountability

Responsibility for economic policy is usually shared between a country's government and its central bank. By reporting their decisions to the public and to democratic institutions, they can be made more accountable to the people.

How it works

Democratic countries typically insist that governments report annually to their legislative bodies about taxation and spending plans for the next year. This annual budget has become the central instrument of government fiscal policy, and its contents are widely scrutinized. Before the 2008 crash, monetary policy had been increasingly left to central banks. However, since then the policy and the banking system's role in it have been subject to more rigorous examination, and taxation and spending plans now tend to dominate the debate during national elections.

Media reports on budget

The media reports on changes to the government budget and how they will affect the public.

Public adjusts its spending habits

Knowledge about the budget may inform decisions by households and firms on spending and saving money.

Legislative body approves budget

A country's legislative body, typically an elected parliament, will debate the budget and potentially make changes.

Auditors inspect public finances
Many countries have an independent body that inspects the government's financial decisions.

FISCAL IMPACT
Government policymakers take a long-term perspective. To achieve the best economic outcomes, central bank policymakers need to be guided by this perspective.

Government draws up a budget

Typically an annual budget allocates spending across different resources.

MONETARY IMPACT
Central bank decisions on monetary policy affect government spending due to the impact of interest rates on employment and inflation in particular.

TRANSPARENCY AND ACCOUNTABILITY IN CENTRAL BANKS

The current trend in many countries is for an independent central bank. It is essential that an autonomous central bank is able to coordinate effectively with the government and keep it, and the public, appraised of plans and projections. To this end, a central bank must demonstrate both transparency and accountability.

Transparency

> **Increased openness** is expected to lead to better-informed decisions.

> **Political, economic, and procedural policies** should all be clearly outlined.

> **Regular and comprehensive reports** must be made available to the public and the government.

Accountability

> **Rigorous standards of conduct** for the central bank's staff should lead to higher-quality decisions.

> **Audited financial statements** should be made publicly available.

> **Operating expenses and revenue** should be disclosed.

EXTERNAL FACTORS
Central bank decision-making must also take into account factors such as social attitudes, business considerations, and the volatility of the financial markets.

Central bank also oversees commercial banks Oversight of commercial banks gives the central bank large power in shaping the economy.

Report justifies and explains decisions

The central bank governor appears before the committee to give further explanation when required.

Minutes of policy meeting published

Reports of the central bank's decision-making process are publicly available.

Central bank sets interest rates

Having consulted a range of financial indicators, the central bank decides on a target rate of interest.

Impact of policy is monitored and quantified

Financial institutions and the specialty press pay especially close attention to the central bank's decisions.

IMPACT ON THE PUBLIC
Interest rates affect saving, borrowing, and spending decisions. These feed through into output and employment, then producers' costs and prices, and eventually consumer prices.

IMPACT ON MONEY MARKETS
Interest rates affect the price of financial assets and the exchange rate, which affect consumer and business demand and the return on a country's assets relative to their foreign-currency equivalents.

Attempting control

Governments can attempt to manage the economy by adjusting policies such as taxes and influencing interest rates. Each adjustment can affect a small part of the complete economic machine. However, the economy is usually beyond the direct control of a country's government, and its different elements interact with each other in different ways. Forecasting its behavior is difficult, and attempting to balance competing demands for resources requires clear political judgment.

Economic machine

This design is based on a real machine, the MONIAC, a hydraulic simulation of the UK economy built in 1949 by economist Bill Phillips. Based on the theory of national income, it showed the connections between the different parts of the economy using a system of tanks, pumps, and tubes, and could be used to make simple forecasts resulting from policy changes.

ECONOMIC INDICATORS
Each part of the machine has a reading associated with it. In an actual economy, the indicators these readings represent are collected and produced by the country's national statistical bureau, generally using survey data to assess levels of spending, employment, and so on. One problem for the government is the delay between actual events in the economy, and processing and receiving indicators. *See pp.116–119*

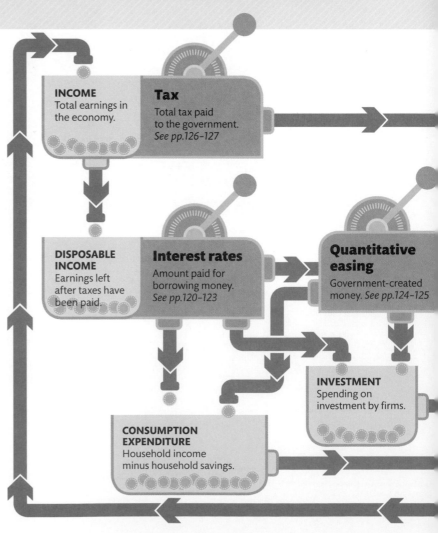

INCOME
Total earnings in the economy.

Tax
Total tax paid to the government. *See pp.126–127*

DISPOSABLE INCOME
Earnings left after taxes have been paid.

Interest rates
Amount paid for borrowing money. *See pp.120–123*

Quantitative easing
Government-created money. *See pp.124–125*

INVESTMENT
Spending on investment by firms.

CONSUMPTION EXPENDITURE
Household income minus household savings.

NATIONAL INCOME ACCOUNTING

National income

National income is the total amount earned by every sector of the economy and from the foreign balance (also known as the balance of payments). National income accounting is a method that a national government uses to measure the level of a country's economic activity in a given time period.

Income equals expenditure

The idea of national income means that every penny spent in one part of the economy must equate to a penny earned elsewhere, and the total earnings of the economy must match the total spending of the economy. This idea allows economists to build models such as the MONIAC machine.

$4.29 trillion
Japan's Gross National Income (GNI) in 2015

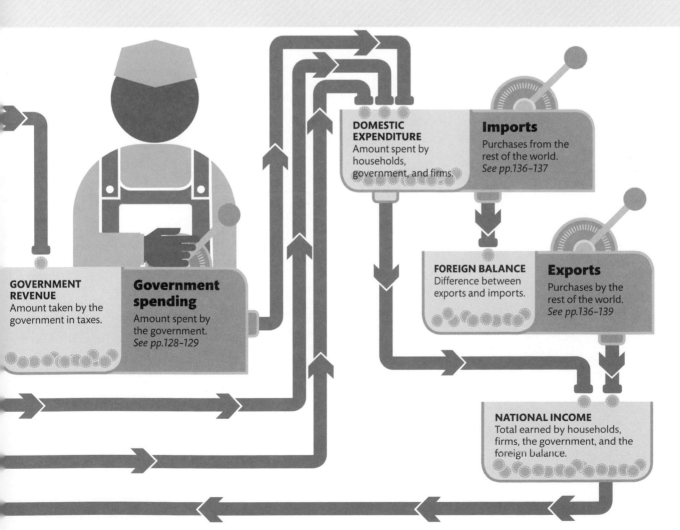

DOMESTIC EXPENDITURE
Amount spent by households, government, and firms.

Imports
Purchases from the rest of the world.
See pp.136–137

GOVERNMENT REVENUE
Amount taken by the government in taxes.

Government spending
Amount spent by the government.
See pp.128–129

FOREIGN BALANCE
Difference between exports and imports.

Exports
Purchases by the rest of the world.
See pp.136–139

NATIONAL INCOME
Total earned by households, firms, the government, and the foreign balance.

Reading economic indicators

Using a few key indicators of performance, governments can monitor how parts of the economy are working and whether there are potential problems ahead. However, such indicators must be read with care.

Measuring performance

Indicators are usually shown as the rate of change over time, because the economy is very dynamic. But this means indicators are only estimates, based on surveys taken at a particular point in time.

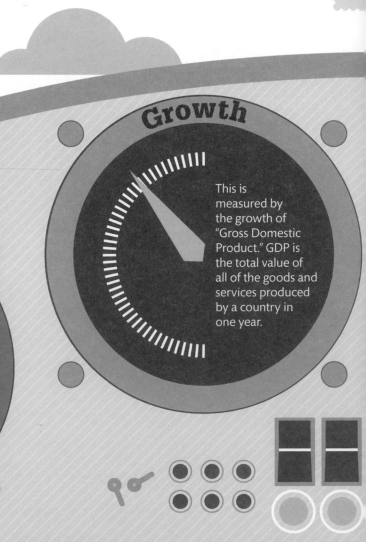

Growth

This is measured by the growth of "Gross Domestic Product." GDP is the total value of all of the goods and services produced by a country in one year.

Inflation

This is how quickly prices are rising on average. Inflation is typically defined according to the percentage increase in price of a "basket of goods," which is selected by looking at what products people typically buy over a year.

How it works

The main indicators governments use to monitor the economy are based on surveys of individuals, businesses, and government departments. A national statistics agency is usually charged with running the survey, and then calculating the figures. The agency will look at the economy, business, industry and trade, the employment and labor markets, and society in general. The "headline indicators" generally relate to parts of the economy that have the most impact on people's daily lives, and might include assessments of the likelihood that individuals will find employment, whether their pay will go up or down, and whether businesses will be able to expand.

1884 the year the US Bureau of Labor Statistics was formed to analyze data

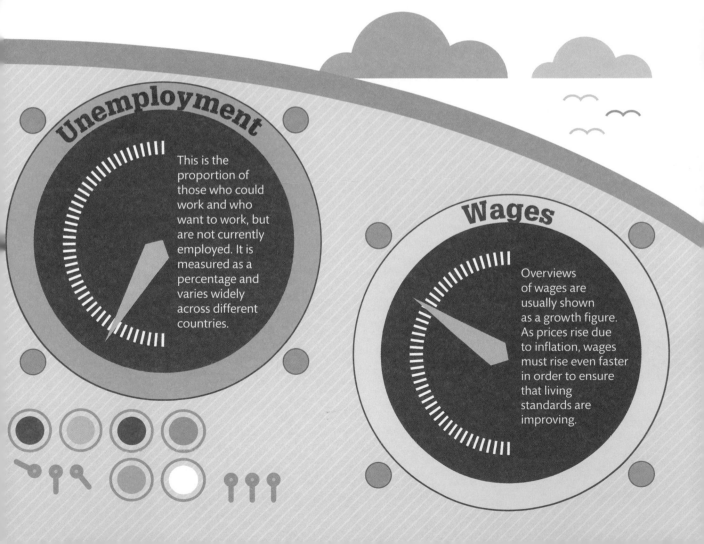

Unemployment

This is the proportion of those who could work and who want to work, but are not currently employed. It is measured as a percentage and varies widely across different countries.

Wages

Overviews of wages are usually shown as a growth figure. As prices rise due to inflation, wages must rise even faster in order to ensure that living standards are improving.

Deciding on economic policy

Governments closely monitor data on the economy to establish which policies might improve its performance. There are numerous ways of intervening, each with their own pros and cons.

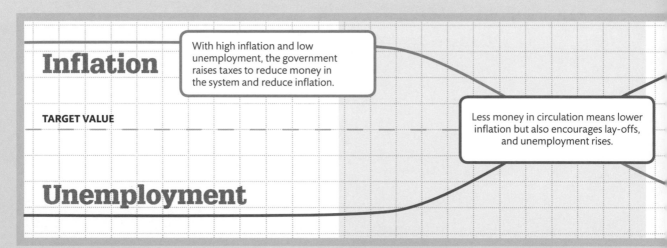

Inflation

With high inflation and low unemployment, the government raises taxes to reduce money in the system and reduce inflation.

TARGET VALUE

Less money in circulation means lower inflation but also encourages lay-offs, and unemployment rises.

Unemployment

Calibrating the economic machine

Governments have a number of different controls they can adjust to help the smooth running of the economy. The biggest are taxes, spending decisions, and interest rates. Each of these controls affects the economy in many different ways, and governments have to consider these when taking action.

> "Inflation **is the one form of** taxation **that can be** imposed **without legislation**"
>
> Milton Friedman

Increasing tax

The government can try to slow down the economy by raising taxes, a measure taken when inflation is a risk. An increase in taxes reduces spending. When spending falls, suppliers are less likely to put up their prices, since they risk losing a market, and inflation therefore slows. Cutting taxes has the opposite effect.

How it works

Economic policy making has been compared to trying to operate a finely balanced machine. By adjusting various policy "dials," the government aims for the best combination of key economic variables—usually, a combination of low inflation and unemployment levels. However, economists point to a trade-off between inflation and unemployment, with low unemployment coming at the cost of high inflation, and vice versa (*see pp.132–135*). More recently, economists have concluded that economies run best by themselves, with limited intervention. Other institutions have control over policy, while the state concentrates on "supply-side policies," such as making markets more efficient.

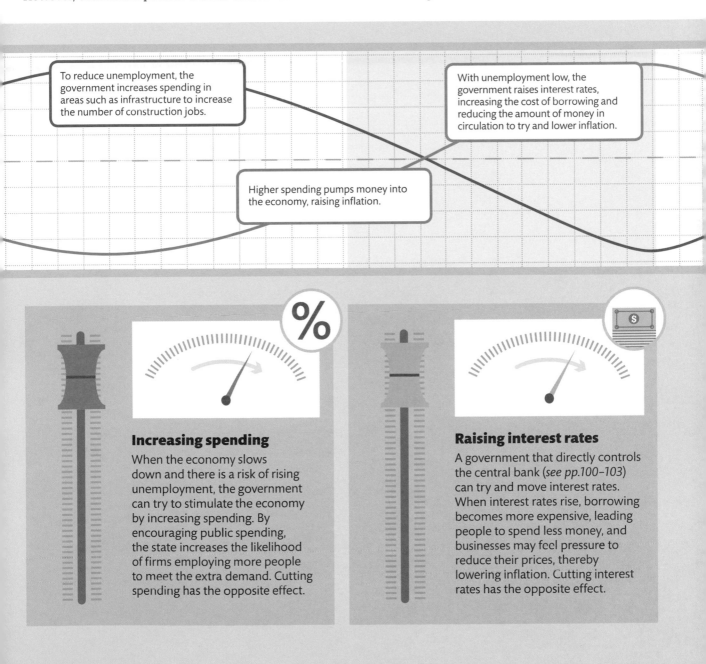

To reduce unemployment, the government increases spending in areas such as infrastructure to increase the number of construction jobs.

With unemployment low, the government raises interest rates, increasing the cost of borrowing and reducing the amount of money in circulation to try and lower inflation.

Higher spending pumps money into the economy, raising inflation.

Increasing spending

When the economy slows down and there is a risk of rising unemployment, the government can try to stimulate the economy by increasing spending. By encouraging public spending, the state increases the likelihood of firms employing more people to meet the extra demand. Cutting spending has the opposite effect.

Raising interest rates

A government that directly controls the central bank (*see pp.100–103*) can try and move interest rates. When interest rates rise, borrowing becomes more expensive, leading people to spend less money, and businesses may feel pressure to reduce their prices, thereby lowering inflation. Cutting interest rates has the opposite effect.

Interest rates

Interest is effectively the price charged by a lender to a borrower for the use of funds. The national reserve interest rate, set by the central bank, affects how easy it is to borrow or lend money in a country.

How it works

Lenders charge interest on the money or other assets that they loan. This is a charge levied to cover risks to the lender, should the borrower fail to repay the loan. Borrowers perceived to present a greater risk of failing to repay a loan may be charged more. Interest charges also compensate lenders for profits that they may have made if the money had been invested elsewhere. Interest charges with banks and other financial or business institutions are normally calculated as a percentage of the borrowed amount and expressed as a yearly figure—the annual percentage rate or APR (*see p.210*). In the US, the Fed plays a key role in setting national interest rates (*see pp.100–103*).

How interest rates are set

The base rate of interest is set by a country's central bank in response to inflation targets set by its government. Commercial banks respond to changes in the base rate by adjusting the interest rates of the different products that they offer.

Government

Each year, the government sets out its goals for economic growth and rates of employment. One such aim is to achieve price stability, as this makes for stable economic growth. Prices are kept steady when inflation occurs at a limited rate, so the government sets an inflation target, beyond which prices should not rise or fall. This is announced annually, expressed as a percentage of the Consumer Price Index (CPI). The CPI is the cost of a basket of representative goods bought by a household, measured periodically. The 2016 inflation target for the US, Eurozone, and Japan was 2 percent.

Central bank

The government's inflation target is noted by the central bank, who then sets the base rate—the interest rate that the central bank charges commercial banks to borrow from it. The central bank does this in order to encourage commercial banks to adjust their rates in line with the base rate, as bank rates determine the ease with which customers and businesses can borrow and so affects investment, spending, employment rates, and wage levels in the wider economy. This in turn influences the prices charged for products, which affects inflation (*see pp.122–123*).

Base rate

Raising the base rate means that commercial banks pay higher interest on money they borrow from the central bank, making it more expensive for them to borrow. Lowering the base rate means that commercial banks pay less interest on reserves they borrow from the central bank, which makes their borrowing cheaper.

HOW INFLATION AFFECTS INTEREST RATES

Interest rates affect inflation and the converse is also true: inflation affects interest rates. Inflation is the decline of a currency's purchasing power due to an oversupply of money (*see pp.132–135*). A limited supply of goods and services, along with an oversupply of money, means that money devalues and more of it is required to obtain products. A loan is a product and the interest rate the price paid for it, so if the value of money decreases, then commercial banks may charge a higher interest rate on their loans. Higher charges will make borrowing more expensive, resulting in fewer loans being taken out. This may ultimately impact spending, causing the money supply to fall, as well as the rate of inflation.

✓ NEED TO KNOW

> **Nominal rate** An advertised interest rate, which does not factor in the effect of inflation (or fees, or the effect of compound interest).

> **Real rate** Of particular interest to investors, this rate takes inflation into account and is calculated by subtracting the inflation rate from the nominal rate.

Commercial banks

Banks need to make a profit, so if the cost for them of borrowing from the central bank increases (as the base rate goes up), or the interbank lending rate increases, they need to reflect this in the interest rates that they charge customers for borrowing. Commercial banks set interest rates according to their own needs so some banks may choose not to pass lower interest rates on to customers taking out loans, while other banks may offer a higher interest rate on savings in order to attract new customers' money.

INTERBANK LENDING RATE

Banks lend to each other at a slightly higher rate than the base rate.

LOANS HAVE HIGHER INTEREST RATES THAN SAVINGS/ DEPOSITS

TYPICAL INTEREST RATES OFFERED BY COMMERCIAL BANKS

Unsecured loans

15% → **CREDIT CARDS**

10% → **PERSONAL LOAN**

Unsecured loans do not have guarantors or assets to act as collateral. This makes them riskier to lenders, who may charge higher interest rates as a result.

Secured loans

4% → **30-YEAR FIXED MORTGAGE**

3% → **15-YEAR FIXED MORTGAGE**

Secured loans are backed by collateral, such as property. Mortgages are secured by houses. Banks do not have to pass base rate changes on unless the borrower has a tracker mortgage (*see pp.214–215*).

Savings

.6% →

Interest paid out on savings is kept lower than the interest rate charged on loans, so that the bank can profit from the difference between them.

The impact of changing interest rates

If interest rates fluctuated all the time, the economy would become volatile. This is why the government and central bank work together to keep inflation and interest at stable rates. Every time the interest rate is changed, it sends a signal to society to either spend or save—and may also increase or decrease confidence in the state of the economy. A rise in interest rates encourages saving, since higher interest will be paid on money in savings accounts, and investments can grow. Meanwhile, borrowing becomes less attractive as interest repayments are steeper, and banks more selective about whom they lend to. This impacts the affordability of obtaining or repaying an existing loan, such as a mortgage. By contrast, a drop in interest rates is intended to cause an increase in spending, since borrowers are able to take out loans more cheaply. For those with mortgages tracking the base rate, interest repayments will drop. At the same time, savers will tend to spend or invest deposits that are attracting little interest. While discouraging saving through very low interest rates might stimulate the economy, this can ultimately negatively impact long-term savings plans, such as pensions.

When interest rates are raised

Higher interest rates make loans less affordable, while high interest on savings accounts encourages saving rather than spending. As spending slows, so does the economy, with demand for goods and services decreasing. This eventually affects businesses and employment levels.

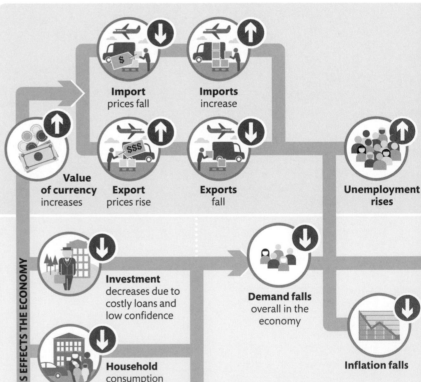

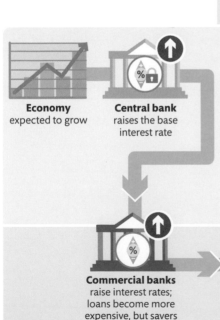

Import prices fall

Imports increase

Value of currency increases

Export prices rise

Exports fall

Unemployment rises

Economy expected to grow

Central bank raises the base interest rate

HOW THIS EFFECTS THE ECONOMY

Investment decreases due to costly loans and low confidence

Household consumption decreases, with less spending and more saving

Demand falls overall in the economy

Inflation falls

Commercial banks raise interest rates; loans become more expensive, but savers are rewarded

Companies may find they are less profitable as it gets harder to find loans and investors

0

TIME (YEARS)

1

2

NEGATIVE INTEREST RATE POLICY (NIRP)

In some countries, the central bank has experimented with cutting base interest rates to a negative figure, for instance, –0.01 percent. If this rate is passed on by commercial banks, it means that depositors must pay a percentage of their deposit to the bank. A central bank might impose a negative interest rate to encourage spending and investment, and discourage savers from hoarding cash. Commercial banks, however, usually tend to be reluctant to pass negative interest charges on to customers, particularly small businesses, as small depositors may be driven to withdraw their savings as cash to avoid fees. Large depositors will pay negative rates to gain security and a stable currency account.

40.5%
Argentina's rate of inflation in April 2016, the world's highest

When interest rates are lowered

Lower interest rates make it cheaper to take out loans, and hence to spend more money. Saving becomes less attractive as interest rates are low. With more money in circulation, demand for products and services rise, stimulating businesses and increasing employment.

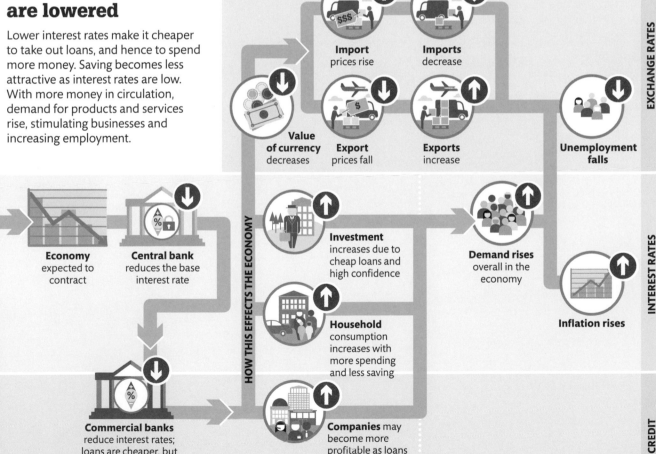

Import prices rise

Imports decrease

Value of currency decreases

Export prices fall

Exports increase

Unemployment falls

Economy expected to contract

Central bank reduces the base interest rate

HOW THIS EFFECTS THE ECONOMY

Investment increases due to cheap loans and high confidence

Demand rises overall in the economy

Household consumption increases with more spending and less saving

Inflation rises

Commercial banks reduce interest rates; loans are cheaper, but saving becomes less rewarding

Companies may become more profitable as loans and investors are easier to secure

EXCHANGE RATES

INTEREST RATES

CREDIT

0   TIME (YEARS)   1   2

Quantitative easing

Quantitative easing is a 21st-century strategy aimed at boosting the economy. It uses central bank's powers to create new money in an effort to reduce interest rates and increase investment and spending.

How it works

Governments use a number of tools to try to manage the growth of the economy in a stable and balanced way. One of their key tools is their influence, via central banks, over interest rates. Lowering interest rates can encourage financial institutions to lend more to businesses and individuals, which encourages those individuals and businesses to spend rather than to save.

In recent times, quantitative easing (QE) has been used when economic activity is sluggish and there is a fear of deflation or recession. QE involves the creation of new money—usually in the form of electronic currency—which the central bank then uses to buy government bonds or bonds from investors such as banks or pension funds. The aim is to increase the liquidity of money in the economy which will in turn lower interest rates and make lending easier and more attractive. This, in turn, should encourage businesses to invest and consumers to spend more, thus boosting the economy.

QE is still very much a monetary policy experiment in progress. There are concerns that it could lead to an inflation problem, and its detractors point out that its benefits are felt only in selected sectors of the economy.

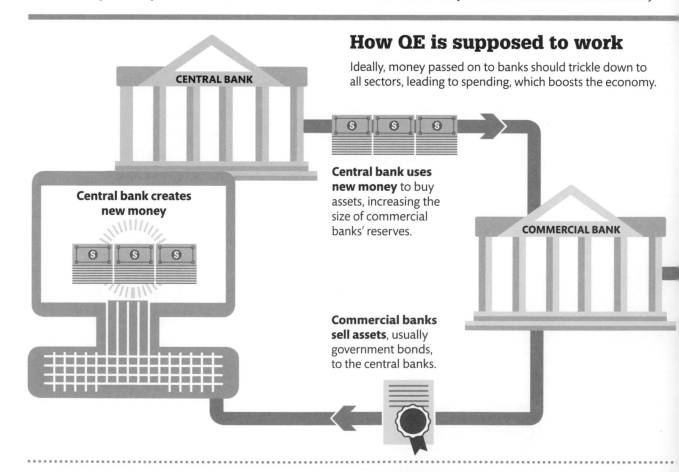

How QE is supposed to work

Ideally, money passed on to banks should trickle down to all sectors, leading to spending, which boosts the economy.

CENTRAL BANK

Central bank creates new money

Central bank uses new money to buy assets, increasing the size of commercial banks' reserves.

COMMERCIAL BANK

Commercial banks sell assets, usually government bonds, to the central banks.

DANGERS OF QUANTITATIVE EASING

QE is a new strategy and its effects are hard to measure. There is still disagreement about whether it can stimulate the economy without taking too many risks.

The economy may not respond as expected even to very large amounts of new money being created.

Inflation may occur due to increased money supply, but it is unlikely to lead to hyperinflation.

Banks don't always pass on the money to businesses in need, but hoard it or invest it elsewhere.

CASE STUDY

UK

The UK began a QE program in early 2009, after interest rates were cut to almost zero. Most of the new money has been used to purchase government debt. The effects of QE depend on what sellers do with the money they receive from selling assets, and what banks do with the additional liquidity they obtain. The Bank of England believes QE has boosted growth, but at the cost of higher inflation and increasing inequality of wealth, as prices rise.

$3.5 trillion
spent on QE purchases by the US government

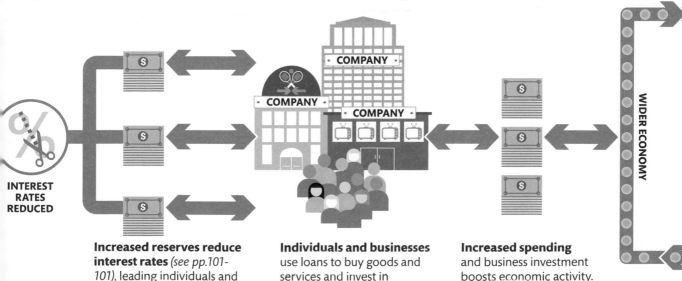

INTEREST RATES REDUCED

WIDER ECONOMY

Increased reserves reduce interest rates (*see pp.101-101*), leading individuals and businesses to borrow more.

Individuals and businesses use loans to buy goods and services and invest in businesses.

Increased spending and business investment boosts economic activity.

The level of taxation

It is difficult for governments to establish how much tax to levy. Too low, and the government cannot provide the services people want. Too high, and people will be unwilling to pay the tax.

How it works

Governments can impose taxes on a person's earnings, their buildings and homes, savings and investments, pensions, inherited property, or on what they spend. Most governments rely heavily on income taxes, usually with different proportionate levels for different levels of earnings. This makes the tax system fairer, but introducing more complexity also increases the chances of tax avoidance. However, some taxes are levied in order to change behavior. By taxing something viewed as bad, such as tobacco or alcohol, the government can help to persuade people to consume less of those things.

Pigouvian taxes

Standard economic theory says that if consuming a good or service causes harm, a tax should be applied to it until the value of the tax matches the cost of the harm done. As shown to the right, a government could impose a tax on sugar to match the cost to public health services of obesity. In the US, some states tax sugary drinks, but the percentage varies.

✓ NEED TO KNOW

> **Effective tax rate** Many tax systems allow different "reliefs"—such as investment relief to encourage investment. More than one tax may also be levied at once, for example income and corporation tax. As a result, the effective (average) tax rate may differ from the headline (basic) rate.

> **Marginal tax rate** Describes the additional tax paid from undertaking a small amount of extra activity—for example the extra tax paid in earning $1 more. Decisions made "at the margin" influence the behavior of individuals and businesses, such as whether it is worth working longer hours.

> **Gray economy** People who work for cash wages or fees and do not declare their income, in order to avoid paying tax.

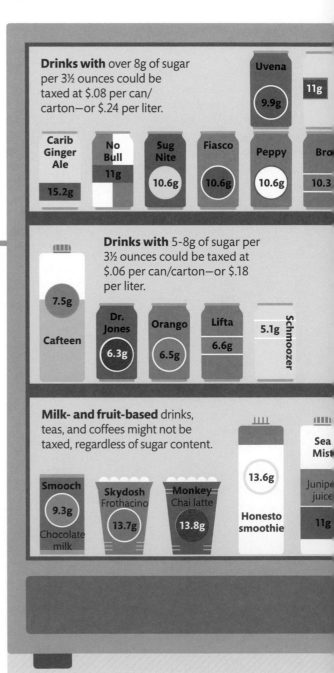

Drinks with over 8g of sugar per 3½ ounces could be taxed at $.08 per can/carton—or $.24 per liter.

Uvena 9.9g
11g
Carib Ginger Ale 15.2g
No Bull 11g
Sug Nite 10.6g
Fiasco 10.6g
Peppy 10.6g
Bro 10.3

Drinks with 5-8g of sugar per 3½ ounces could be taxed at $.06 per can/carton—or $.18 per liter.

7.5g Cafteen
Dr. Jones 6.3g
Orango 6.5g
Lifta 6.6g
Schmoozer 5.1g

Milk- and fruit-based drinks, teas, and coffees might not be taxed, regardless of sugar content.

Sea Mist
Smooch 9.3g Chocolate milk
Skydosh Frothacino 13.7g
Monkey Chai latte 13.8g
13.6g Honesto smoothie
Junipe juice 11g

THE LAFFER CURVE

The Laffer curve, named after US economist Arthur Laffer, illustrates the idea that there is an optimum level of taxation to maximize revenues. This is because at very high rates of taxation, more people will be looking to avoid or reduce the tax than will pay it. So, although tax revenues initially increase with rising tax rates, eventually they will decline. Controversy surrounds the idea because it is very hard to know where this optimum point might be and also because it would seem to legitimize non-payment of taxes by high net-worth individuals, and tax avoidance by ordinary people who start to participate in the "gray economy."

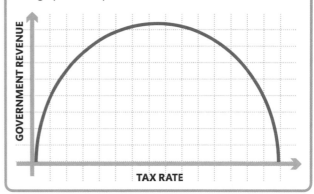

Unintended effects of tax

> Some US cities are assessing the tax by the ounce. This might encourage people to drink less.

> Consumers may turn to sugary untaxed drinks such as milkshakes and smoothies.

> The tax increase may hit poorer consumers harder, making it a regressive tax.

> Share prices and profits of drinks companies may fall, affecting government tax revenue.

> If businesses are affected, this may lead to the loss of jobs.

> In Mexico, a 10 percent tax on soft drinks has raised more than $2 billion since 2014, but sales have started to rise again after an initial drop.

24%
estimated percentage of economic activity in Greece that went undeclared and untaxed in 2013

Government spending and cuts

Governments today spend a large part of what an economy produces, using taxes to prioritize political commitments and potentially boosting their country's economy in the process.

How it works

Modern governments are expected to pay for a range of services that typically includes education, healthcare, pensions, and welfare payments. The electorate may also expect them to invest in roads, airports, water, electricity and gas supply, and other infrastructure.

However, governments cannot simply spend whatever they want. Healthy tax revenues are dependent on a thriving economy. Most governments attempt to prioritize their spending depending on their political commitments, setting an annual budget to allocate spending from taxes they expect to receive.

Typical government spending

How a government spends money depends on its political priorities, the size of the government relative to the economy, and its level of debt. For instance, Scandinavian countries famously prioritize significant welfare spending. Government spending can also boost the economy. By spending on infrastructure, governments can help to sustain economic activity. Funding scientific research aids product invention, feeding into economic growth, while spending on education can provide the training to make a workforce more productive.

SPENDING VS CUTS

Government spending can directly support the economy, such as expenditure on transportation and communications. Scientific research is often funded by the government, and spending on education helps to train workers. Some governments also subsidize and support key industries. However, many governments since the 2008 financial crash have tried to cut their spending to reduce their deficits (*see pp.146–147*). These decisions are controversial, as the long-term effects on the economy are still unknown.

$4.15 trillion
the United States federal government's budget for 2017

Medical programs 25%

Interest payments 6%

Transport 2%

Defense 16%

Social security 24%

Other 24%

...ation 3%

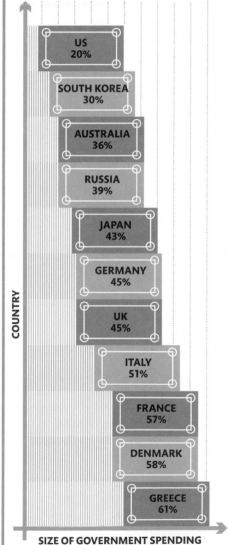

GOVERNMENT SPEND RELATIVE TO ITS ECONOMY

The size of a government's budget, relative to its economy, can vary. Typically, governments spend around 40 percent of GDP. The graph below shows some of the variation. South Korea's government spends 30 percent of GDP, but Denmark's spends 58 percent.

COUNTRY

US 20%
SOUTH KOREA 30%
AUSTRALIA 36%
RUSSIA 39%
JAPAN 43%
GERMANY 45%
UK 45%
ITALY 51%
FRANCE 57%
DENMARK 58%
GREECE 61%

SIZE OF GOVERNMENT SPENDING AS % OF TOTAL ECONOMY

How governments provide for the future

Government spending can help to shape how an economy develops. By investing in productive activities, as well as day-to-day items, governments can help their economies to grow.

How it works

As well as providing services like education and healthcare, governments also usually take responsibility for providing the buildings public services use, and for essential infrastructure like railways, electricity and gas supplies, and roads. Sometimes, governments will also invest in housing.

Spending on this is government investment, and appears as its "capital" spend in the national budget. It is equivalent to spending by private companies and

Government investment and returns

Governments can invest in many different areas of economic activity. The returns, such as those below, can benefit the government, or wider society.

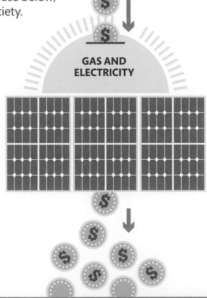

Returns to government

> **Direct** Passenger fares
> **Short-term** Tax on increased spending near stations
> **Long-term** New businesses move in
> **Indirect** Economic growth

Returns to government

> **Direct** Energy bills paid
> **Short-term** Lower energy costs
> **Long-term** More investment in infrastructure by business
> **Indirect** Economic growth

Returns to government

> **Direct** Utility bills paid
> **Short-term** Cheaper utility costs
> **Longer-term** Health and environmental benefits
> **Indirect** Growth of cities

individuals on things such as machinery and buildings, and in the same way the investment will produce a return over its lifetime. Sometimes this return is paid directly (for instance in passenger fares) and sometimes it appears indirectly (for instance in the economic benefits of a new road, helping businesses to trade and resulting in more tax revenues). Governments justify spending by showing the returns it will produce.

CAPITAL SPENDING AND BORROWING

To fund their capital spending, governments (just like businesses) will often borrow money. This means adding to their overall debt, so governments concerned with cutting debts will often look first at ways of reducing capital spending. However, this means missing out on the returns of an investment, so in order to lower the costs, many governments have used private funding. This allows the private investors to share in the returns. In some cases this means full privatization, in which a government allows a private firm to build and run the investment outright. When this is not possible or desirable, private investment may take the form of a deal between government and private investors to split the costs, risks, and profits of building and running the investment.

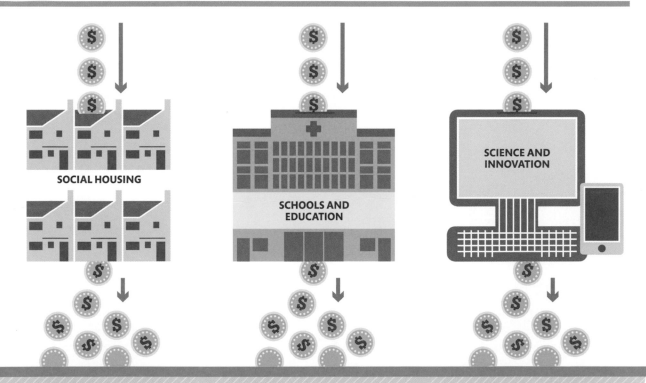

Returns to government
> **Direct** Rent from tenants
> **Short-term** Cheaper rents; less homelessness; more stable society
> **Longer-term** Growing towns
> **Indirect** Economic growth

Returns to government
> **Direct** None
> **Short-term** Public opinion
> **Longer-term** More productive workforce; better social cohesion
> **Indirect** Economic growth

Returns to government
> **Direct** Revenue from research
> **Short-term** Tax revenues
> **Longer-term** New markets; investment in business
> **Indirect** Faster economic growth

Inflation

The general increase of average prices in an economy, accompanied by a decrease in the purchasing power of money, is called inflation. This leads to a rise in the cost of living.

How it works

Inflation is the year-on-year rise in general prices. This increase is usually measured by the cost of a basket of representative household goods. As more money is needed to buy the same goods and services, the value of money decreases, and day-to-day living becomes more expensive. There are various factors that influence inflation, but changes in the supply and demand of goods and services, and of money, have a major impact. There are two main types of inflation: "cost-push" and "demand-pull." Cost-push inflation is driven by rising costs to businesses, which are then passed on to their customers. A business's costs might go up for a number of reasons, such as a rise in the price of a raw material or the need to raise the wages of employees. Demand-pull inflation happens when a high demand for goods exceeds the company's ability or willingness to provide them. Rather than increasing supply to match demand, businesses instead raise their prices. This alone would not cause demand-pull inflation, but if there is also an oversupply of money in the economy, consumers will continue to pay elevated prices, increasing them further—a case of too much money chasing too few goods.

Cost-push inflation

Several factors can cause costs to rise. An increase in the price of a raw material, for instance, can have a ripple effect, leading to a rise in prices throughout the economy. Increased energy and transportation costs can also push prices up. Higher salaries and taxes are other examples of expenses that are ultimately passed on to customers in the form of rising prices.

Cost of raw materials increases

The availability of an essential commodity, oil, becomes limited, raising its price and the cost of transportation, heating, and manufacture. This has an immediate and widespread impact on basic costs for businesses, particularly those that require the commodity for production, such as this car factory.

Cost of components increases

The rising price of oil increases the costs involved in making the components that are used to manufacture cars, raising the business's production costs.

"Inflation is always and everywhere a monetary phenomenon"

Milton Friedman

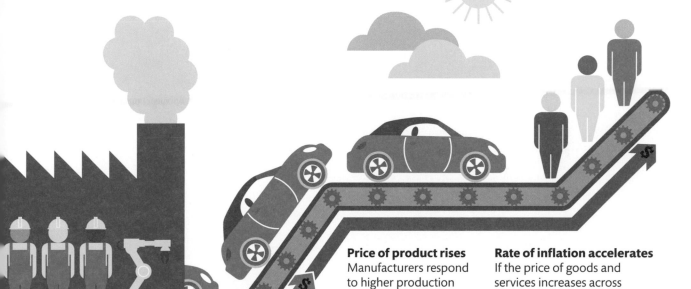

Price of product rises
Manufacturers respond to higher production costs by passing some of this on to customers.

Rate of inflation accelerates
If the price of goods and services increases across the economy, a higher rate of inflation results.

Higher wages
The employees demand better pay, as it appears that prices are rising. The company agrees and their overall costs increase.

Indirect tax increase
The government raises the sales tax on the car. The company offsets this by passing the cost on to consumers.

CAUSES OF COST-PUSH INFLATION

Cost-push inflation is driven by a rise in running costs for businesses. This can have a number of causes.

> **Costs of raw materials** Increases might be due to a scarcity resulting from a natural disaster, or an artificial limit imposed by a monopoly—for instance, the oil embargo in the 1970s, which tripled prices.

> **Labor costs** Strikes, low unemployment—meaning that companies need to pay more in order to attract skilled labor—strong unions, and staff expectation that general prices will rise can all result in the company's increasing wages and shifting the cost to customers.

> **Exchange rates** When a country's currency drops against a trading partner, more money is required to purchase goods from abroad, which can cause inflation.

> **Indirect taxes** A rise in excise taxes or other tax on a product might be passed on to the customer.

✓ NEED TO KNOW

> **Nominal values** Prices, wages, and other economic variables that are not adjusted in order to take account of inflation.

> **Real values** Figures adjusted for inflation and used when looking at economic variables over a period of time to determine whether increases are influenced by inflation or economic growth.

Inflation and the velocity of money circulation

It is not just the supply of money that affects growth in an economy, but also the rate at which money changes hands. This is called the "velocity" of money. It is a measure of how many times a unit of money has been used in transactions for goods and services over a period of time. For instance, if the same unit of money, such as $1, is spent three times in one year in three separate transactions, the velocity of money will be three. If the money supply increases rapidly, as well as the velocity of money, the supply of goods and services may not be able to keep pace with demand—there will be more money buying fewer goods. This can happen if the economy expands too rapidly, perhaps due to a sudden increase in money supply as a result of monetary policy. Companies respond by raising their prices, kickstarting demand-pull inflation.

However, a higher money supply may not necessarily result in an increase in velocity. If confidence in the economy is low, banks may limit loans, while individuals and businesses may hoard rather than spend their money. If there is less money pumping around an economy, inflation reduces.

Demand-pull inflation

In an expanding economy, a phone company experiences a sudden increase in demand for their product. However, since the company's resources are already at full capacity, they cannot increase their supply. Instead, they raise their product's price.

Demand rises
With more money available in the economy, there is a willingness to spend more money on products in general. This brand of mobile phone, a market leader, is particularly in demand.

Manufacture at maximum capacity
The factory is already producing at full capacity, with full employment. Without investment to increase production, which takes time, the supplier is unable to produce more.

Demand outstrips supply
Suppliers cannot increase output in the short term so consumer demand exceeds the number of products that can be supplied.

2%
the US federal government's target level of inflation

CAUSES OF DEMAND-PULL INFLATION

When an economy expands too rapidly, or unsustainably, an excess money supply can cause customer demand to overtake the supply of goods and services. An increase in spending is caused by several factors.

> **Monetary policy** A cut in interest rates leading to a relaxation of loan restrictions can increase money supply, leading to more borrowing and spending.

> **Government spending** Increased investment and spending by the state can expand the money supply, resulting in consumer activity.

> **Lower tax** A decrease in direct or indirect taxes can increase income.

> **Consumer confidence** If consumers and companies feel confident about the future, they may spend money they would otherwise have saved.

> **Property prices** High house prices can cause home owners to feel more wealthy, increasing their willingness to spend and thus their demand for consumer goods.

> **Rapid growth abroad** High export sales can increase the amount of money flowing into the country, with a ripple effect on inflation.

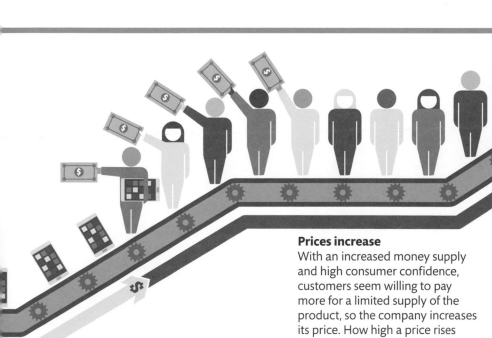

Effective demand
The rise in customer demand has an impact on the product's price, as it is an "effective demand": customers have the income to meet a higher price point and are willing to pay more for a product they perceive as valuable.

Prices increase
With an increased money supply and high consumer confidence, customers seem willing to pay more for a limited supply of the product, so the company increases its price. How high a price rises depends on consumer demand for the product; if price elasticity of demand is inelastic—the item is something that customers need and cannot do without—the price point may be pushed higher.

Rising rate of inflation
If consumer spending increases generally across the economy, and businesses respond by raising prices, rather than output, then a higher rate of inflation will result.

Balance of payments

A country's balance of payments (BOP) is a record of its international transactions over a set period of time. This record tracks goods, services, and investment into, and out of, the country.

COUNTRY

How it works

A country's balance of payments account provides a record of all of its international credits and debits. Transactions that result in money flowing into a country will appear as a credit, while transactions moving money out of the country will appear as a debit. The BOP account has three parts: the current account, which measures goods and services; the capital account, which tracks the movement of capital and nonfinancial assets; and the financial account, a subdivision of the capital account, which looks at investment.

In theory, a country's BOP should total zero, as each credit to the current account will correspond with a debit to the capital account, and vice versa. Realistically, as a result of variations in accounting practices and exchange rate fluctuations, this rarely happens.

International flow

A country's balance of payments includes transactions by individuals, businesses, and the government. Tracking these transactions helps the government determine how much money is coming into and leaving the country, and in which economic areas there is a deficit or surplus.

THE THREE PARTS OF A BOP ACCOUNT

A balance of payments account is separated into three main accounts, each of which track different types of international transactions into and out of the country. The three main accounts are, in turn, divided into subaccounts, to chart specific areas of expenditure.

Current account
❯ Raw materials and merchandise
❯ Services, such as business, tourism, or transportation
❯ Income, including from property and shares

❯ Unilateral or one-way transfers, such as foreign aid or gifts

Capital account
❯ Capital transfers, such as money transfers or assets of migrants
❯ Nonproduced, nonfinancial assets, such as natural resources and land

Financial account
❯ Assets held abroad, such as bonds, investment, and foreign currency
❯ Foreign-owned assets at home, including bonds, investment, and local currency

COUNTRY'S BOP		
CURRENT ACCOUNT	CAPITAL ACCOUNT	FINANCIAL ACCOUNT
Credit	Debit	Debit
+$2bn	–$1bn	–$1bn
TOTAL: 0		

REST OF THE WORLD

Goods and services
$3bn

IMPORT

Current account

The current account is mainly concerned with the international exchange of goods and services.

$3bn - $1bn = $2bn

EXPORT

Goods and services
$1bn

Money transfers and land
$1bn

Capital account

This account is chiefly for recording the movement of money and nonfinancial, nonproductive assets.

$1bn - $2bn = $-1bn

Money transfers and land
$2bn

Currency and stocks
$1bn

Financial account

This account monitors international positions in local and foreign currency, bonds, and investment.

$1bn - $2bn = $-1bn

Currency and stocks
$2bn

Zero

Current account
$2bn

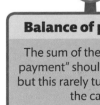

Balance of payment

The sum of the "balance of payment" should equal zero, but this rarely turns out to be the case.

Capital and financial accounts
−$2bn

International currency fluctuations

Exchange rates fluctuate according to supply and demand. If one country has a stronger, more stable economy than its trading partners, then its currency will be valued more highly.

How it works

A country's economic conditions change from day to day, which is why exchange rates also fluctuate continuously. These currency fluctuations are determined in foreign exchange markets around the globe when currencies are traded (a buyer selling one currency to buy another).

Buyers base their trading decisions primarily on the performance of a country's economy. They examine real-time data such as interest rates, and political and commercial events that will affect economic performance—such as elections, the crash of a financial institution, or news of increased investment in manufacturing facilities. Four key economic factors—gross domestic production (GDP), inflation, employment, and interest rates—indicate how well a country's economy is performing, and determine its exchange rates.

Political stability is also crucial. If investors fear that a government is not capable of managing its country's economy, they will lose confidence, sell their investments in that country, and exchange the local currency for other currencies. This in effect pushes down the value of the local currency by increasing the supply of it and reducing the demand for it.

Weak currency

These economic factors—either by themselves or combined with each other—can trigger a fall in the value of a country's currency.

LOW INTEREST RATES
Low rates encourage domestic growth, but do not attract investors to buy currency.

HIGH INFLATION
Inflation increases the cost of export goods, lowering demand for them and for the exporter's currency.

FALLING GDP
Shrinking production indicates that demand for a country's exports, and so for its currency, has fallen.

HIGH UNEMPLOYMENT
Rising unemployment may signal falling production and a lack of competitiveness.

LOW CONFIDENCE
Nervous investors sell local currency and so depress the exchange rate.

✔ NEED TO KNOW

❯ **Dovish** A cautious government monetary policy that encourages lower interest rates.

❯ **Hawkish** An aggressive government monetary policy that is likely to lead to higher interest rates.

❯ **Capital flight** The movement of money invested in one country's currency to another; usually caused by a drop in investor confidence.

Currency fluctuations

The state of the economy in any country will dictate whether its currency will rise or fall against other currencies. Interest rates, inflation, productivity, and employment will all have a bearing on currency. Investor confidence also affects exchange rates—investors favor countries with a sound political regime, efficient infrastructure, educated workforce, and social stability.

$5.3 trillion

the typical value of foreign exchange trades made each day

Bank counteractions

When a country's central bank expects the currency's value to drop, it tries to shrink the money supply.

Bank

INCREASING INTEREST RATES
Increasing interest rates attracts investors to buy the country's currency as they will be rewarded with high rates of interest.

SELLING FOREIGN RESERVES
Selling foreign reserves and retaining domestic currency increases demand for the domestic currency.

Strong currency

These factors signal a booming economy, and boost demand for the country's currency as well as increasing its value.

HIGH INTEREST RATES
Higher rates attract foreign investors and increase the value of the currency.

STABLE INFLATION
Stable or falling inflation can help to boost the value of the local currency.

RISING GDP
High production rates demonstrate demand for a country's products, and thus its currency.

LOW UNEMPLOYMENT
Employment is linked to GDP, indicating that a country's products are in demand.

HIGH CONFIDENCE
Confidence in a nation's economy can be enough to keep its currency buoyant.

THE IMPORTANCE OF RESERVE CURRENCY

Reserve currency is a recognized safe foreign currency held by a country's central bank and financial institutions and used to make trade payments. Using the reserve currency avoids the need to change payments into local currency, minimizing the exchange-rate risk for both countries. Many central banks set a reserve ratio—the percentage of domestic currency that the bank must hold. The US dollar is the currency most commonly held in reserves worldwide.

Managing state pensions

Most governments use taxpayer money from current workers to fund pensions for those who have retired. Some governments invest taxpayer money to increase the overall pension fund.

How it works

In most countries, it is the current working generation that is funding the pensions of those who have reached retirement age, as well as the pensions of those who are due to retire. This is the case in the US, where Social Security contributions from current workers fund retirement benefits for those who reach the age for Social Security. Governments need to ensure there is enough money to go around, a task that is all the more challenging because in most developed countries the population is aging, which means that fewer and fewer workers will be funding the pensions of an increasing number of older people.

Measuring how well pension funds are likely to meet current and future liabilities is key to the successful management of state pensions.

Managing investments

In countries with sovereign wealth fund the government invests taxpayers' contributions to increase the available money in the fund. Investment is usually core assets, which are less risky but can fluctuate. If stock markets rise, so do pension funds, and vice versa.

Managing contributions

In some countries, such as Chile and Japan, and at a state level in the US, pension managers invest the funds collected from taxpayers with the aim of keeping the amount of available money high enough to meet predicted demand. In other countries, any surplus in the pension fund (such as the National Insurance Fund in the UK) may be lent to the government, but in general it is simply used to pay for the pensions of people who have already retired.

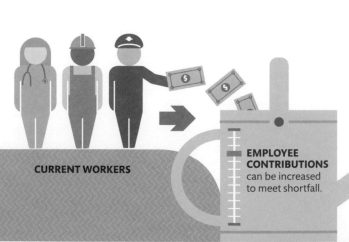

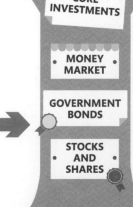

CURRENT WORKERS

EMPLOYEE CONTRIBUTIONS can be increased to meet shortfall.

Assets

CORE INVESTMENTS

MONEY MARKET

GOVERNMENT BONDS

STOCKS AND SHARES

INFRASTRUCTURE ASSET INVESTMENT

"A pension is nothing more than deferred compensation"

Elizabeth Warren

⚠ WARNING

> **Overinvestment in equity** (stocks and shares), which can promise high returns, poses a potential risk to any pension fund, and can be especially damaging to state pension funds. Japan discovered this after the nation's Government Pension Investment Fund lost 5.6 percent of its value in the third quarter of 2015 due to stock market investments.

> **Government priorities** can influence the way pension contributions are invested—not necessarily in the best interests of the pension pool or its future ability to make payments. In some countries, a percentage of pension contributions are lent to the government for other purposes, or invested in public projects such as housing.

LIABILITIES

Payments to pensioners will appear as a liability on the government balance sheet. Demographics influence the amount of money needed to meet this liability. For example, if the population is projected to live longer in old age, the amount needed for future payments will rise.

Increased assets from investments

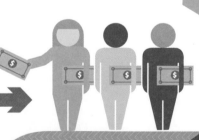

SOCIAL SECURITY BENEFITS

Measuring health

Sufficient money must come in to the pension fund to maintain or improve it. The fund's performance can be assessed in two ways:

> **Funding level** The amount of money in a pension fund compared to the amount of pension that needs to be paid out. This can be expressed as a percentage or as a ratio (the assets divided by the liabilities). A funding level of 100%, or a ratio above 1, means that there will be enough money in the pension fund to meet the payment obligations. A funding level below 100%, or a ratio below 1, means there is not enough.

> **Deficit** The difference between the liabilities and assets in a pension fund—i.e. the shortfall between the money coming in and the money due to be paid out. This is also known as unfunded liability.

Why governments fail financially

It is possible for a government to fail financially, and there are two main ways this can happen. The first is when it loses the ability to meet its obligations to repay its debt, potentially leading to a default. The second is when it fails to reassure the public that the value of its currency, or money itself, can still be trusted, potentially leading to hyperinflation. Fundamentally both causes are due to a loss of public trust. So, if a government cannot be trusted, it is more likely to fail.

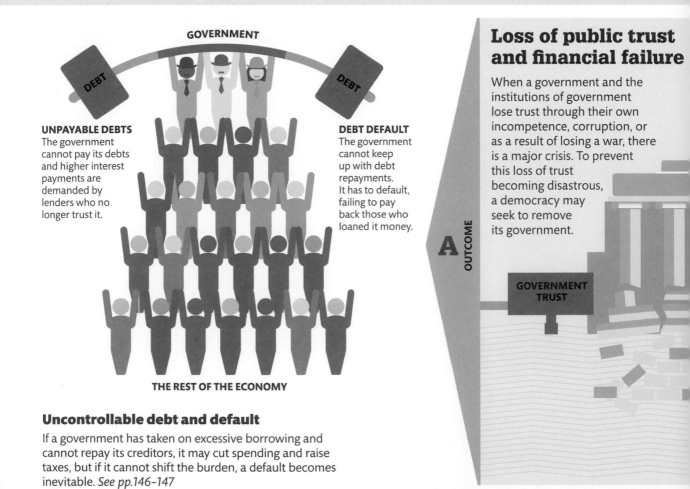

GOVERNMENT

DEBT

DEBT

UNPAYABLE DEBTS
The government cannot pay its debts and higher interest payments are demanded by lenders who no longer trust it.

DEBT DEFAULT
The government cannot keep up with debt repayments. It has to default, failing to pay back those who loaned it money.

THE REST OF THE ECONOMY

Uncontrollable debt and default

If a government has taken on excessive borrowing and cannot repay its creditors, it may cut spending and raise taxes, but if it cannot shift the burden, a default becomes inevitable. *See pp.146–147*

A OUTCOME

Loss of public trust and financial failure

When a government and the institutions of government lose trust through their own incompetence, corruption, or as a result of losing a war, there is a major crisis. To prevent this loss of trust becoming disastrous, a democracy may seek to remove its government.

GOVERNMENT TRUST

6 countries have never defaulted on their debt: New Zealand, Australia, Canada, Thailand, Denmark, and the US

THE IMPORTANCE OF TRUST

Gaining trust

Trust is critical to making money and for governments to work properly. It is necessary for economic growth. If people do not believe a government's financial promises, it may lose control of the economy. Trust is hard to win, and usually comes from political stability over a period of time.

Losing trust

Governments can lose trust in many different ways. A weak government might decide to issue more money to meet the demands made on it, instead of raising taxes. A government unable to repay its own debts, especially those owed to other countries, may decide that defaulting on the debt is easier than trying to levy taxes to pay. In both cases, trust in the government and its money will be undermined.

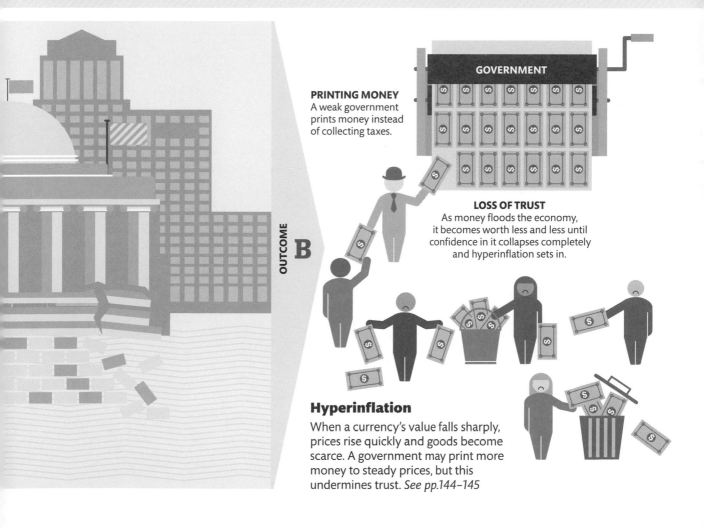

OUTCOME **B**

PRINTING MONEY
A weak government prints money instead of collecting taxes.

GOVERNMENT

LOSS OF TRUST
As money floods the economy, it becomes worth less and less until confidence in it collapses completely and hyperinflation sets in.

Hyperinflation
When a currency's value falls sharply, prices rise quickly and goods become scarce. A government may print more money to steady prices, but this undermines trust. *See pp.144–145*

How governments fail: hyperinflation

Public confidence in a country's currency can collapse, resulting in exceptionally high rates of inflation. These episodes of hyperinflation are comparatively rare, but always very serious.

How it works

Trust in the value of a currency is essential to maintain price stability in modern economies. Governments therefore seek to control money supply in order to prevent dramatic price fluctuations that could erode trust. But when governments are weak or not trusted, these controls can break down. A weak government, for example, may be unwilling to raise taxes to pay for public spending, printing money to pay for it instead. Prices can thus rise very rapidly as citizens refuse to believe that money has any value, and so they demand more of it in any sale. Governments can subsequently feel pressured to issue more and more money in order to keep the economy moving. When this happens, hyperinflation sets in, and it can be very hard for governments to regain control.

 Case study: Hyperinflation in Germany, 1921–24

Germany experienced an infamous period of hyperinflation after World War I.

COLLAPSE IN TRUST

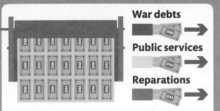

1. Following war defeat, Germany's new government is unstable. It prints money to pay for war debts, reparations, and public services.

2. The German government starts using the money it prints to purchase foreign currency, causing a collapse in the value of the German mark.

3. By 1922, Germany cannot pay reparations. France and Belgium occupy the Ruhr to enforce payment in goods instead of money.

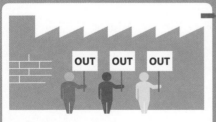

4. German workers in the Ruhr go on strike. The government prints more money to pay their wages.

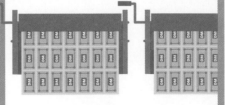

5. As the economy collapses, the German government continues to print money.

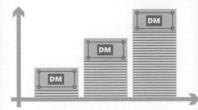

6. Domestic prices in Germany explode as confidence in the currency evaporates.

HYPERINFLATION

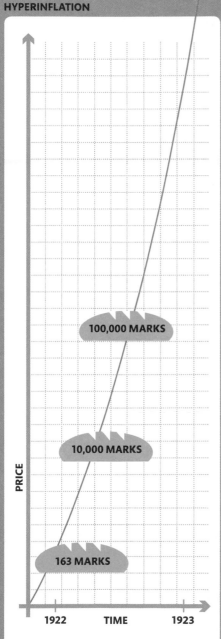

200,000,000,000 MARKS

100,000 MARKS

10,000 MARKS

163 MARKS

PRICE

1922   TIME   1923

7. Hyperinflation sets in and prices rise faster than people can spend their money. In 1922, a loaf of bread cost 163 marks—by November 1923 this had risen to 200,000,000,000 marks.

STOPPING HYPERINFLATION

Credibility

Because hyperinflation is based on expectations about the future, with people believing prices will carry on rising rapidly, it can also be halted rapidly (in theory). If the government can credibly commit to ending inflation (for example, by introducing a new currency and tight rules on issuing it), it can stop hyperinflation with limited costs. However, fulfilling that commitment can be challenging, particularly for weak governments.

Dictatorship

One controversial argument is that because hyperinflation results from weak governments, ending hyperinflation requires a strong government—even one that ends democracy. Economist Thomas Sargent has made this argument for central Europe in the 1920s, where a series of hyperinflationary episodes were halted by authoritarian governments.

460 septillion

the number of Hungarian pengö to 1US$ at the height of hyperinflation in July 1946

NEW GOVERNMENT

8. A new government is formed in November 1923, with a new president of the German central bank. The central bank stops paying government debts with printed money. A new currency, the Rentenmark, is introduced, replacing the near-worthless paper mark. The Rentenmark is backed by mortgages on land, while the new central bank president promises to fix its exchange rate against the dollar. These measures restore public confidence in the currency. Some of Germany's war debts are written off and reparations reduced in 1924–25. The situation is stabilized.

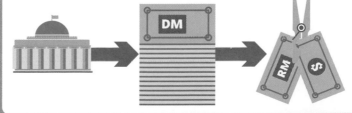

How governments fail: debt default

A government can find its debts spiraling out of control, as interest payments rise faster than it can raise taxes. Once this happens, the government is on the path to default.

How it works

Ideally, government borrowing should remain stable. Sometimes, however, even a well-run government can be hit by an unexpected and costly event, such as a currency crisis or a sharp recession. When this happens, the government may find itself borrowing increasing amounts to try and keep up with interest payments due on its existing debt.

To alleviate this pressure, a government may increase taxes and cut public spending to bring in money. In practice this may mean government employees accepting payment as an IOU in lieu of cash, or a reduction in public services. If these measures fail, a government may eventually be forced to default on the debt and admit that it cannot pay. Governments that default on a debt will find it very difficult to borrow in the future, since trust in the country's economic stability will be low. However, countries that default on their debts do sometimes recover very rapidly.

INTEREST PAYMENTS

Those lending money to countries will charge more if they think the risk of a default is high, to compensate for that risk. The danger for any country with large amounts of debt is that this means a debt spiral can become a self-fulfilling prophecy. As lenders lose confidence and demand more in interest payments, the debt becomes more difficult to control, and default is more likely.

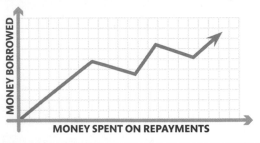

Argentina 1998–2001

The debt spiral in which Argentina found itself from 1998 until 2001 resulted in what was the largest default in history at that time (it has since been dwarfed by the 2012 "restructuring" of Greece's debt). Argentina owed a large amount of money, and was borrowing more from other countries and the International Monetary Fund (IMF), until a recession prevented it from repaying its debts fully and the country defaulted.

Borrowing increases

DEBT RISES

Recession

IMF World Bank US

DEBT

1. Following a period of hyperinflation during the 1990s, Argentina attempts to implement IMF rules. It finds itself having to borrow substantially from official institutions such as the IMF, and from other countries such as the US.

6. The economic downturn in the country worsens.

5. Argentina's government implements austerity measures in an attempt to cut costs.

€107 billion amount of Greek debt written off in 2012

7. Argentina's repayments are still too small to control rising levels of debt.

Borrowing increases
DEBT RISES

9. The IMF withdraws its economic support.

8. Argentina fails to meet conditions set out by the IMF on deficit targets.

10. Argentina cannot repay its $120 billion debt, and defaults.

3. Its repayments fail to bring debt under control.

Argentina defaults

11. The value of the currency plummets.

12. Argentinian unemployment reaches 20%.

2. Argentina borrows heavily from elsewhere in the world.

13. A run on the banks leads to the government freezing deposits.

DEBT

Borrowing increases
DEBT RISES

14. Civil unrest and rioting break out.

15. A period of political instability sets in.

4. The countries it has borrowed from lose faith in Argentina's ability to pay.

Argentina enters a debt spiral

16. Agreements on repayments in 2002 help promote a boom.

PERSONAL FINANCE

> Worth, wealth, and income > Investments for income
> Wealth-building investments > Managing investments
> Pensions and retirement > Debt > Money in the digital age

Worth, wealth, and income

Wealth is a measure of the value of the assets owned by an individual, group, or country. An individual's net worth is the value of any assets owned, minus any debt owed or personal liabilities. Income is earned through working and can also be gained from assets owned. Being aware of their net position can make it much easier for individuals to set financial goals, establish effective investment strategies, and achieve financial independence on or before retirement.

Planning for financial independence

To gain financial independence a person must have sufficient money to be able to pay their living expenses without work, for example after retirement. This can be achieved by saving and investing well, so accumulating enough wealth to live on, or by generating a passive income that will continue paying out when retirement age is reached.

Assess situation
Calculate the value of assets such as cash, stocks, bonds, property, and retirement funds. Then subtract liabilities—loans, credit card debts, and mortgage. *See pp.152–153*

Set financial goals
Start by establishing retirement age. Assess how much income will be needed to maintain a good standard of living in retirement.

Increase savings from income
Save from income and evaluate savings regularly to ensure they are performing efficiently—the higher the yield, the better chance of reaching the financial goal.
See pp.154–155

PROS AND CONS OF A FINANCIAL ADVISOR

Pros

A financial advisor assesses their client's circumstances and identifies mortgage, pension, and investment products that best meet their financial goals. This is useful for people who do not have time to research markets. It is possible to take action against an advisor if poor advice was given or a person feels that a product has been mis-sold.

Cons

Financial advisors have a limited role and do not advise on day-to-day money issues, such as finding the best savings rates or reducing household expenses, but this information can be easily found in newspapers or online. Financial advice can also be expensive—advisors might charge an hourly fee or based on commission—or both.

52%
number of pre-retirees who use a financial advisor

Manage debt
Pay off credit cards and loans as quickly as possible. Look for cheaper interest rates that can bring down the cost of loans and that can also help reduce mortgage debt more quickly. *See pp.156–157*

Use investment payouts
When investments produce additional income, use the funds to reduce any debt, as well as reinvesting to build up assets. *See pp.160–161*

Financial independence
Effective investment over a lifetime builds up wealth or passive income. If successful, an individual can maintain a good standard of living without the need to work.

Calculating and analyzing net worth

A person's wealth—or net worth—can be calculated by adding up all of the assets they own and subtracting from this total the amount of any debt that they owe.

Net worth statement

Individuals can calculate their net worth at any given time by subtracting debts from assets. They can then compare statements over months or years to track any changes.

ASSETS – DEBT = NET WORTH

Assets

Liquid assets

Easily accessible sources of cash

> Cash in hand
> Cash held in current account
> Cash value of life insurance
> Money market funds
> Certificates of deposit
> Short-term investments

Investment assets

Convertible to cash in the short or long term

> Term deposits held at the bank
> Securities, stocks, shares, or bonds
> Investment real estate
> Endowment policies
> Retirement funds

Debts

Short-term liabilities

Payable within the next 12 months

> Credit card interest and capital repayments
> Repayments on a personal or student loan
> Current monthly household bills (e.g., for utilities, communications, and insurance)
> Unpaid personal income tax for the year

Long-term liabilities

Payable over more than 12 months

> Mortgage or rental payments
> Child support or alimony if separated or divorced
> Children's education through to college
> Payments to a pension fund
> A hire-purchase contract or lease for a car

How it works

The net worth figure tells financial institutions a lot about an individual's financial status. Over time, a person's net worth can fluctuate—for example, total assets will be boosted if bank deposits earn interest, or the level of debt will increase if a new mortgage is taken out. If a person's net worth figure increases, it means they are enjoying good financial health; if the figure decreases, the opposite is true.

Net worth is a more relevant indicator of financial health than income or wealth because it takes into account any debt that may be owed or that will accrue.

$30 million
liquid asset value of ultra-high net worth individuals

Personal assets

Can be sold for cash but may take time

> Home, which can be sold if downsizing
> Additional property such as a vacation home
> Art, jewelry, and other valuables
> Furniture, especially collectable pieces
> Vehicles (although they lose value quickly)

✓ NEED TO KNOW

> **Positive net worth**
  When assets are greater than debts.

> **Negative net worth**
  When debts are greater than assets.

High net worth individual (HNWI)
A person with very high levels of liquid assets, commonly viewed as over $1 million.

Net worth

This figure—assets minus debt—can be used by anyone to assess an individual's wealth at any point in time.

> If the figure is negative, debts are greater than the value of assets and financial health is poor.

> If the figure is positive, assets are greater than the value of debts and financial health is OK or good.

> Financial advisors suggest calculating net worth once a year.

? Contingent liabilities

May be owed in the future

> Taxes such as capital gains
> Car or other loan guarantees for children who may fail to pay
> Damage claims such as lawsuits
> Attorney fees for personal legal disputes

LIQUIDITY AND NET WORTH

Although net worth is a useful measure of current wealth, liquidity tells savers and investors how much cash they could access in an emergency. It is worth keeping a proportion of investments in a form that can be easily converted into cash.

Income and wealth

Two of the key concepts of personal finance, income and wealth, represent different states of an individual's finances. Income is moving and often unstable, while wealth is mainly static and stable.

Income

Income is money that flows into a household. It is used to pay for housing, bills, food, and other essential needs as well as nonessentials such as vacations.

Turning income into wealth

Unless they inherit a large sum of money, or win it in a lottery, most people need to rely on creating wealth through savings. The formula is simple but requires patience and discipline. The amount of money going out each week or month (outgoings) must be kept lower than the amount coming in (income) over the same period, and the difference should be saved and invested as soon as possible.

INCOME (AFTER TAX)

Earnings

Income also includes any benefits or tax allowances as well as returns on investments.

SALARY

RENTAL INCOME

INTEREST

SHARE DIVIDENDS

OUTGOINGS

Costs

Household expenditure can be regulated via a budget, which will help pinpoint where economies can be made.

FOOD

HOUSING

TRANSPORTATION

CLOTHES

How it works

Wealth is the value of a person's assets, savings, and investments, while income is the money received regularly in return for work, from investments, or as a benefit or pension. Recognizing the difference between the two concepts is key to both building and protecting wealth. Income that is closely managed and carefully invested can create wealth over time.

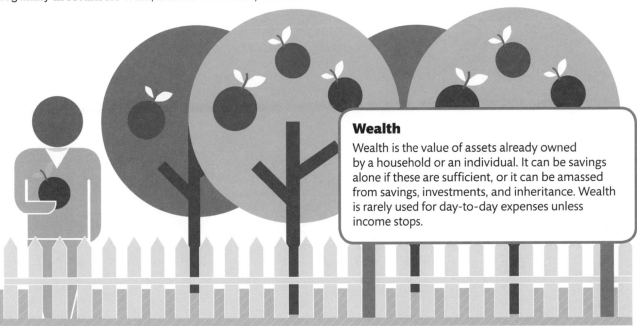

Wealth

Wealth is the value of assets already owned by a household or an individual. It can be savings alone if these are sufficient, or it can be amassed from savings, investments, and inheritance. Wealth is rarely used for day-to-day expenses unless income stops.

WEALTH

 ### Debts

Debt should be paid off as quickly as possible unless there are tax advantages in spreading repayments.

CREDIT CARD

LOANS

MORTGAGE

EDUCATION

Savings

The amount left after costs and debt commitments are met is savings. This should be invested into assets as soon as possible.

INVESTED INTO ▶

Assets

The most efficient investments generate income and boost savings as well as increasing in value over time.

PROPERTY

SHARES

ART

JEWELRY

Converting income into wealth

High earnings alone do not guarantee wealth. Keeping outgoings lower than income, accruing savings, and investing them wisely are key to long-term financial security.

How it works

There is no formula to determine how much wealth is enough, or how much income is needed to build wealth. It depends on the individual. High earners tend to have higher lifestyle expectations than those on lower incomes. They must therefore save more, and invest more, to generate the wealth they need to maintain their lifestyle during retirement. The danger for this group is that high wages can lead to a false sense of affluence, resulting in big spending on lifestyle but little set aside in savings.

In order to start building wealth, a proportion of after-tax income should be saved regularly. Some financial advisers suggest a goal of one-third.

When a high income fails to produce wealth

A top salary will not ensure a secure retirement if saving habits are poor. To set aside a third of after-tax income each month might seem an impossible target, but even saving as little as 10 percent can create a decent stockpile of cash for investment over time.

Spending levels

High-income earner **A** is accustomed to spending money on goods with little long-term value.

High-income earners

Two senior managers at the same company earn identical salaries. However, they use their money differently, with contrasting results.

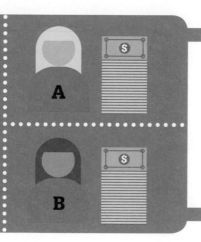

A

B

B

Earner **B** invests in a retirement fund and shares, and saves in a high-interest account.

70% of the richest Americans claim to be self-made

A PERSONAL BUDGET

There are many ways in which household spending can be curtailed in the pursuit of wealth—even the smallest changes can be significant when continued year after year because any reduction in spending can be invested in savings. Setting and sticking to a budget will help meet savings goals. Other savings strategies include:

> **Setting financial goals**, such as buying a house or funding a masters' degree.

> **Drawing up a spending plan** for expenditures such as housing, food, transportation, and debt repayments.

> **Monitoring budgets** weekly or monthly to keep track of spending.

> **Deciding on a percentage** of income to save each month, and setting up a direct debit for that amount to go straight into a savings account.

> **Finding cheaper accommodation**, or refinancing a mortgage to achieve a cheaper rate.

> **Comparing insurance rates** and switching to a cheaper insurer; comparing deals from different energy suppliers to cut utility bills.

> **Shopping with a list** to eliminate impulse buys, and buying in bulk in order to take advantage of cheaper prices or sales.

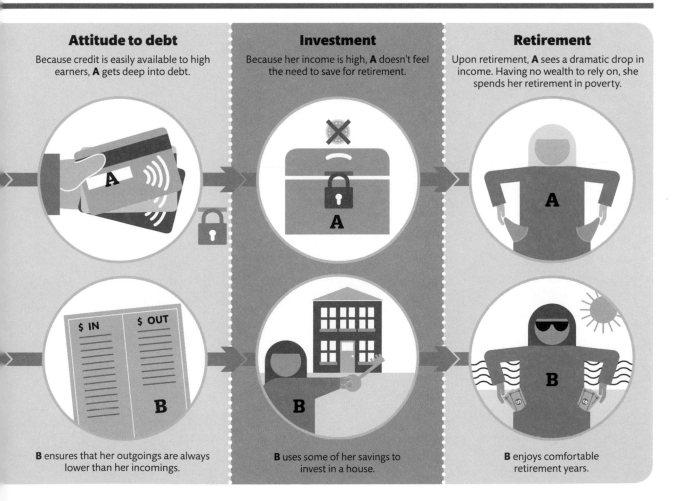

Attitude to debt

Because credit is easily available to high earners, **A** gets deep into debt.

B ensures that her outgoings are always lower than her incomings.

Investment

Because her income is high, **A** doesn't feel the need to save for retirement.

B uses some of her savings to invest in a house.

Retirement

Upon retirement, **A** sees a dramatic drop in income. Having no wealth to rely on, she spends her retirement in poverty.

B enjoys comfortable retirement years.

Generating income

Earning sufficient income to ensure regular savings and investments is the basis of building wealth. The more sources of income the better, especially if some of those sources are passive, or unearned.

How it works

Wealth can be built in various ways, almost all of which rely on income. Inheriting money, property, or other assets is the fast track to wealth, but for anyone who does not have an inheritance, savings and investments are the two principal strategies. Income can be earned in two main ways. The more common route is via active or earned income, such as wages, which usually involve a degree of exertion to generate.

Passive income includes rent from property and portfolio income, such as dividends from stocks and shares or interest from bonds. Regardless of the source of income, if an individual's earnings are not high enough to cover expenses and still have some left over, it becomes almost impossible to build wealth. With this in mind, any goal of becoming wealthy must be underpinned by a strategy for generating and sustaining enough income to allow savings.

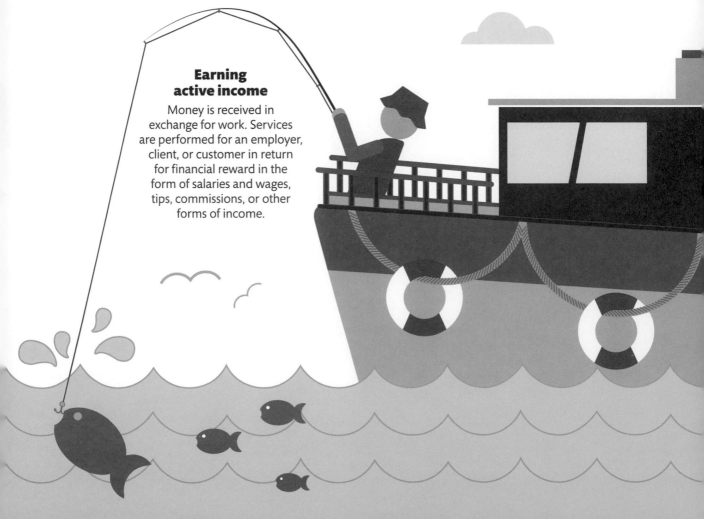

Earning active income

Money is received in exchange for work. Services are performed for an employer, client, or customer in return for financial reward in the form of salaries and wages, tips, commissions, or other forms of income.

EARNING PASSIVE INCOME

 Savings accounts can offer modest to high returns, but savers should know their other terms before investing.

 Blogging on a popular subject can be monetized in various ways.

 Royalty payments can be negotiated for photography, writing, or other creative work.

 Rent from a house or spare room can provide individuals with a regular source of funds.

 Online market places, garage sales and auctions can raise funds through selling unwanted items.

 Focus and market research groups pay individuals to test new products.

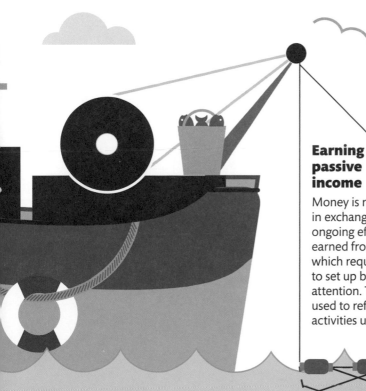

NEED TO KNOW

❯ **Portfolio income** Money earned from interest, dividends, or capital gains. This is recognized as a separate type of income by tax authorities in some countries, such as the US.

❯ **Capital gain** The profit earned from the sale of an asset, such as a house or art, that has gone up in value since it was first bought.

❯ **Unearned income** Money from investments, pension funds, alimony, interest, or rental property.

Earning passive income

Money is received in exchange for little ongoing effort. It is earned from investments, which require some work to set up but then need less attention. The term can also be used to refer to money-making activities undertaken on the side.

Generating wealth

The billionaires who appear on annual lists of the world's wealthiest individuals may have built their empires in different ways, but almost all relied on starting with at least a little cash to invest.

Building wealth

Most people begin by earning an income and saving a portion of it to build wealth, ensuring they have financial security in the future. Generating enough money for business ventures or investments goes hand in hand with creating wealth. Making small changes in lifestyle can cut spending and increase savings so even people on the lowest incomes can take their first steps on the road to affluence.

2. Store and save

A strict household budget will reduce outgoings, which can then be reinvested.

❯ **Track spending** Monitoring money going out will indicate where costs can be cut.

❯ **Set a budget** Sticking to a plan makes it easier for individuals to see the path to personal wealth.

❯ **Build credit** High savings and low debt ensure a better credit rating, as does paying your bills on time, allowing options for future investment borrowing.

1. Earn income

Converting income to wealth is crucial. Working to earn an income, whether actively, passively, or a combination of the two, brings essential money into the household on a regular basis.

❯ **Active earnings** Saving can maximize money received and workers can relocate for a potentially higher income.

❯ **Passive income** Income can be boosted with investments, and by buying and selling possessions.

How it works

Building wealth requires discipline and a long-term strategy for optimum results. For most people wealth is amassed over time using funds saved from income, which are then invested to make even more money. It is a good idea to spread investments over a variety of financial instruments and if a person is not confident initially, it is worth seeking professional guidance.

3. Invest wisely

Investing is a balancing act—the nearer a person is to retirement the less risk they can afford.

> **Factor in retirement age** Starting early gives savers greater flexibility.

> **Consider options** Cash savings, shares, property, and pensions offer differing returns.

> **Assess the risk factors** It is important to balance the yield versus risk of each option.

4. Maintain and manage wealth

Decisions made at the start will determine how quickly a person can build wealth.

> **Reevaluate investments** Moving funds may mean better returns and lower fees.

> **Time decisions** Global political and economic events affect when to sell, cash in, or reinvest.

> **Make a will** A tax-efficient will ensures that wealth can be passed on.

70%
of US families lose wealth by the second generation

DIFFERENT ROUTES TO BUILDING WEALTH

The aim of investing is to make money and there are ways to do it to suit your lifestyle and interests.

Traditional investment Asset values fluctuate with economic changes, so many investors watch events closely to try to time their investments.

Through property Residential property can provide capital growth or a steady rental income. Vacation homes generate less capital growth, but a potentially high income.

In businesses Ideas require little to no investment and there can be long-term potential. Investing in a start-up can result in big gains, but many fail so it can be risky.

Investments for income

The main aim of personal finance planning is to ensure that there is enough money to buy a larger house if an individual's family grows, to provide for children's education, and ultimately to have a healthy income in retirement. To achieve this, individuals should invest in assets that will generate a stream of cash in the future. Many investors use a management service to look after their money in return for a percentage of returns; others prefer to research and invest directly on their own.

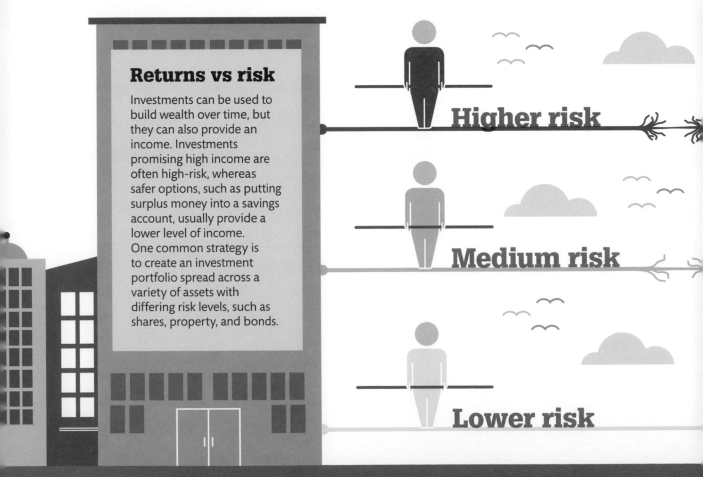

Returns vs risk

Investments can be used to build wealth over time, but they can also provide an income. Investments promising high income are often high-risk, whereas safer options, such as putting surplus money into a savings account, usually provide a lower level of income. One common strategy is to create an investment portfolio spread across a variety of assets with differing risk levels, such as shares, property, and bonds.

Higher risk

Medium risk

Lower risk

> "Risk **comes** from not knowing **what** you're doing."
Warren Buffet

LIFESTYLING

This is an investment strategy that changes the ratio of different assets according to an individual's age. For example, when young, the investor may put 100 percent of assets into high-risk investments such as futures. But funds are increasingly transferred into less risky investments such as bonds as a person nears retirement. Moving money from higher-risk to lower-risk investments can be preset to happen automatically, for example 10 years before a person retires.

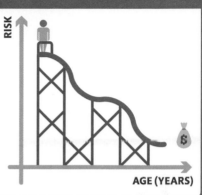

RISK / AGE (YEARS)

Shares
Higher risk, potential for higher income

> **Ordinary** See pp.246–247
> **Preference** See pp.246–247
> **Options** See pp.246–247
> **Futures** See pp.246–247
> **Units in managed share funds** See pp.168–169

Property
Medium risk, potential for steady income

> **Rent from residential, commercial, industrial** See pp.170–171
> **Profit from buying and selling** See pp.176–179

Interest-paying
Lower risk, potential for some income

> **Savings accounts** See pp.166–167
> **Term deposits**
> **Debentures**
> **Bonds** See pp.166–167

✓ NEED TO KNOW

> **Investment income** A regular flow of money from investments such as rent, interest, dividends, and capital gains.
> **Net income** The money left after tax and business expenses.
> **Equities** An alternative term for stocks and shares.
> **Diversification** The investment of money in a variety of ways to minimize risk and maximize returns by spreading the risk across different investments.

Dividends from shares

A dividend is a regular payment made to a company shareholder that is usually based on the amount of profit the company has made that year. Dividends provide a reliable stream of income for many investors.

How it works

Investors buy shares for two main reasons. The first is in anticipation of the share price going up in value, meaning that it can be sold for profit. The second is to earn an income from dividend payouts. For investors who rely on dividend income, it is important to choose shares in companies that prioritize generous dividend payments for shareholders, and to consider the type of shares bought, since not all shares guarantee a dividend. Investors may choose preference shares (*see "Need to know"*) or rely on judgment and research to pick dividend-producing shares.

3%
plus—the average
S&P 500 yield

Generous dividends likely

> **The amount** of the company's income that it pays as a dividend (dividend payout ratio) is steady.

> **The company's dividend** payouts have grown by more than 5% year on year.

> **The dividend yield**—the dividend price divided by the share price—is above 2%.

> **The company** has a comfortable profit barrier (enough to pay dividends without borrowing).

> **The company's additional** profit is sufficient to preserve its current dividend level.

What makes a company likely to pay dividends?

Investors can use several measures to work out which shares will provide the safest bet, with likely regular income now and in the future. Generally speaking, they will look for companies in good financial health with a history of steady dividend payouts over several years.

INVESTOR

Company A
> A history of paying decent cash dividends with no dramatic rises or falls in payout.
> Healthy cash reserves to fall back on.

Can a company afford the dividends it promises?

By comparing a company's profit with the amount it pays in dividends over several years, investors can judge if that company is a good long-term bet for providing a future income stream. Older, larger, and more established companies with steady earnings tend to pay healthy dividends, although their share value may not rise by much.

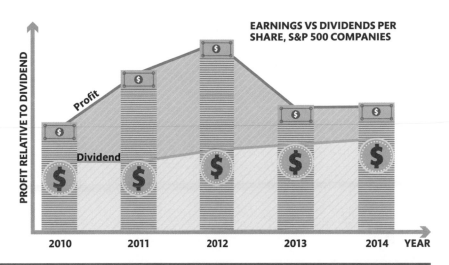

EARNINGS VS DIVIDENDS PER SHARE, S&P 500 COMPANIES

PROFIT RELATIVE TO DIVIDEND

Profit

Dividend

2010   2011   2012   2013   2014   YEAR

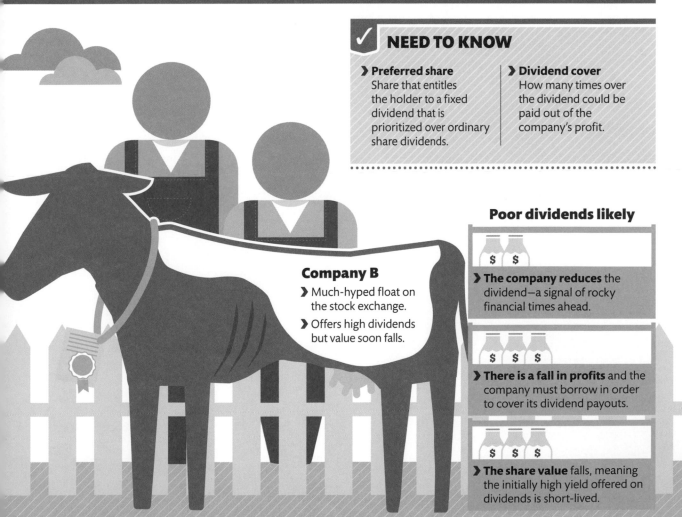

✓ NEED TO KNOW

> **Preferred share**
> Share that entitles the holder to a fixed dividend that is prioritized over ordinary share dividends.

> **Dividend cover**
> How many times over the dividend could be paid out of the company's profit.

Company B
> Much-hyped float on the stock exchange.
> Offers high dividends but value soon falls.

Poor dividends likely

> **The company reduces** the dividend—a signal of rocky financial times ahead.

> **There is a fall in profits** and the company must borrow in order to cover its dividend payouts.

> **The share value** falls, meaning the initially high yield offered on dividends is short-lived.

Earning income from savings

Putting money into savings accounts and fixed-term deposits is low-risk, making them safer options for wary investors. But investors also need to consider if their money is likely to "earn" enough income to live on.

Which savings or deposit account?

All investment products offer a trade-off between risk and return, and savings or deposit accounts are no exception. As a rule, such investments carry the least risk, but the downside is that they may not provide a very good return; the products with the best return tend to be the most risky. New products such as peer-to-peer lending show the strongest potential for gains.

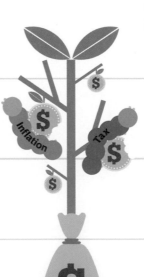

INSTANT ACCESS SAVINGS ACCOUNTS

❯ Low return, low risk

❯ No minimum investment

❯ Cash can be withdrawn on demand

NOTICE SAVINGS ACCOUNTS

❯ Low to medium return, low risk

❯ May require minimum deposit

❯ Cash withdrawals must be arranged in advance

MINIMUM MONTHLY DEPOSIT ACCOUNTS

❯ Low to medium return, low risk

❯ Higher interest rates, but with restrictions

❯ Significant deposit needed to earn decent income

CERTIFICATES OF DEPOSIT

❯ Low to medium return, low risk

❯ Fixed interest rate

❯ Cash not instantly accessible as held for fixed term (from one month to five years)

How it works

Savings accounts and fixed-term deposits traditionally provide a guaranteed return with little of the risk associated with more volatile investment products such as shares or managed funds. However, when interest rates are low, it can be hard to find a savings or deposit product that offers high enough returns to provide a decent income. Many investors use fluctuating interest rates to their advantage, continually monitoring the latest offers to ensure their money is always earning the maximum interest possible. With a substantial deposit, even small changes in the interest rate can make a significant difference to earnings.

66 million
US adults have no savings

MONEY MARKET DEPOSITS

❯ Medium to high return

❯ High risk, but some banks offer FDIC-insured accounts

❯ High interest but high deposit and often limited term

TAX-FREE DEPOSITS

❯ Medium to high return

❯ Advantage of tax saved on certain types of bonds, which means earnings not depleted

FIXED-RATE BONDS

❯ Medium to high return

❯ Can be high risk, but some banks insure deposits

❯ High interest rates; some funds reinvest interest

PEER-TO-PEER LENDING

❯ Medium to high return

❯ Medium risk, but strong potential for gains

❯ Provides capital and interest payments

Investing in managed funds

Investors in managed funds do not have direct control over what happens to their money. Instead they rely on an investment manager to invest on their behalf.

How it works

When an investor puts money into a managed fund, the money is pooled with money from other investors. An investment fund manager then invests the money in the fund in shares or other assets, such as bonds or property loans. As the funds earn interest, the interest money is paid out to the different investors relative to their original investment.

Investors can choose from either a single asset fund or a multisector fund, in which their money is invested across different assets. This has an advantage as poor performance by one asset will be balanced out by high returns from another *(see pp.188–189)*. Funds may be actively or passively managed. An actively managed fund tries to outperform the market, while a passive one aims to perform in line with the market at low cost.

The process

Investors who decide to invest in a managed fund need to make a series of decisions to ensure their investment is as profitable and safe as possible.

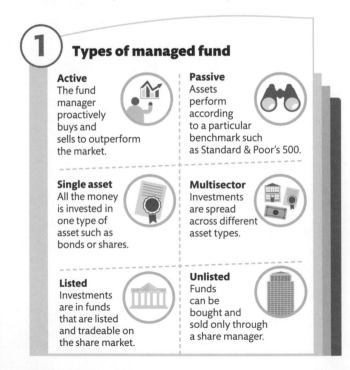

1 Types of managed fund

Active The fund manager proactively buys and sells to outperform the market.

Passive Assets perform according to a particular benchmark such as Standard & Poor's 500.

Single asset All the money is invested in one type of asset such as bonds or shares.

Multisector Investments are spread across different asset types.

Listed Investments are in funds that are listed and tradeable on the share market.

Unlisted Funds can be bought and sold only through a share manager.

2 Choosing a fund

Risk Investors must decide how much of their investment they are prepared to risk losing.

Time frame The period of time over which the investment is made will affect the terms of the investment.

Product disclosure Details of fees and penalties, insurance against loss, and performance guarantees must be understood in advance of investment.

Long-term performance Investors research the market to identify funds that consistently perform well.

RISK AND REWARD OF MANAGED FUND SECTORS

Generally, the more volatile the asset, the better the return. Spreading investments helps achieve high returns while minimizing risk.

VOLATILITY

SHARES

LISTED PROPERTY

FIXED INTEREST

CASH

RETURNS

✓ NEED TO KNOW

> **Market index** A statistical measurement reflecting the performance of stocks, shares, and bonds in a single market.

> **Index arbitrage** An investment strategy of profiting from the price difference in buying and selling futures in the same stock index. *See pp. 68–69.*

> **Index fund** An investment fund consisting of stocks in one particular market index, such as Standard & Poor's 500.

Indexes to know

> **FTSE 100** Top 100 UK companies.

> **FTSE All-share** All companies on London stock exchange.

> **Dow Jones** Top 30 US companies.

> **Standard & Poor's 500** Top 500 US companies.

> **Wilshire 5000** Total US stocks.

> **MSCI EAFE** Equity markets in 21 European and Pacific countries.

③ Buying a fund

The fund manager should be registered with the SEC under the Advisor's Act.

Direct investment through an online platform is possible via a broker.

How many units to buy and how much to spend is best determined with expert advice.

Diversification should be kept within limits to spread risk, but not over-diversify.

Fees will affect returns: the greater the fee, the lower the return.

Withdrawal rights should be checked: there may be penalties for early termination.

④ Managing a fund

Regular performance reports Figures received every month or quarter should be reviewed.

Warning signs These might include the promise of high returns with little or no risk and should be investigated.

Statements Brokerage receipts, annual summaries, and other statements should be filed.

Rental income from property

Potentially one of the most lucrative investments for generating income, property can also be risky because, unlike financial products such as bonds, it also generates expenses, and requires maintenance.

Rental income **Landlord expenses**

High rental yield

SOLD $200,000

RENT $14,400

$1,200 expenses

An investor buys a house and becomes a landlord in an industrial town with a high population of seasonal workers. Demand for short-term rentals is strong.

In the first year, the investor-landlord has to repair the heating system, on top of meeting insurance costs and mortgage interest payments.

Low rental yield

SOLD $500,000

RENT $17,000

$2,000 expenses

An investor buys a house and becomes a landlord in a booming city. House prices are high, but people are only renting in the short term before they buy.

The investor-landlord has to pay for repainting. Their interest payments are high because the deposit amount was minimal and the loan amount is large.

How it works

Buying property to rent has become a popular choice for investment in many parts of the world thanks to low interest rates on mortgages and comparatively high rents. However, landlords will need to spend money on a regular basis on mortgage interest, insurance, agency fees, maintenance, and repairs, and may also need to spend time managing the property. There is also the risk that the landlord can lose out financially if their property remains empty, or if tenants default on their rental payments or cause damage the property. Landlords base the success of their investment on the value of the regular rental yield it produces.

Property cost		**100**		**Rental yield**

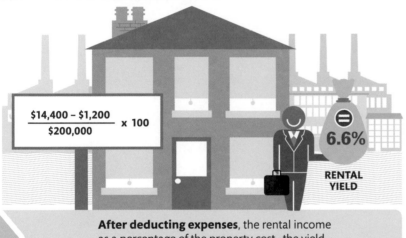

$$\frac{\$14{,}400 - \$1{,}200}{\$200{,}000} \times 100$$

6.6%
RENTAL YIELD

After deducting expenses, the rental income as a percentage of the property cost—the yield—is high compared with the national average.

High rental yields can indicate:

❯ **The presence of large immigrant** or transient populations, who seek short-term housing while they take advantage of local opportunities, and are unwilling or unable to purchase property.

❯ **Rents are steady and property prices** have fallen—for example, in a booming town offering high wages, which attracts new residents who fuel local rental demand.

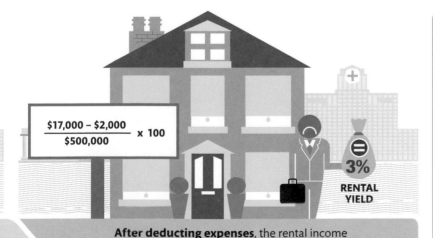

$$\frac{\$17{,}000 - \$2{,}000}{\$500{,}000} \times 100$$

3%
RENTAL YIELD

After deducting expenses, the rental income as a percentage of the property cost—the yield—is relatively low compared with the national average.

Low rental yields can indicate:

❯ **Rents are steady** and property prices have risen—for example, when low interest rates fuel a property bubble, driving up the cost of houses relative to rent and income.

❯ **Rental demand has fallen, so that rents** have risen more slowly than property prices—for example, in a city with low unemployment when interest rates are low, encouraging renters to buy.

Life assurance

Although life assurance will not usually produce income for the policyholder until after their death, it will benefit family members, who can receive regular payments or a lump sum.

How it works

Although the two terms are sometimes used interchangeably, life assurance is different from life insurance. Assurance protects the holder against an inevitable event—their death—while insurance protects against the possibility that their death might happen within a set timeframe—for example, 50 years from the date the policy was purchased. So if a policyholder with 50-year life insurance dies before the term is up, their beneficiaries receive a payout. If, however, they die 51 years after the policy was taken out, there is no payout at all.

In contrast, a life assurance policy will pay out when the policyholder dies, whenever that happens, or provide a lump sum if the holder outlives the policy term.

SELLING A LIFE INSURANCE POLICY

❯ **Life settlement** The sale of a policyholder's life insurance policy to a third party for more than its cash value, but less than its net death benefit, providing a lump sum. People may sell a policy because they no longer want it, they wish to purchase a different policy, or they cannot afford the premiums.

❯ **Viatical settlement** This is the same as a life settlement, only the policyholder sells their policy because they have a terminal or life-threatening illness.

Life insurance

Decreasing term life
The payouts reduce over time, which means that the premiums are lower than for level-term insurance.

Family income benefit
This pays out an agreed monthly income from the date of the claim to the end of the term. Premiums are lower, but this type of policy would not clear a mortgage.

Life insurance
Also called term insurance, this covers the holder for a fixed period of time, with their estate receiving a payout if they die within the term stated in the contract. Premiums are cheap but if they outlive the agreed period they get nothing. Most mortgage agreements stipulate that the borrower must have a life insurance policy in place.

Variable life
This is a permanent life insurance policy with an investment component. The policy has a cash value account—a tax-sheltered investment which is invested in sub-accounts.

Level-term life
This policy pays out a fixed lump sum if death occurs during the policy term. The sum does not change over time so the holder knows exactly what funds will be left in the event of their death.

Life assurance

Endowment

These are effectively investment plans with life coverage attached. They used to be popular with interest-only mortgage holders who used them to build up savings to repay their mortgage capital.

With profit

A with-profit whole-of-life policy includes an investment element, so that the payout on death is the sum assured, plus any investment profits allocated to the policy.

Final expense

This type of policy includes some coverage for burial, funeral, and bereavement costs. It has a relatively low cost and lacks prescreening for health conditions.

Both

Whole of life

This policy provides coverage for the holder's entire lifetime with no set term, guaranteeing a lump sum at whatever age they die as long as premiums have been paid continuously from the start.

Life assurance

A life assurance policy promises the holder a payout—either when they die, or when the term of the policy comes to an end. It can also be used to pay any future inheritance tax. The fact that a payout is guaranteed inevitably means that monthly or annual premiums are higher for life assurance than with life insurance. It is an investment for the long term.

Maximum coverage

This policy offers a high initial level of coverage for a low premium, until a review. Premiums will probably greatly increase to provide the same level of coverage.

Universal
This gives flexible coverage with a savings element that is invested to provide a cash value. Policyholders can use interest from their accumulated savings to help pay the premiums over time.

Balanced cover
This has a premium set high enough by the provider so as to stay the same for the length of the policy. Some of the premium is invested to give additional coverage over time.
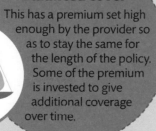

Wealth-building investments

The purpose of investing is either to generate an income (for example in retirement), or to build wealth, although the two functions often overlap. When an investment asset produces income—in the form of interest, dividends, rent, and so on—the money can be reinvested in order to build wealth, instead of being taken as cash for living expenses. Other types of wealth-building investments do not produce income, but grow in value over time and can be sold for profit.

Building wealth through investments

Financial advisors agree that the best way to build wealth is by investing savings to make more, and by buying investments that will generate income and/or gain in value over time. To build wealth, investments need to match or outstrip the cost of living, so investors need to watch the markets closely and keep up to date with economic news, especially changes in interest rates and inflation.

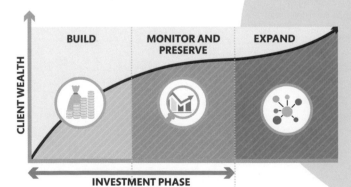

BUILD

MONITOR AND PRESERVE

EXPAND

CLIENT WEALTH

INVESTMENT PHASE

Income-producing investments and other investments that will grow in value over time provide the building blocks.

Close monitoring of investments, and selling those that fail to perform, helps to maintain and enhance wealth.

Reinvesting income from investments that pay interest, dividends, or rent, maximizes returns.

Investments that produce income

Some investments produce income in the form of annual, quarterly, or monthly revenue. If this income is reinvested, rather than spent, then the asset's value will continue to grow, building greater wealth in the long term.

CASH IN BANK ACCOUNTS
Long-term accounts, many of which have penalties for withdrawing cash early, generally pay higher rates of interest.

SUPERANNUATION
Purpose-designed to generate income at retirement, these plans also often offer tax-saving incentives, adding to income potential.

MANAGED FUNDS
These carry higher risk than bank savings, but can produce greater income if fund managers invest successfully.
See pp.184–185

7.2%
average annual gain made by a stock portfolio held for over 20 years

BUILDING WEALTH THROUGH INVESTMENT

> **An early start** Investors who start young generally have more flexibility to take risk—and more time to recover from any errors.

> **A measured approach** Individuals must ascertain their financial situation and investment goals before they begin to construct a portfolio.

> **A simple plan** The less complex the plan, the easier it is to monitor and manage, and the more likely to succeed in its objectives.

> **A balanced portfolio** Regular buying and selling of portions of the portfolio "rebalances" it, helping to keep risk levels and goals in line with the investor's original design. This may incur fees.

SHARES
Those that pay regular dividends (income) and are likely to appreciate in the long term offer the best wealth-building potential. *See pp.182–183*

ANTIQUES
Investors must be confident they can recognize a genuine article, and be willing to spend time scouring markets.

ART
Works by up-and-coming artists who are still early in their careers are good starting points for investment in art.

Investments that appreciate

These investments do not produce income, but their value can increase significantly over time.

PROPERTY
Property can appreciate in value and, in the case of rental property, produce a regular source of income too.
See pp.176–181

GEMS
These generally appreciate at the rate of inflation. Best bought as loose stones from a wholesaler, they are not easy to sell quickly.

GOLD
This precious metal generally holds its value over time, but is best viewed as a long-term investment. Unlike gems, it is easy to sell quickly.

Investing in property

There are various ways to make money from property, but each involves a lot of research and management and, potentially, risk.

How it works

Unlike many other types of investment, such as buying shares or bonds, the investor does not need to come up with the full sum to buy property, just enough for a deposit. Most lenders require, on average, 20 percent of the value and a loan (mortgage) can be obtained to pay for the balance.

The aim of investing in property to build wealth is to buy when the value is low and sell for a profit, then use any profit to finance additional property purchases. There are several ways to do this. A person can buy and remodel a house then sell it for a profit, or buy in an inexpensive area and wait for the area to rise in value. Buying in a depressed market can reap rewards when conditions improve. Buying to rent a property can generate an income that pays the mortgage and excess can be used for a deposit for another property when prices have risen.

30%
the value lost on house prices in the US from 2004 to 2009

How to invest

Making money from property is a game of ups and downs that can entail short-term setbacks as well as gains on the road to the finish line. Success in the long run relies on the investor's strategy. There are several factors to consider: careful financial planning; good timing (to take advantage of rises and falls in the property market); thorough research of locations; appraisal of commercial versus residential investment options; and a clear understanding of economic indicators such as interest rates.

✓ NEED TO KNOW

- **Market value** The amount that a buyer would be willing to pay for a property (or other asset) at any given time.
- **Below market value (BMV)** The pricing of a property that is much lower than the average price of other similar type properties in the area (i.e. those priced at market value).
- **Buy-to-rent (BTR) mortgage** A mortgage for investors who are buying a property with a plan to rent it out for a period of time.
- **Buy-to-sell mortgage** A mortgage designed for investors who are buying property that will be sold shortly afterward.
- **Capitalization rate** The rate of potential return on an investment property; the higher the better.
- **Operating expenses** The cost of the day-to-day administration of a property (or business).
- **Capital gains** The increase in value of a property (or other asset) from its purchase price; this can be short-term (under one year) or long-term.

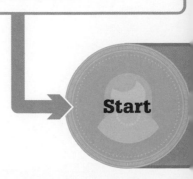

Start

Keep?   or   Sell?

When prices stagnate or increases are minimal, it is worth keeping a property until the market improves.

Whether investing long- or short-term, selling at the right time releases equity for further purchases.

Sell

Finish

HOUSE PRICES DROP

Reinvest

HOUSE PRICES PEAK

Maintain the property

Maintenance is essential to preserve the capital investment. A property must be inspected on a regular basis. Receipts need to be kept as proof of work as well as for tax purposes.

Buy

Buyers should compare prices, risks, and returns for a variety of properties—both apartments and houses—and consider numbers of bedrooms.

Build a good team

A mortgage broker and solicitor are essential from the outset. In addition, it is important to find an accountant and a team of tradespeople—even a property manager can be useful.

Specialize in a type

It is a good plan to concentrate on one type of property, such as student housing.

SOLD

GOOD MORTGAGE BROKER HELPS FIND A SUITABLE MORTGAGE

DEFAULT ON PAYMENTS—LENDER REPOSSESSES

Research

Undervalued areas with signs of growth, such as new shopping centers, can be a good investment.

Look at budget

Operating expenses and cost of mortgage repayments need to balance rental income and/or capital gain.

CAN'T AFFORD MORTGAGE REPAYMENTS

Interest

Rises (and falls) in interest rates can affect cost of mortgage repayments.

INTEREST

Choose mortgage

Before beginning, a buyer must look at mortgage options, confirm their eligibility, and find out what can be borrowed.

INHERIT MONEY FOR INVESTMENT

Save

The bigger the deposit the better the chance of a good mortgage offer with preferential interest rates.

Protect credit rating

A buyer should get a copy of their credit report—free at www.annualcreditreport.com—and find out how to improve it if necessary.

Buying and selling for profit

Knowing when to buy and sell is the key to amassing wealth through property. As with the financial markets, prices in the property market are cyclical, going up or down depending on the state of the economy. Factors such as interest rates and inflation, GDP growth, employment, infrastructure, and immigration can all affect property prices. The trick to successful property investing is knowing how to assess the market and identify the right time to invest, the right type of investment, and the right time to sell.

The property cycle

Economics experts who have studied real estate trends over more than a century have concluded that property prices rise and fall in distinct patterns, triggered by economic and social events and trends. A property boom is followed by a slowdown and a slump. Eventually the housing market recovers and begins to boom again.

COMMERCIAL VS RESIDENTIAL

Commercial property

As an investment, commercial property can offer much higher rental returns than residential property and longer leases, but capital growth is less likely. It can be harder to obtain a mortgage on a commercial property, but investment can also be made via commercial property funds.

Residential property

Investing in residential property generally offers a more predictable return than commercial property, both on rentals and resale, although location is key as always. Residential property can be valued more easily than commercial property, which can help when selling.

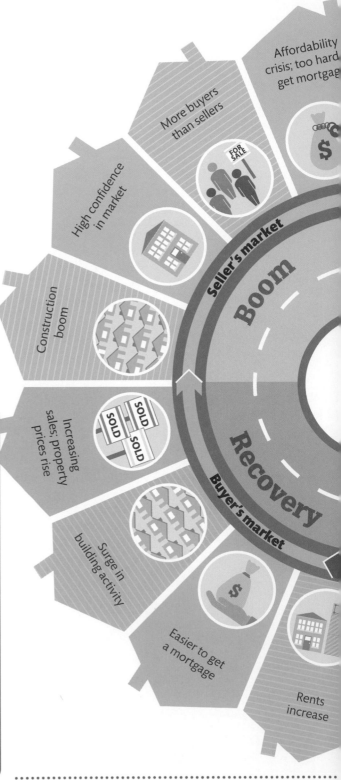

Affordability crisis; too hard get mortgage

More buyers than sellers

High confidence in market

Construction boom

Seller's market

Boom

Recovery

Buyer's market

Increasing sales; property prices rise

Surge in building activity

Easier to get a mortgage

Rents increase

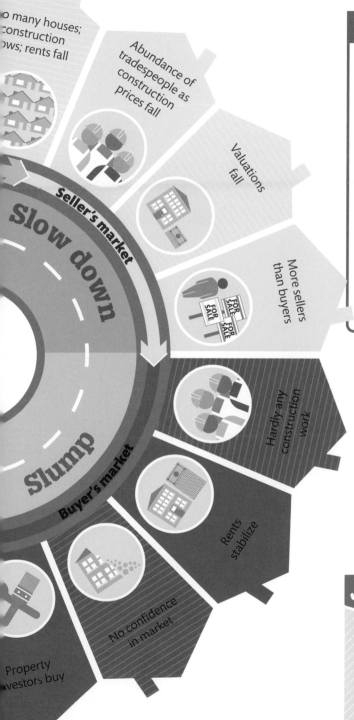

o many houses;
construction
ows; rents fall

Abundance of
tradespeople as
construction
prices fall

Valuations
fall

More sellers
than buyers

Seller's market

Slow down

Slump

Buyer's market

Hardly any
construction
work

Rents
stabilize

No confidence
in market

Property
vestors buy

THE 18-YEAR REAL-ESTATE CYCLE

The idea that ups and downs in the real estate market run in an 18-year cycle is based on US studies of the property market over two centuries by economic forecaster Phillip J. Anderson. He demonstrated that land sales and property construction peak on average every 18 years—14 years up and four years down.

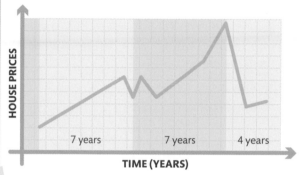

HOUSE PRICES

7 years   7 years   4 years

TIME (YEARS)

5%
annual housing price increase in US in 2015

✓ NEED TO KNOW

❯ **Appreciation** Rise in the value of a property over time.

❯ **Depreciation** Fall in the value of a property over time.

❯ **Capital gain** The increase in value of a property (or other asset) from its purchase price; this can be short term (under one year) or long term.

❯ **BRR** Buying, Refurbishing, and Refinancing strategy.

Home equity

The amount of equity in a home is a measure of a property's value. It is the realizable amount an owner could expect if, after taking debts against it into account, a property was sold.

How it works

The equity of a property is calculated by subtracting all debts incurred on behalf of that property from its actual value. The amount of equity rises as the mortgage (loan) is paid down, and/or the property's value increases.

Financial institutions work out home equity as a loan-to-value (LTV) rate, which is arrived at by dividing any remaining loan balance by the current market value of the property. A low LTV (less than 80 percent) is seen as lower risk for further lending.

✓ NEED TO KNOW

› **Collateral** A property or asset that a lender will take if a borrower fails to pay a loan.

› **Home equity loan** A loan that uses equity in a property as collateral.

› **Equity** A property's equity is equal to the current value of the property minus the outstanding loan amount.

$11.9 trillion
US mortgage debt at the end of 2008

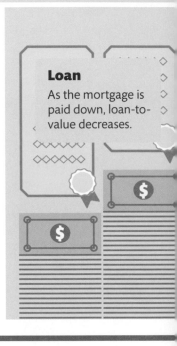

Loan
As the mortgage is paid down, loan-to-value decreases.

Positive equity

If the actual market value of a property is greater than the amount of debt owed on it in the form of a mortgage, then the property is said to be in positive equity.

Equity = house value - loan

$160,000 Loan

$40,000 Equity

House value = **$200,000**

$13,000 of loan paid off over five years

$100,000 increase in market value

$147,000 Loan

$153,000 Equity

New house value = **$300,000** minus new loan value = **$147,000**

LOANS, VALUE, AND EQUITY

Equity fluctuates depending on the market value of a property and the amount of any mortgage held against it. If a house is bought for $500,000, with a loan of $400,000, the equity in it is $100,000. If after five years, the loan has been paid down to $300,000, but the value falls below $300,000, then the house is in negative equity as the loan is greater than the market value.

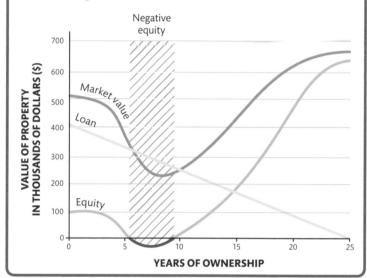

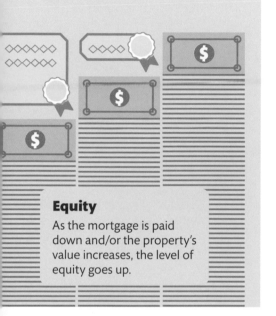

Equity

As the mortgage is paid down and/or the property's value increases, the level of equity goes up.

Negative equity

If the value of a property falls, generally as the result of a real estate slump, to the point where it is lower than the amount of loan owed on it, then the property is said to be in negative equity, or "under water."

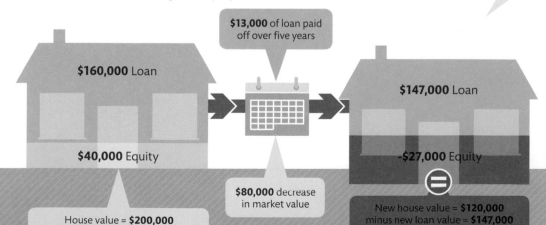

$13,000 of loan paid off over five years

$160,000 Loan

$40,000 Equity

House value = **$200,000**

$80,000 decrease in market value

$147,000 Loan

-$27,000 Equity

New house value = **$120,000** minus new loan value = **$147,000**

Shares

When individuals invest in shares, they are buying "a share" of a business, meaning that they have part ownership of that company. Shares can be bought and sold, and their price can go up or down.

How it works

Companies issue shares (or equities) to raise money. Investors buy shares in a business because they believe the company will do well and they want to share in its success.

It is not necessary for a company to be listed on the stock market to issue shares. Some start-ups raise money from a small number of outside investors, who are given a share of the company in return.

When a company wants to raise money more widely, it can apply to become publicly listed—or quoted—on a stock exchange, such as the New York Stock Exchange. The company will need to go through an approval process in order to be listed. Once listed, the company's shares are described as "quoted" because their prices are quoted daily on the stock exchange. Trading in shares is executed by stockbrokers, who buy and sell shares on behalf of investors.

Shareholders are entitled to a say in the running of the business in which they own shares: for example, they can vote on directors' appointments and their pay packages.

How to buy shares

Investing in the stock market can be a good way for individuals to grow their wealth. There are a number of ways in which shares can be bought and held.

Online share dealing platform

Low-cost online, discount, or execution-only stockbrokers allow investors to buy and sell shares simply, and usually without receiving any specific guidance or advice on investments.

Employee stock option plan

Some companies offer their employees the opportunity to purchase shares in the business. The shares might be offered at a discount to the market price, and are often paid for via deductions from employees' monthly salaries.

BULL AND BEAR MARKETS

Bull market

Several months or years of rising stock prices characterized by high sales volumes and a generally strong economy. Investors are optimistic, and buy stocks expecting the price to keep rising.

Bear market

A general decline in the stock market over a period of time, with falling prices, stagnant sales volumes, and little optimism. This leads to a weak economy, falling business profits, and high unemployment.

Through a stockbroker

A "full service" broker offers advice on what to buy and sell, as well as executing the trade. They are more expensive than online brokers and typically charge a percentage of the purchases as a fee.

Initial Public Offering

When a company first floats on the stock market, it is not always possible—or may be very difficult—to apply for shares directly because the company is looking for investors to buy large amounts.

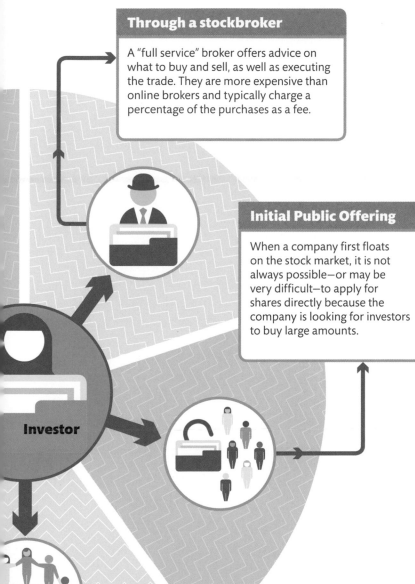

Investor

Invest in a fund

Shares can be purchased indirectly by individuals buying units in a managed fund. Funds may focus on certain industry sectors or geographical areas, and are often used as a way to diversify an investment portfolio or manage risk.

WHY SHARE PRICES MATTER

> **Investors focusing** on capital growth will only make a profit if the share price of their stock increases. They may also lose money if the share price falls.

> **A falling share price** can impact the reputation of a company and its management, and also on its ability to borrow money.

> **Public traded companies** with a falling share price can become takeover targets for wealthy shareholders or rival companies.

> **The value of pension** savings pots linked to the stock market will fall if the underlying share prices fall. This is bad news for those nearing retirement.

> **When stock markets** in a country fall, foreign investors often remove money from that country altogether, reducing the value of its currency.

1987

marked the beginning of the longest US bull market to date, lasting 13 years

Managed funds

Inexperienced or time-poor individuals often opt to invest in a managed fund, where numerous people pool their money and invest in a variety of markets. The fund is managed by an expert.

How it works

Managed funds offer a simple way for investors to access a variety of investment markets. As well as the advantage of having the fund managed by investment professionals, investing via a fund is a straightforward way of diversifying investments.

In many cases only a small initial amount of money is required to get started and further investments can either be made by lump sum or regular (monthly) contributions. Managed funds are traditionally set up as "unit trusts," with each investor owning a number of units (or shares).

Unit trusts

When an individual invests in a managed fund, they are usually allocated a number of units based on the amount they invest and the current unit price. The unit price reflects the value of the fund's investments and rises, or falls, in line with those investments. Investors realise gains from managed funds by selling units.

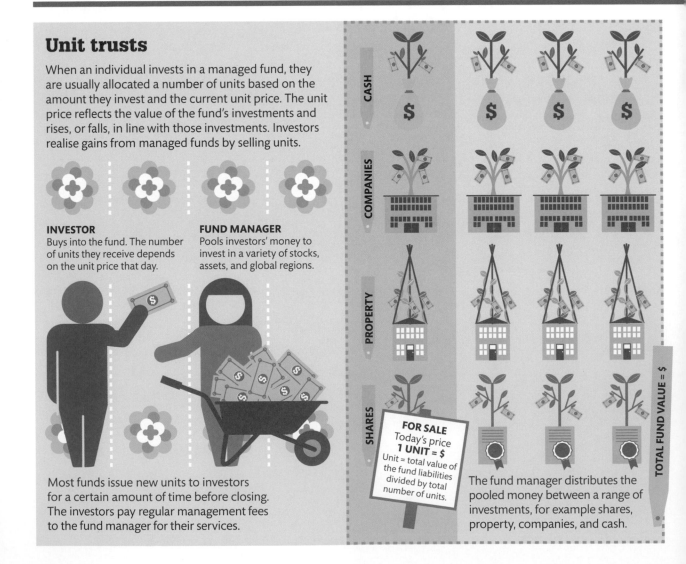

INVESTOR
Buys into the fund. The number of units they receive depends on the unit price that day.

FUND MANAGER
Pools investors' money to invest in a variety of stocks, assets, and global regions.

Most funds issue new units to investors for a certain amount of time before closing. The investors pay regular management fees to the fund manager for their services.

CASH

COMPANIES

PROPERTY

SHARES

FOR SALE
Today's price
1 UNIT = $
Unit = total value of the fund liabilities divided by total number of units.

TOTAL FUND VALUE = $

The fund manager distributes the pooled money between a range of investments, for example shares, property, companies, and cash.

MANAGED FUND STRATEGIES

Index funds

These funds aim to match the performance of a particular financial index, such as the FTSE 100.

Actively managed funds

These aim to deliver higher than average returns. Active managers analyze, research, and forecast markets to make investment decisions on which securities to buy and hold, or sell off.

Absolute return funds

These funds aim to deliver consistent returns regardless of whether the stock market rises or falls.

WARNING

> **The value of investments** will fluctuate depending on the stock market, which will cause fund prices to fall as well as rise.

> **Fluctuations** mean that investors may not get back the original amount of capital invested.

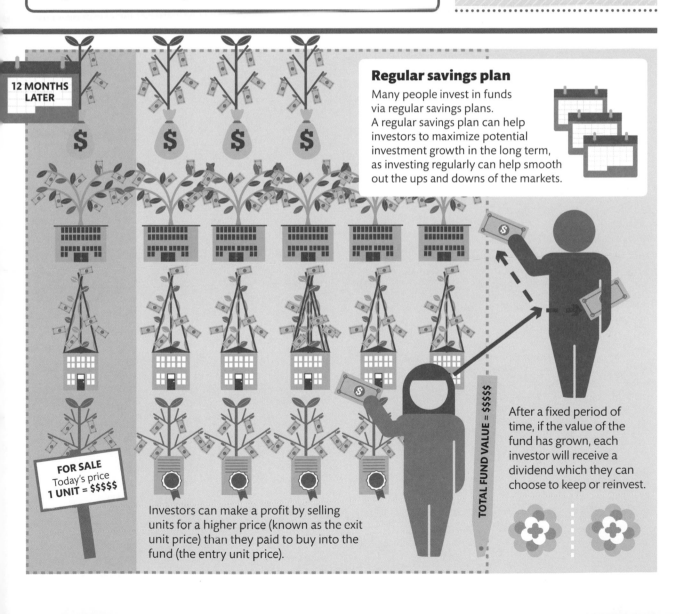

12 MONTHS LATER

Regular savings plan

Many people invest in funds via regular savings plans. A regular savings plan can help investors to maximize potential investment growth in the long term, as investing regularly can help smooth out the ups and downs of the markets.

FOR SALE
Today's price
1 UNIT = $$$$$

Investors can make a profit by selling units for a higher price (known as the exit unit price) than they paid to buy into the fund (the entry unit price).

TOTAL FUND VALUE = $$$$$

After a fixed period of time, if the value of the fund has grown, each investor will receive a dividend which they can choose to keep or reinvest.

Managing investments

Investments are something individuals buy or put money into in order to make a profit, or "return." There are different types of investments—known as asset classes—each of which offers a different type of return. Investors may receive interest (from cash or bonds), dividends (from shares), rent (from property), or capital gains when they sell the asset (the difference between the purchase and sale price). Investors can manage their own investments or pay someone else to do it.

Personal investment basics

Investing money for the first time is a big step, and it is essential to prepare well. Investing means taking a risk with money, and it is possible to lose some or all of the capital invested. Before deciding what to invest in, anyone looking to invest must assess the state of their personal finances. They should pay off any outstanding debts and loans first, and maintain access to a source of cash in case of emergency.

Asset allocation

Asset classes are simply different categories of investments. The four main asset classes are cash, bonds (or fixed-interest securities), shares (or equities), and property.

CASH
Money held in savings accounts is secure and accessible. However, returns are low and could be wiped out by inflation.

BONDS
Fixed-interest securities such as bonds and gilts provide regular income and are generally a lower risk than investments such as shares.

SHARES
Buying shares means investing in a company and thereby owning a part of it. Shares may pay regular dividends or gain capital value.

PROPERTY
Residential housing and commercial units can provide a good rental income and high returns when sold, but property is relatively illiquid.

Asset diversification

Diversification means investing in different asset classes. It helps to spread risk because there is less potential to lose everything if things go wrong if money invested is spread across assets and not channeled into one class.

2,175
S&P 500 record high, July 2016; S&P 500 closes above 100 for the first time on June 4, 1968

HOW TO INVEST

⟩ **Take a DIY approach** This is an investment method in which an investor, without professional advice, builds and manages his or her own investment portfolio.

⟩ **Consult a financial advisor** This is a professional who can give advice on which assets to buy and when, based on goals and risk tolerance.

⟩ **Buy from a fund supermarket or discount broker** These financial companies offer "execution-only" services, without advice, allowing individuals to buy and sell shares or funds.

⟩ **Invest in a fund company** These investment firms spread risk by pooling investors' money and buying units in a fund that invests in a number of companies.

Dollar cost averaging

Also known as unit cost averaging, dollar cost averaging is the practice of buying a fixed monetary amount of an investment gradually over time, rather than investing the desired total in one lump sum. This strategy can reduce the average cost per share of an investment as more units may be purchased when the price is low, and fewer when the price is high. *See pp.190–191*

⟩ Dollar cost averaging is also known as "drip feeding" money.

⟩ Using this approach means that investors don't have to monitor market movements and time their investments strategically.

⟩ Most investment companies offer regular savings plans that allow investors to take advantage of dollar cost averaging, also enabling them to save a little at a time.

MONTH 4

MONTH 3

MONTH 2

MONTH 1

INVESTMENTS

Risk tolerance/risk-return trade-off

The possibility of losing some or all of a capital investment is risk. An acceptable level of risk must be decided before investments are chosen. *See pp.192–193*

⟩ All investments carry a degree of risk, but some have the potential to be much riskier than others.

⟩ A financial advisor can help to build a portfolio to match an investor's risk tolerance.

The optimal portfolio

A portfolio in which the risk-reward combination yields the maximum returns possible is known as an optimal portfolio. Optimal portfolios differ between investors with different attitudes to risk. *See pp.194–195*

Risk   Reward

⟩ Portfolio "weight" is the percentage of a particular holding in a portfolio.

⟩ Investors should reassess and rebalance their portfolios annually.

Asset allocation and diversification

To reduce the risk of their investment, investors often try to diversify their portfolio, spreading the risk they are exposed to by investing in different assets, sectors, or regions.

Strategic asset allocation

A defensive investor may choose to use strategic asset allocation. This involves investing in a combination of assets, taking into account the expected returns for each asset class, and therefore the overall expected return of the investment. In the illustration on the right, the expected returns of stocks are 10 percent, so by allocating 20 percent of the portfolio to stocks, the investor will expect them to contribute 2 percent to the returns.

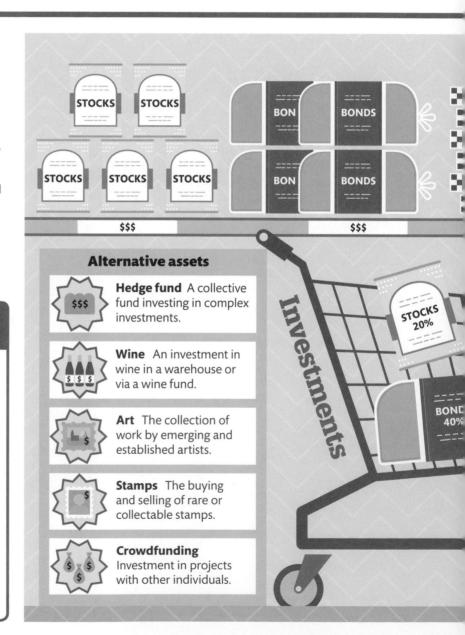

Alternative assets

Hedge fund A collective fund investing in complex investments.

Wine An investment in wine in a warehouse or via a wine fund.

Art The collection of work by emerging and established artists.

Stamps The buying and selling of rare or collectable stamps.

Crowdfunding Investment in projects with other individuals.

MARKET CAPITALIZATION

The total value of a company—its market capitalization—is equal to the total number of its shares multiplied by the price of one of those shares. For example, if a company had 100 shares and one share in that company was worth $50, its market capitalization would be $5,000 (100 x $50).

The investment industry refers to the size of market capitalization when it talks about large- (or "blue chip"), medium- and small-cap companies. Large caps are usually more stable but offer limited growth opportunities. Medium and small caps can be riskier, but can grow quickly.

How it works

Asset classes are different categories of investment. Investors diversify by investing in different asset classes, or investing in different companies, industries, markets, regions, or countries, within an asset class. Another strategy, known as asset allocation, attempts to balance risk versus reward by setting the percentage of each asset class in an investment portfolio—stocks, bonds, property, cash, and alternative assets—according to the investor's risk tolerance, goals, and investment time frame. The percentage of a particular holding in a portfolio is known as the "portfolio weighting." Diversification helps reduce the risk of each asset class in the portfolio.

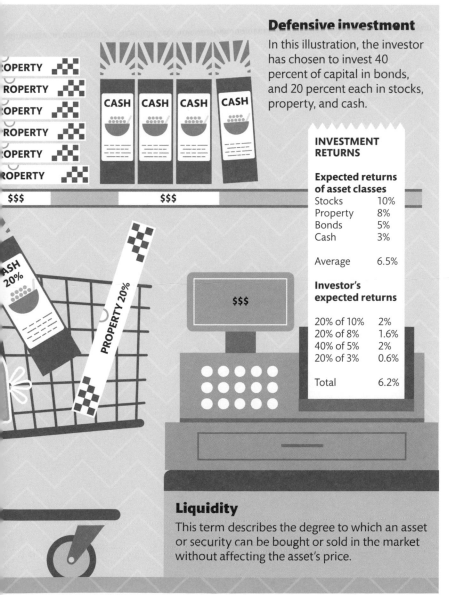

Defensive investment

In this illustration, the investor has chosen to invest 40 percent of capital in bonds, and 20 percent each in stocks, property, and cash.

INVESTMENT RETURNS

Expected returns of asset classes

Stocks	10%
Property	8%
Bonds	5%
Cash	3%
Average	6.5%

Investor's expected returns

20% of 10%	2%
20% of 8%	1.6%
40% of 5%	2%
20% of 3%	0.6%
Total	6.2%

Liquidity

This term describes the degree to which an asset or security can be bought or sold in the market without affecting the asset's price.

> "Have a strategic asset allocation mix that assumes you don't know what the future holds."
>
> Ray Dalio

ASSET ALLOCATION MODELS

❯ **Defensive** A small proportion of equities (stocks and shares) with the bulk of the capital invested in less volatile asset classes such as bonds and cash.

❯ **Income** Most of the investment is in bonds and alternative assets. This model is designed for income-seeking investors willing to take on a reasonable degree of risk.

❯ **Income and growth** Around half of the fund is in equities, with the remainder in bonds and alternative assets. This model focuses on a return composed of both capital growth and income.

❯ **Growth** Most of the investment is in equities, but some in bonds and alternative assets. This model aims for longer-term capital growth.

Dollar cost averaging

Dollar cost averaging (DCA) is the practice of building up investment capital gradually over time, rather than investing an initial lump sum.

How it works

Catching the bottom of the market to get the best unit price is difficult, and even the experts get it wrong sometimes. One way for investors to smooth out the market's highs and lows is to spread or drip-feed money into investments instead of investing it all in one go. This is known as dollar cost averaging. For example, if $100 a month is invested into a fund, the sum of money would buy fewer fund units when the cost is high and more units when the cost is low. The average cost per share over time is the mean of highs and lows. As well as freeing investors from having to second-guess market movements, this approach encourages regular investing each month. Dollar cost averaging can be especially beneficial in a falling market, as the cost per unit is then lower.

Dollar cost averaging vs lump-sum investing

One key argument for regular drip-feed investing is the effect of dollar cost averaging. Dollar cost averaging allows savers to benefit from market volatility because by investing a small amount regularly, it allows them to buy units more cheaply on average.

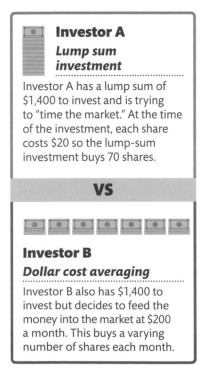

Investor A
Lump sum investment

Investor A has a lump sum of $1,400 to invest and is trying to "time the market." At the time of the investment, each share costs $20 so the lump-sum investment buys 70 shares.

VS

Investor B
Dollar cost averaging

Investor B also has $1,400 to invest but decides to feed the money into the market at $200 a month. This buys a varying number of shares each month.

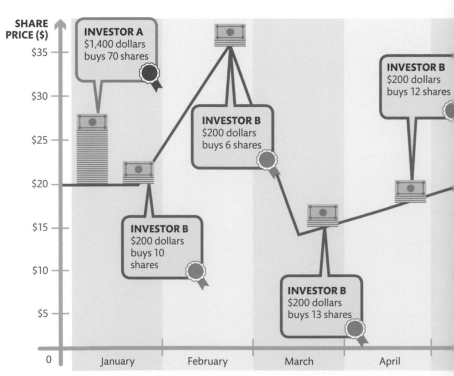

WHAT IS MARKET VOLATILITY?

Volatility is the degree of variation in a trading price over time. It is measured by looking at the standard deviation of returns—that is how spread out returns are from an average value. Lower volatility means a share's price does not fluctuate dramatically, but changes in value at a steady pace.

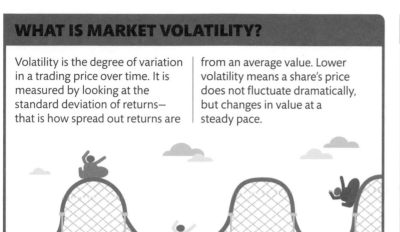

✓ NEED TO KNOW

> **Lump-sum investing** Although high returns are possible, putting large single sums into the market tends to require a more impulsive, or short-term approach, which may be counterproductive.

> **Market conditions** Dollar-cost averaging means investors do not have to study the details of market behavior to maximize their returns.

> **Investments from income** By regularly investing directly from regular income, investors can keep cash on hand for other purposes or emergencies.

"**The** individual investor **should act** consistently **as an** investor **and not as a** speculator."

Benjamin Graham

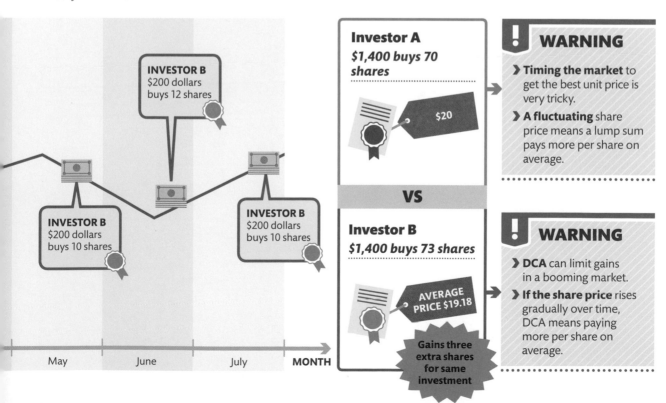

INVESTOR B
$200 dollars buys 12 shares

INVESTOR B
$200 dollars buys 10 shares

INVESTOR B
$200 dollars buys 10 shares

May   June   July   **MONTH**

Investor A
$1,400 buys 70 shares

$20

! WARNING

> **Timing the market** to get the best unit price is very tricky.

> **A fluctuating** share price means a lump sum pays more per share on average.

VS

Investor B
$1,400 buys 73 shares

AVERAGE PRICE $19.18

Gains three extra shares for same investment

! WARNING

> **DCA** can limit gains in a booming market.

> **If the share price** rises gradually over time, DCA means paying more per share on average.

Risk tolerance

Assessing risk tolerance is an important consideration when investing. Investors should have a realistic understanding of their ability to cope with large swings in the value of their portfolio.

How it works

To assess risk tolerance, investors should review worst case scenarios for different asset classes to see how much money they might lose in bad years, and gauge how comfortable they feel about such losses. Factors affecting risk tolerance include timescales, future earning capacity, and personal circumstances. In general, the longer the timescale the more risk an investor can take. Investors also need to assess how much money they can afford to lose without it affecting their lifestyle. Even for high net worth individuals with very large sums available as liquid assets, investing a small percentage of capital is wiser than investing a large one.

Investor types

Fund managers and financial advisers often provide risk-profile questionnaires to individual investors to help them determine which investments best suit them. The questionnaires examine an investor's tolerance to risk, time frame, objectives, and investment knowledge.

Conservative

Investors who are unwilling to take much risk and are happy to accept lower returns as a result might prefer a portfolio that has a significant proportion in cash or assets with guaranteed returns such as bonds.

5 KEY FACTORS THAT AFFECT RISK TOLERANCE

Investors need to consider these factors and choose investments to fit the risk–return trade-off that they are comfortable with.

Time frame The period over which investment will be made. More risk may be taken over a longer time frame.

Risk capital The money available to invest or trade which, if lost, should not affect an investor's lifestyle.

Investment goals Objectives such as funding for education or retirement.

Experience An investor's understanding of assets and risk, and experience of past investments.

Risk attitude An investor's stance on losing his or her investment capital.

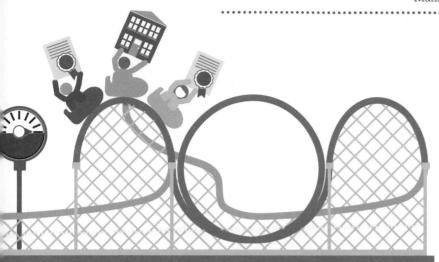

> ✓ **NEED TO KNOW**
>
> ❯ **Capital risk** The possibility of losing the initial capital (money) invested. With more risky investments, capital could grow significantly but it could also be dramatically reduced.
>
> ❯ **Inflation risk** The threat of rising prices eroding the buying power of money. If the returns on investments do not match or beat inflation, they will effectively be losing value each year.
>
> ❯ **Interest risk** The possibility that a fixed-rate debt instrument, such as a bond, will decline in value as a result of a rise in interest rates. If new bonds are issued with a higher interest rate, the market price of existing bonds will decrease.
>
> ❯ **Negative interest** Currently tens of billions are invested in Europe at negative interest rates simply to provide low risk and security.

High risk

Investors who are willing to accept more risks for potentially higher returns might consider including emerging markets and alternative asset classes in their portfolios.

Balance

Investors who are happy to invest in more shares and property are likely to want only a small proportion of their capital in cash in fixed-interest accounts.

Cautious

Investors who are more willing to take some risk in return for a profit are likely to go for a mix of growth and defensive assets, and invest more in shares than in bonds.

"The only strategy that is guaranteed to fail is not taking any risks."

Mark Zuckerberg, founder of Facebook

The optimal portfolio

A portfolio consists of a selection of different assets. The optimal portfolio achieves the ideal trade-off between potential risk and likely reward, depending on an investor's desired return and attitude to risk.

How it works

The optimal portfolio is a mathematical model that demonstrates that an investor will take on increased risk only if that risk is compensated by higher expected returns, and conversely, that an investor who wants higher expected returns must accept more risk.

The optimal portfolio reduces risk by selecting and balancing assets based on statistical techniques that quantify the amount of diversification between assets. A key feature of the optimal portfolio is that an asset's risk and return should not be assessed on its own, but by how it contributes to a portfolio's overall risk and return. The main objective of the optimal portfolio is to yield the highest return for a given risk or the lowest risk for a given return, these being investors' most common goals.

Efficient frontier

The efficient frontier is considered the optimum ratio between risk and reward—that is, the highest expected return for a defined level of risk, or the lowest risk for a given level of expected return. Portfolios that lie below the efficient frontier are suboptimal, either because they do not provide enough return for that risk level, or because they have too high a level of risk for a defined rate of return. Asset correlation, a measure of the way investments move in relation to one another, is important to the efficient frontier. A portfolio is better balanced if the prices of its securities move in different directions under similar circumstances, effectively balancing risk across the portfolio.

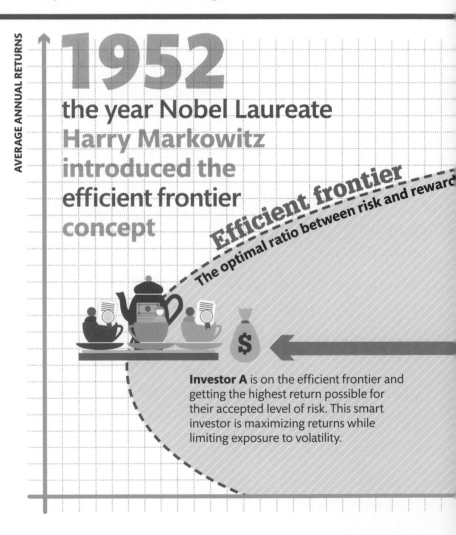

AVERAGE ANNUAL RETURNS

1952 the year Nobel Laureate Harry Markowitz introduced the efficient frontier concept

Efficient frontier
The optimal ratio between risk and reward

Investor A is on the efficient frontier and getting the highest return possible for their accepted level of risk. This smart investor is maximizing returns while limiting exposure to volatility.

REBALANCING A PORTFOLIO

Investments in a portfolio will perform according to the market. Over time this will cause the portfolio's asset allocation, which was originally tailored to the investor's preferred level of risk exposure, to shift. If left unadjusted, the portfolio will either become too risky or too conservative. In order to maintain a portfolio's risk profile reasonably close to an investor's level of risk tolerance, it should be reviewed regularly and rebalanced when necessary.

The goal of rebalancing is to move the asset allocation back in line with the original plan. This approach is one of the main dynamic strategies for asset allocation and is known as a constant-mix strategy.

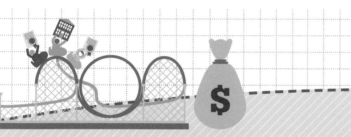

Investor C is also on the efficient frontier. C has a high-risk portfolio but is compensated by receiving higher returns.

The efficient frontier flattens as it goes higher because there is a limit to the returns that investors can expect, so there is no advantage in taking more risk.

Investor B has a suboptimal portfolio. If happy with the risk level, B should rebalance the portfolio closer to C's position to achieve higher returns. Alternatively, to lower the risk for the same rate of return, B should adjust the asset allocation closer to A's position.

RISK, MEASURED BY THE STANDARD DEVIATION OF ANNUAL RETURNS

✓ NEED TO KNOW

❯ **Weighting** The percentage of a portfolio consisting of particular assets. Calculated by dividing the current value of each asset by the total value of the portfolio.

❯ **Variance** The measure of how the returns of a set of securities making up a portfolio fluctuate over time.

❯ **Standard deviation** A statistical measurement of the annual rate of return of an investment that can give an indication of the investment's volatility.

❯ **Expected return** The estimated value of an investment, including the change in price and any payments or dividends, calculated from a probability distribution curve of all of the possible rates of return.

❯ **Asset correlation** A statistic that measures the degree to which the values of two assets move in relation to each other. A positive correlation means that assets move in the same direction; a negative correlation means that they diverge.

Pensions and retirement

A pension plan is a type of savings plan to help save money for retirement. Pensions enable workers to save a proportion of their income regularly during their working life so that they can have an income when they retire. It is important for workers to think about starting to make pension contributions when they are young, rather than when they are approaching retirement age. In many countries, pensions have certain specific tax benefits in comparison with other forms of savings.

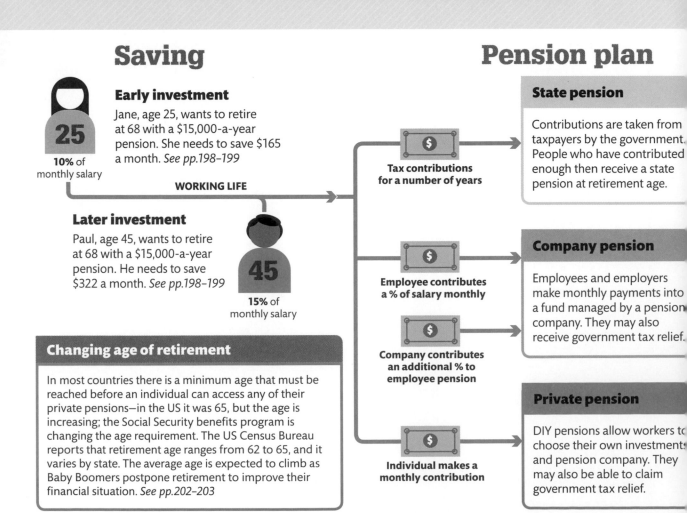

Saving

Early investment

25

10% of monthly salary

Jane, age 25, wants to retire at 68 with a $15,000-a-year pension. She needs to save $165 a month. *See pp.198–199*

WORKING LIFE

Later investment

Paul, age 45, wants to retire at 68 with a $15,000-a-year pension. He needs to save $322 a month. *See pp.198–199*

45

15% of monthly salary

Changing age of retirement

In most countries there is a minimum age that must be reached before an individual can access any of their private pensions—in the US it was 65, but the age is increasing; the Social Security benefits program is changing the age requirement. The US Census Bureau reports that retirement age ranges from 62 to 65, and it varies by state. The average age is expected to climb as Baby Boomers postpone retirement to improve their financial situation. *See pp.202–203*

Pension plan

Tax contributions for a number of years

State pension

Contributions are taken from taxpayers by the government. People who have contributed enough then receive a state pension at retirement age.

Employee contributes a % of salary monthly

Company pension

Employees and employers make monthly payments into a fund managed by a pension company. They may also receive government tax relief.

Company contributes an additional % to employee pension

Individual makes a monthly contribution

Private pension

DIY pensions allow workers to choose their own investments and pension company. They may also be able to claim government tax relief.

ACCESSING YOUR PENSION OR SOCIAL SECURITY (SS)

Different countries have different rules about when, and how, to access pensions or IRAs. In the US, SS can be accessed at 62, and access to an IRA begins at 59½. There are three main options:

》 **Option 1** Take 100% (also called a lump-sum payout) of the pension as cash to spend or invest. With a lump-sum payment, the employer is required to hold back 20% of the payment for federal income taxes.

》 **Option 2** Buy an annuity. This is an insurance product that provides a fixed amount of cash every year for life. An annuity means the money won't run out, but the rate of income will be lower.

》 **Option 3** Use income drawdown. This means withdrawing invested money as and when it is needed. There is the risk of running out of cash if the fund performs badly.

> "You can be young without money, but you can't be old without it."
>
> Tennessee Williams, US playwright

Retirement

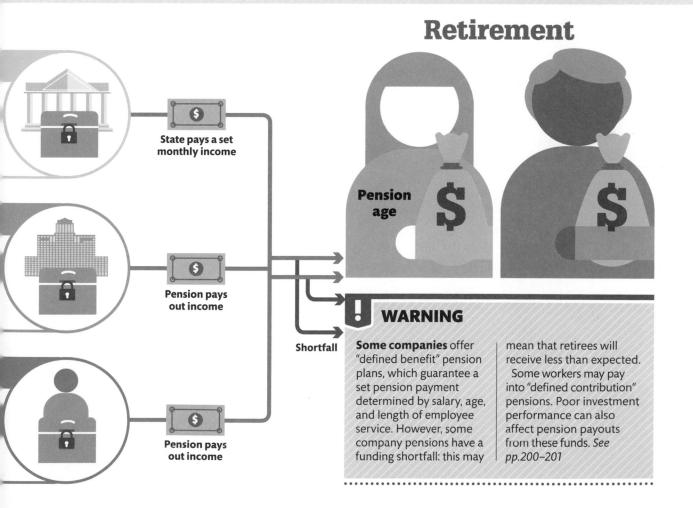

State pays a set monthly income

Pension age

Pension pays out income

Pension pays out income

Shortfall

WARNING

Some companies offer "defined benefit" pension plans, which guarantee a set pension payment determined by salary, age, and length of employee service. However, some company pensions have a funding shortfall: this may mean that retirees will receive less than expected.
Some workers may pay into "defined contribution" pensions. Poor investment performance can also affect pension payouts from these funds. *See pp.200–201*

Saving and investing for a pension

A pension is a savings plan or investment designed to provide a retirement income, based on how much has been saved and how well the investment performs.

How it works

Some countries pay retirees a state pension based on taxpayers' contributions. However, a state pension only provides enough money for a very basic standard of living, and many countries encourage people to save money while they are working to provide them with additional income for a more comfortable retirement.

Saving into a private pension is the most common way of doing this. A pension is a long-term savings plan in which the money is invested in shares, bonds, or other types of assets with the aim of providing a return on the money invested. The more money saved while working, and the better the investments perform, the more money there will be to live on in retirement.

Early investment for maximum return

The earlier a saver starts saving for a pension, the better. Firstly, the saver will need to save less each month to reach their desired sum for retirement. Secondly, some employers also contribute to employees' pension savings, while some governments offer tax advantages on pension savings. Thirdly, investments will have more time to ride out the ups and downs of the capital markets, and savers will benefit from more interest as it accrues over the years.

Saving at 25
25-year-olds may struggle to save $165 a month but they should still aim to save a little, increasing the amount if earnings increase.

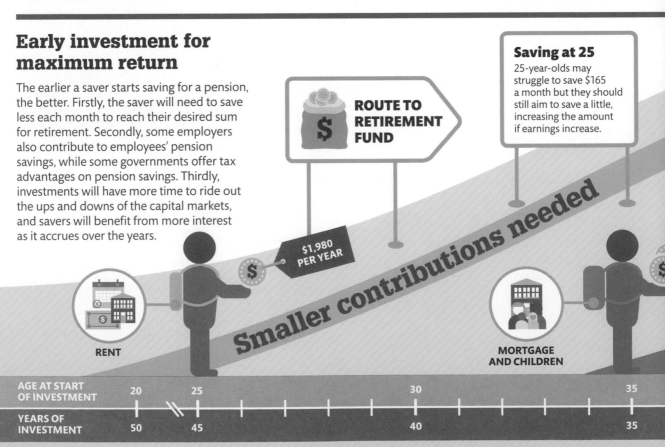

ROUTE TO RETIREMENT FUND

$1,980 PER YEAR

Smaller contributions needed

RENT

MORTGAGE AND CHILDREN

AGE AT START OF INVESTMENT	20	25		30		35
YEARS OF INVESTMENT	50	45		40		35

PENSION CONTRIBUTIONS

Calculations by a British consumer association reveal that to achieve an annual pension income of $15,000 by age 68, savers starting at age 25 need to save $165 a month. Starting at 35 would mean having to save $215 a month.

A professional financial advisor can calculate exactly how much an individual needs to save to meet their retirement goals, and offer advice on the different types of pensions and investments available.

50% of one's age when **starting to save** is the percentage of salary to save for retirement.

RETIREMENT FUND

Saving at 50+

Savers over 50 may no longer be paying a mortgage but may still need to balance pension contributions with other financial burdens, such as paying their children's college fees or caring for elderly parents.

$2,580 PER YEAR

Larger contributions needed

$3,864 PER YEAR

Very large contributions

MORTGAGE AND CHILDREN

Very late starters will need to contribute large percentages of their salaries—20% if age 40 compared to 10% age 20.

40   45   70

30   25   0

Defined benefit vs defined contribution

Company pension plans that promise a fixed monthly pension are known as defined benefit plans. These are risky for employers, who have to pay out regardless of how the pension investments perform. This "pension promise" has led to some pension funds having insufficient funds to meet their commitments as a result of poor financial management of the pension plans. With defined contribution plans, it is the employee who carries the investment risk. The success of both plans hinges on the investments in the pension performing well, but if defined contribution funds lose money, an individual's pension pot may be smaller than expected when they retire.

Why pensions fail

It is important for individuals to take professional financial advice at various stages in their lives to ensure that their pension is on track to pay out the desired level of income. A financial adviser can provide guidance on how much to save, the best way to pay money into a pension fund, and any steps that can be taken to reduce the risk of a pension failing. In some cases it may be advisable for savers to increase their contributions or diversify their pension investments.

5. High inflation

Increases in the cost of living need to be reflected in the value of the pension pot to ensure it will provide adequate income in retirement.

3. Taxes

Pensions are usually taxed as income, so relevant taxes should be factored in when a pension is designed.

1. Business failure

Company pension funds can be lost if an employer goes bust and the money is not ring-fenced (financially separate from other assets and liabilities).

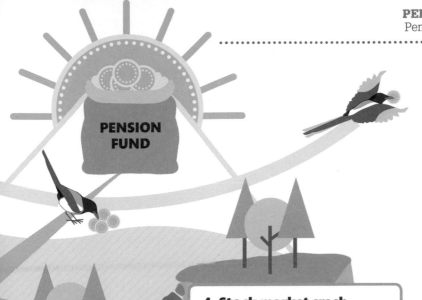

2030
the **year by which**
one in six people
will be aged 60+

AGING POPULATION

The population is aging in most countries. According to global averages, a child born in 1960 could have expected to live for 52 years. But if that child were born today, he or she could expect to live to the age of 69. By the middle of the century, average lifespan is likely to be higher still: well over 70. An aging population has dramatic consequences for state pensions, as current workers' contributions are not invested by the state to pay for future pensions but are instead used to simply pay the pension benefits of current pensioners. As the number of pensioners increases, the shortfall between tax income and pension payouts will increase.

4. Stock market crash

Investments losing value over the long term or in a crash can mean that the value of a pension fund will also fall.

2. Pension fund management

Poor decisions by the pension fund managers can lead to low returns, as with any investment.

Pension pathway

Converting pensions into income

On retirement, savers can invest the money in their pension to give themselves a fixed regular income, withdraw cash in one or more lump sums, or arrange a combination of both options.

How it works

There are two main options for turning pension savings into income. The first involves buying an insurance product that will provide a fixed sum as either a monthly or annual income for life. This is called an annuity, and may also be known as "steady payments" or "a retirement income stream."

The second option is to take out pension savings as cash, in one or more lump sums, with the rest of the money remaining invested. Withdrawing money and leaving some invested in this way is called income drawdown. Savers may combine an annuity with cash withdrawals.

Pension fund options

The options available to retirees will depend on the type of pension they have (defined benefit or defined contribution), the size of their pension pot, and the laws and tax rules of the country they live in.

PENSION POT AT RETIREMENT AGE

Cash lump sum

Some pension plans allow savers to take some or all of their pension fund as a cash lump sum on retirement. Retirees can then spend, invest, or save their pension money as they see fit. However there is the risk with this approach that, sooner or later, the fund will run out, especially if they live a long life.

TAXMAN

Tax-free percentage

%

The way in which pension savings are taxed varies from country to country. In the US, individuals can roll the lump sum into an IRA account to avoid paying taxes on a large amount. Taxes are assessed on the amounts withdrawn. There are penalties if the money is withdrawn before 59½ unless a personal hardship is proven.

TAXMAN

HOW TO CONSOLIDATE PENSIONS

Most people will have paid into different workplace pensions over the years as they move from employer to employer. As a result it can be hard to keep track of how each pension fund is being run, how much has been saved into it, and how it is currently performing. Consolidating pensions into one plan makes it easier for savers to keep track of their pension savings—and it may save money too, through reduced fees and administration costs. But some older pension plans have better benefits that may be lost if all pension plans are consolidated into a single pot.

⚠ WARNING

All pension plans have very strict rules, so if a saver receives a letter, call, or email suggesting they can break these rules penalty-free, they should be very suspicious. Fraudsters try to tempt savers into handing over their pension funds by talking about:

> A money-making investment or other business opportunity
> New ways to invest their pension money
> Accessing their pension money before retirement age

59.5
the minimum age at which savers can unlock their pensions in the US

Annuities

An annuity is an insurance product that offers a fixed monthly or annual income for life. Use of annuities varies from country to country. For example, about 80 percent of pension funds are converted to annuities in Switzerland, but far fewer are in Australia. A rule change in the UK means that savers are no longer legally obliged to buy an annuity on retirement.

Income drawdown

Some pension plans offer the option of keeping money invested—and hopefully producing decent returns—with cash sums withdrawn as necessary. If too much cash is withdrawn, or the investments perform badly, however, there is a risk of the saver running out of money.

Debt

This is an amount of money borrowed by one party from other parties. Borrowing is the way in which corporations and individuals make large purchases that would otherwise be unaffordable. They pay interest, a fee charged for the privilege of borrowing money, which is normally a percentage of the money borrowed. Banks and other financial institutions offer various different types of consumer debt products, ranging from bank overdrafts and credit cards to mortgages and loans.

Ways to borrow money

There are various institutions willing and able to lend consumers money, and each will offer a number of different financial products. Borrowers need to research the best options for their circumstances.

Loans

Personal loans allow consumers to borrow a lump sum of money that will be repaid at set intervals over a pre-agreed period of time. Loans can be secured or unsecured. *See pp.210–211*

❯ **Types of loans** There are many types such as car, student, debt consolidation, and payday loans.

❯ **Who offers loans** Banks, credit unions, and other financial institutions all offer loans.

Credit cards

These allow a type of revolving credit that allows users to make purchases without using their own money, which can be paid back monthly, or later for an additional fee. Transactions are processed by global payment networks. *See pp.218–219*

❯ **Installment credit** The opposite of revolving credit—the money is paid back in installments.

❯ **Dual-purpose cards** In some countries, banks issue cards with both debit and credit facilities.

Statement

TRANSACTIONS

DESCRIPTION

MORTGAGE

CREDIT CARD

CAR LOAN

SALARY

CASH

OVERDRAFT FEE

CURRENT TOTAL
CLOSING BALANCE

$12.29 trillion the debt owed by US consumers at the end of July 2016

CREDIT RATING

A credit rating is an estimate by a lender of the ability of a person or organization to fulfill financial commitments, based on their credit history. It can be used to help lenders decide who to lend money to, how much to lend them, and in some cases how much interest to charge.

High levels of existing debt, missed or late payments on a loan or credit card, and a history of multiple applications for credit can all negatively affect an individual's credit rating.

Individuals can check their credit report via a number of different websites, such as myFICO.com, and if necessary, take steps to improve their credit rating.

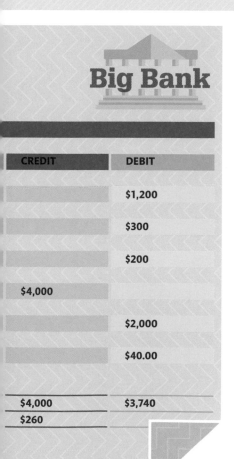

Big Bank

CREDIT	DEBIT
	$1,200
	$300
	$200
$4,000	
	$2,000
	$40.00
$4,000	$3,740
$260	

Mortgages

A mortgage is a longer-term loan used to purchase a property, which is secured against it. The lender can repossess the property if the mortgage is not repaid as agreed. *See pp.212–215*

> **Mortgage payments** These consist of the capital repayments—against the amount borrowed—plus the interest charged.

> **Loan-to-value (LTV)** This is the mortgage value as a percentage of the property's purchase price.

Credit unions

Credit unions are not-for-profit community organizations that provide savings, credit, and other financial services to their members. Borrowers need to be members of a credit union to be able to borrow money from it. *See pp.216–217*

> **Size and assets** Credit unions vary.

> **Ownership** Credit unions have no shareholders, only members.

Why we use debt

People use debt to buy things they could not normally afford. As well as for purchasing consumer goods, debt can be used to make investments, however, debts have to be repaid in full with interest.

How it works

Countries, companies, and individuals all use debt in order to function. Debt can be a useful way of spreading the cost of purchases, make investments, or manage finances. However, it is dangerous if it cannot be repaid. Taking out a mortgage to buy a property is an example of "good debt," as few people are able to buy a house outright.

There are plenty of examples of "bad debt" where people borrow money, often at high interest rates, to make arguably unnecessary purchases. Those who do can find that simply paying the interest on their loans is more than they can manage. This can lead to taking out more loans just to pay off the interest, and the borrowers never make an indent into the capital borrowed in the first place.

! WARNING

> **Cost of borrowing** The costs can be higher than the income from the assets purchased.

> **Asset value can fall** If this happens, the sale of the assets will not repay the original debt.

> **Interest rates can increase** This can mean the borrowing costs being greater than the value of the assets even if it rises.

Leverage

Leverage, or gearing, is the use of borrowed money to multiply gains (or losses). It is used on the stock market, by companies, as well as by individuals.

$50,000
TO INVEST

CASH PURCHASE

Buyer A buys an E-type Jaguar

Buyer A pays seller the full $50,000

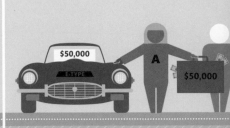

$50,000

A

$50,000

USING BORROWED MONEY

Leverage involves buying more of an asset by using borrowed funds, with the belief that the asset will appreciate in value by more than the cost of the loan. In this example, Buyer B buys 10 E-type Jaguars by splitting his $50,000 cash (equity) into ten $5,000 down-payments and borrowing the extra $450,000. This means the buyer is "highly geared" as there is a high proportion of debt to equity. This is risky as the $450,000 borrowed (plus any interest) will have to be repaid regardless of the sale prices of the cars.

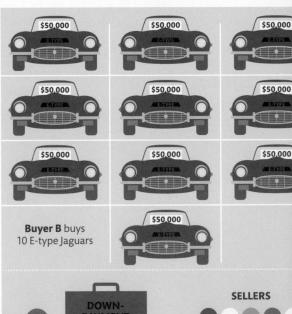

Buyer B buys 10 E-type Jaguars

$50,000 (×10)

B

DOWN-PAYMENT
10 X $5,000

BANK
$450,00
BORROWED

SELLERS

$50,000
TO INVEST

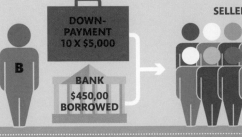

One year later

Buyer A
Sells E-type Jaguar for $55,000, making profit of $5,000

$55,000

E-TYPE

A

$5,000

$729 billion

credit card debt owed by US consumers

One year later

$55,000 · E-TYPE
$55,000 · E-TYPE
$55,000 · E-TYPE
$55,000 · E-TYPE
$55,000 · E-TYPE
$55,000 · E-TYPE
$55,000 · E-TYPE
$55,000 · E-TYPE
$55,000 · E-TYPE
$55,000 · E-TYPE

CARS INCREASE IN VALUE
Buyer B makes a larger profit as the gains are multiplied when selling the cars at a profit of $5,000 each. His gross profit is $50,000; net profit can be calculated by deducting interest payments. However, there is also the possibility of losing money.

Buyer B
makes a gross profit of $50,000

B

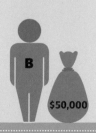

$50,000

INTEREST AND BANKRUPTCY

Interest
This is the cost paid to borrow money. It is expressed as a percentage of the capital borrowed. Various debt products have different interest rates. The rate might be fixed for a set period of time or "variable," meaning it can change. It is important for individuals to take interest costs into account when borrowing to invest.

Bankruptcy
This is a legal process that releases a person (or company) from almost all of their debts. People (and companies) can declare bankruptcy if they do not have a realistic chance of repaying their debts depending on the type of bankruptcy filed. Although it can offer a fresh start, the financial consequence can be that it adversely affects a person's credit rating, and therefore their ability to borrow in the future.

Interest and compound interest

When money is saved it "earns" interest. Compound interest accrues if the investor reinvests it, as opposed to withdrawing the interest.

The snowball effect

If a snowball is rolled down a hill, it gets bigger and bigger as it gathers more snow. In addition, the rate at which the snowball grows increases as it rolls down the hill because there is a greater surface area for the snow to stick to. So, given enough time, a tiny snowball can become a giant one. Compound interest has been described as a "snowball effect" as it works in much the same way, meaning that a small investment can provide bigger returns than an investment where the interest sum is paid out to the investor annually.

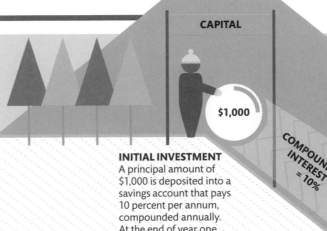

CAPITAL

$1,000

INITIAL INVESTMENT
A principal amount of $1,000 is deposited into a savings account that pays 10 percent per annum, compounded annually. At the end of year one, $100 (10 percent of $1,000) is credited to the account.

COMPOUND INTEREST = 10%

INTEREST PAID = $100

$1,100

END OF YEAR 1

INVESTMENT GROWS
The savings account now has $1,100, then earns $110 (10 percent of $1,100) interest in the second year. By the end of year two the account has a balance of $1,210.

NEED TO KNOW

> **Principal amount** The original capital sum invested or borrowed.

> **Compounding frequency** The number of times that interest is added to the principal amount in one year. For example, if interest is added monthly, the compounding frequency is 12.

> **Annual percentage rate (APR)** The annual rate of interest payable on mortgages, credit cards, etc. It includes the rate as well as fees, such as annual fees. APR can be referred to as the annual equivalent rate (AER), effective interest rate (EIR), or effective annual rate (EAR).

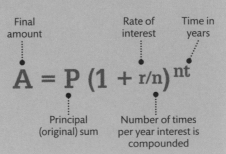

Compound interest formula

"A" is the final amount in the savings account after "t" years' interest compounded "n" times, at interest rate "r" on the starting amount of "P".

Final amount   Rate of interest   Time in years

$$A = P\left(1 + r/n\right)^{nt}$$

Principal (original) sum   Number of times per year interest is compounded

How it works

Interest is the cost of borrowing money, for example from a bank, and it is calculated as a percentage of the capital. When money is saved it is effectively being lent to the institution, which then pays interest to the investor, so the capital "earns" interest.

With simple interest, money is paid out to the investor each year. Compound interest is interest paid on reinvested simple interest, and works for both saving and borrowing. The interest from the first year is added to the initial sum, so in the second year interest is paid on the capital plus the interest accrued. In the third year it is paid on the capital plus the first two years' interest, and so on.

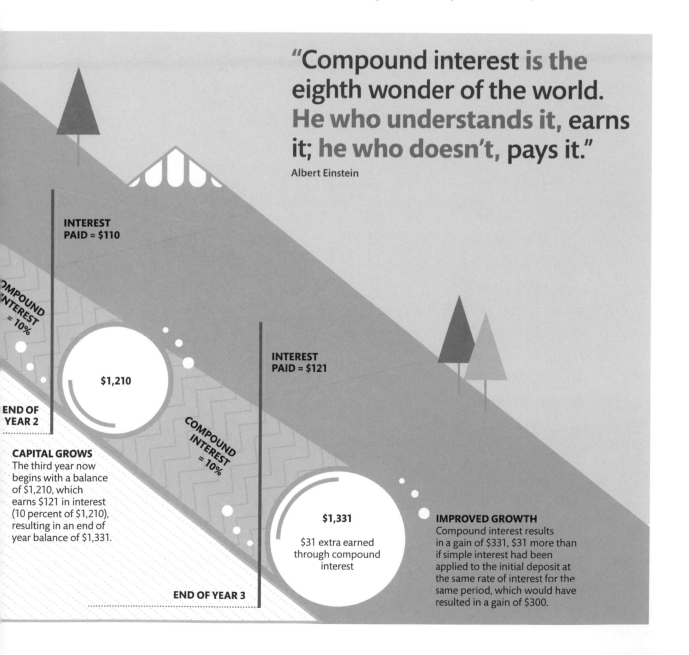

"Compound interest is the eighth wonder of the world. He who understands it, earns it; he who doesn't, pays it."
Albert Einstein

INTEREST
PAID = $110

COMPOUND INTEREST = 10%

$1,210

END OF YEAR 2

CAPITAL GROWS
The third year now begins with a balance of $1,210, which earns $121 in interest (10 percent of $1,210), resulting in an end of year balance of $1,331.

INTEREST
PAID = $121

COMPOUND INTEREST = 10%

$1,331

$31 extra earned through compound interest

IMPROVED GROWTH
Compound interest results in a gain of $331, $31 more than if simple interest had been applied to the initial deposit at the same rate of interest for the same period, which would have resulted in a gain of $300.

END OF YEAR 3

Loans

Loans offer a fixed sum of money to be repaid, plus interest, over a fixed period of time. Personal loans can be used at the borrower's discretion but some other loan types have a defined purpose.

How it works

Loans allow individuals to borrow a lump sum to use in the short term, which they then repay in installments at set intervals over an agreed longer-term period. For example, a person might borrow $10,000 to be repaid over five years. As well as repaying the capital, the borrower also pays interest on the loan. Periodic repayments are calculated so that the borrower repays some of the capital and some of the interest with each payment.

Loans can be used as a cheaper alternative to other borrowing facilities such as overdrafts and credit cards. If a loan is "secured" on an asset (such as a house), and the loan is not repaid on time, the lender is entitled to take the asset. Typically a secured loan is less expensive to the borrower than an unsecured loan. A mortgage is a type of secured loan used to buy a property without paying the entire value of the purchase up front.

Various institutions including banks, payday lenders, credit unions, supermarkets, and peer-to-peer lenders sell loans. Loan brokers may also offer loans from a range of different providers.

5,583%

APR of UK payday loan company Wonga before new rules applied in 2014

 CASE STUDY

Loan repayments

For loans with a fixed monthly repayment of principal plus interest, payments will first consist mainly of interest. This is because the amount of interest paid each month is a percentage of the outstanding balance of the loan. As each payment also repays some of the principal, the outstanding balance (and interest) decreases each month while more of the payment goes to reducing the loan. Final payments will consist of a larger proportion of principal to interest (as interest is paid on ever smaller outstanding balances).

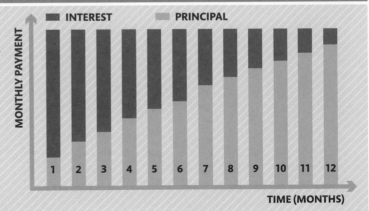

Loan agreement

Abank

A loan agreement is a formal document provided by the lender that sets out the terms and conditions of the loan.

This Loan Agreement ("Agreement") is made and will be effective on **04-04-17**.

BETWEEN   Lender: ("A Bank")   **AND**   Borrower: ("A Person")

TERMS AND CONDITIONS

1. PROMISE TO PAY

Within **60 months** from today, the Borrower promises to pay the Lender the sum of **$20,000** and interest and other charges stated below.

2. DETAILS OF LOAN

The Borrower agrees to repay the full amount of capital borrowed, plus fees and charges, the interest rates, the monetary amount of interest, and the total amount repayable.

Amount of loan:	$20,000.00
Other (such as arrangement fee):	$200.00
Amount financed:	$19,800.00
Total of payments:	$23,533.94
Annual rate:	6.8%

3. REPAYMENT

The Borrower will repay the amount of this loan in **60** equal continuous monthly installments of **$392.23** each on the **4th** day of each month preliminary on the **4th** day of April 2017, and ending on the **4th** day of April 2022.

4. PREPAYMENT

The Borrower has the right to pay back the whole amount at any time, but a charge may be levied for early repayment: **$1,360.00**

5. LATE CHARGE

Any installment not paid within **15** days of its due date shall be subject to a late charge of 4% of the payment: **$15.69**

6. DEFAULT

If for any reason the Borrower fails to make any payment on time, the Borrower shall be in default. The Lender can then demand immediate payment of the entire remaining unpaid balance of this loan without giving further notice.

Term of loan The length of time over which the loan will be repaid in regular installments. This is normally expressed in months.

Amount The capital originally borrowed and advanced to the borrower. It is expressed in the currency of the loan, such as pounds, euros, or dollars.

Total amount repaid The total capital, interest, and fees paid by the borrower to the lender over the whole term.

APR The annual percentage rate: a calculation that takes into account the interest rate plus fees and charges such as arrangement fees.

Regular payments The periodic installments in which the loan will be repaid, for example, weekly, monthly, or quarterly.

Early repayment charge An additional charge applied if the borrower redeems (repays) the loan before the end of the term.

Late fees An additional charge applied if the borrower does not pay the installment on the agreed date. The borrower continues to be charged until the original payment schedule is restored.

Default The failure to meet the legal conditions of a loan puts the borrower in default. A loan agreement sets out the consequences of a default.

Mortgages

A mortgage is a long-term loan that enables the borrower to purchase property or land. A mortgage is made up of the amount borrowed—the principle—plus the interest charged on the loan.

How it works

The word mortgage is derived from an old French term used by English lawyers in the Middle Ages, literally meaning "death pledge," because the deal dies when the debt is paid or a payment fails. A mortgage is secured on the borrower's property, which means that a legal mechanism is put in place that allows the lender to take possession in the event that the borrower defaults on the loan or fails to abide by its terms. This is known as repossession or foreclosure. Most mortgage lenders require borrowers to put down a percentage of the property value as a deposit (or down payment) before they will be given a mortgage, and the bigger the deposit is, the less they will need to borrow.

Fixed rate mortgages

❯ This is the most common type of mortgage in the US.

❯ First, the bank checks the borrower's background to ensure they can afford the loan repayments.

❯ The borrower then puts down a deposit, and the bank lends them the remainder of the purchase price. For example, if the purchase price of a property is $300,000, the borrower may put down a 5% deposit ($15,000) and borrow the remaining

$285,000 from the bank. This amount is known as the principle, or capital.

❯ The bank charges the specified interest rate and the buyer makes monthly payments. The payment includes the principle plus the interest amount.

❯ The borrower pays back both the principle and the interest via monthly repayments. When they have repaid the total amount borrowed, plus the interest, they own the property outright.

Mortgage types

Different countries have different types of mortgage, and different rules governing their issue. The amount that can be borrowed will depend on the property, individual circumstances, and prevailing economic conditions, but all loans will eventually need to be repaid with interest. Islamic law prohibits interest being charged on home loans so sharia-compliant mortgages involve a lease agreement, with the property given to the owner as a "gift" at the end of the term.

Adjustable-rate mortgage (ARM)

❯ This loan doesn't have a fixed interest rate. The interest rate and the monthly principal and interest (P&I) remains the same for a set number of years. After that, the rate is adjusted annually.

❯ While the rate is difficult to predict in the long-term, ARMs can be appealing because the rate is usually lower than a traditional mortgage.

❯ There are different types of ARMs. For instance, a hybrid ARM has an initial fixed rate for a period of time and then the interest rate is

adjusted manually. Another type is the Payment-Option ARM. With this mortgage, you choose among several payment options. Choices with a payment-option ARM include paying only the interest or paying an amount that covers both the principal and the interest.

❯ Be aware that some of these loans come with a prepayment penalty. If the house will be sold or refinanced, then this penalty could apply. Be sure to read the contract and ask that the penalty be removed.

13 the average number of years between house moves

Interest-only mortgage

❯ Interest-only mortgages allow borrowers to repay just the interest on the amount they have borrowed, and not the principle itself.

❯ The bank gives the borrower a mortgage, for example $240,000, to purchase a property, and the borrower repays the interest on this amount via monthly repayments.

❯ Borrowers will need to ensure that they will be able to repay the mortgage at the end of the term.

❯ The amount paid each month will be lower than for repayment mortgages, but borrowers will usually need to put down larger deposits, demonstrate higher earnings, or have a better-than-average FICO score, in order to be given an interest-only mortgage.

❯ At the end of the loan period, the borrower either pays back the entire principle loan amount, in this case $240,000, or the property is sold in order to raise the money needed to repay the loan.

✓ NEED TO KNOW

❯ **Loan-to-value ratio (LTV)** Percentage of a property's value borrowed as a mortgage.

❯ **Security** Collateral for the loan; for mortgages, the property.

❯ **Remortgage** A different or additional loan taken out on a property.

❯ **Term** Years over which the mortgage is repaid.

❯ **Equity** Value of the property over the mortgage amount.

❯ **Negative equity** Value of the property being less than the mortgage amount.

❯ **Guarantor** A person who agrees to be responsible for meeting the mortgage repayments if the borrower fails to do so.

Reverse mortgages

❯ This type of mortgage allows a homeowner to access the value of a property that they fully own.

❯ People who opt for a reverse mortgage are usually elderly—in the UK, borrowers must be at least 55 years old to qualify for this type of mortgage, whereas in the US they must be at least 62.

❯ The bank lends the homeowner money against the value of their property (the equity) but there are usually high fees involved.

❯ The bank then pays this money to the homeowner in monthly installments, or occasionally in a lump sum.

❯ When the homeowner dies, their property is sold in order to repay the loan amount.

❯ Any remaining money from the sale of the property, after the loan amount has been repaid, goes to the beneficiaries in the homeowner's will.

ISLAMIC MORTGAGES

The basic principle of an Islamic mortgage is that no interest should be paid. There are three types of Islamic mortgage:

❯ **The bank purchases** a property on behalf of a buyer, and leases it to them. At the end of the lease term, ownership is transferred to the buyer/tenant.

❯ **A buyer purchases** a property jointly with the bank, and pays rent on the portion they do not own. They then buy shares in the remaining portion of the property, and as their share increases, their rent decreases.

❯ **The bank buys** a property and sells it to a buyer, who makes fixed monthly repayments at a higher price than the original purchase cost.

Mortgage rates

Banks offer a range of mortgages with different interest rates, each of which offers a different ratio of risk to affordability.

Fixed-rate mortgages offer the borrower fixed monthly payments for a set period of time. In the US, fixed rates of 10, 15, or 30 years are common. The borrower either then remortgages to a new fixed-rate mortgage product or the original mortgage defaults to a variable rate. Fixed rates are not altered by changing interest rates or other economic conditions. This means the lender, not the borrower, carries the main interest rate risk.

Variable rates

Variable- or adjustable-rate mortgages have rates that can change during the mortgage term, sometimes tracking a market index such as the country's central bank base rate. Monthly mortgage payments will therefore increase or decrease depending on fluctuations in the base rate. This means the interest rate risk is carried by the borrower, who will need to be sure they can still afford the mortgage should the interest rate increase. Incidences of variable-rate mortgages vary from country to country.

Types of mortgage rates

Generally, the greater the guarantee of security for the borrower, the higher the fees involved. Somedeals also lock borrowers in to a particular rate, offering less flexibility.

Fixed-rate mortgages

❯ The interest rate is set for a period or for the life of the loan, regardless of the base rate. This offers certainty, as borrowers pay a set monthly amount.

❯ These often have higher down payments and fees, and payments will stay fixed even if the base rate falls.

8%

4%

BASE RATE

FIXED RATE AT 3%

Usually for a set period of time

Adjustable-rate mortgages (ARMs)

❯ The lender can raise and lower interest rates, which may be influenced by the central bank's base rate, but can also be changed regardless of the base rate.

❯ These are usually less expensive than fixed-rate mortgages, but borrowers are vulnerable to interest rate increases.

8%

4%

ARM

BASE RATE

Indefinite time period

Why interest matters

Small variations in the interest rate can make a big difference to the total amount of interest paid over the mortgage term.

Mortgage deal 1

BANK

Loan
$200,000
over 25 years

3% interest

Jan

$948

Monthly repayments
to bank over 25 years

BANK

Total
repayment
= $284,400

Interest =
$84,400

2007

the year that defaults on US subprime loans became a crisis

SUBPRIME MORTGAGES AND CREDIT CRUNCH

The subprime mortgage crisis began in 2007 and led to fundamental changes in mortgage products and their regulation. In the US, mortgages had been sold to people without the income to repay them. When the housing bubble burst, this led to a wave of repossessions and bank losses. Mortgage-backed bonds lost value and several banks went bust.

> **Credit crunch** Banks and other lenders reduced the amount of credit available for mortgages and other loans.

> **Recession** The subprime crisis led to a recession or slowdown in several countries. As well as property repossessions, banks and other businesses collapsed.

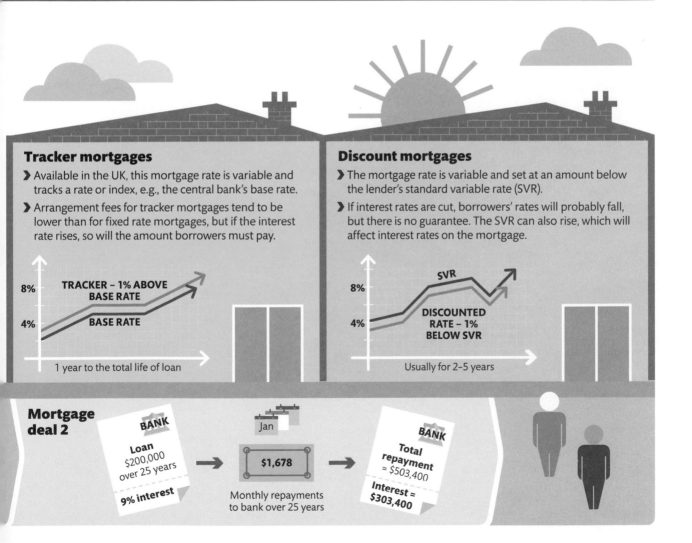

Tracker mortgages

> Available in the UK, this mortgage rate is variable and tracks a rate or index, e.g., the central bank's base rate.

> Arrangement fees for tracker mortgages tend to be lower than for fixed rate mortgages, but if the interest rate rises, so will the amount borrowers must pay.

8%

TRACKER – 1% ABOVE BASE RATE

4%

BASE RATE

1 year to the total life of loan

Discount mortgages

> The mortgage rate is variable and set at an amount below the lender's standard variable rate (SVR).

> If interest rates are cut, borrowers' rates will probably fall, but there is no guarantee. The SVR can also rise, which will affect interest rates on the mortgage.

8%

SVR

4%

DISCOUNTED RATE – 1% BELOW SVR

Usually for 2–5 years

Mortgage deal 2

BANK
Loan
$200,000
over 25 years
9% interest

Jan

$1,678

Monthly repayments to bank over 25 years

BANK
Total repayment
= $503,400
**Interest =
$303,400**

Credit unions

Member-owned, not-for-profit financial organizations, credit unions provide savings, credit, and other financial services to their members.

How it works

Originating in Germany in the mid-19th century, credit unions are nonprofit financial cooperatives set up by members who share a "common bond" for their mutual benefit. The connection between members may, for example, be living in the same town, working in the same industry, or belonging to the same trade union or community group.

Traditionally very small organizations, today around 217 million people worldwide are members of a credit union. Some of the larger unions have hundreds of thousands of members and assets worth several billion dollars.

Credit unions are most prevalent in low-income areas and can be especially useful to those with lower credit scores who fail to qualify for loans from large retail banks, or who are charged increased rates on those loans because of their scores. Unions pool their members' savings deposits to finance their own loan portfolios rather than relying on outside capital. Some unions require members to save with them before they can borrow money. Savings are covered up to set limits by government-backed statutory compensation plans in the event that the credit union ceases trading, and members pay fewer fees on average.

Not-for-profit

Credit unions are owned by their members (customers), who each have one vote to elect a board of directors to run the organization. Unlike large, retail banks, credit unions generally focus on community banking services that benefit members rather than on profit and returns to external shareholders. Surplus revenue is invested back in the credit union to provide personalized service, financial advice, better products, and rates that are as competitive as possible.

Not-for-profit
The aim is to serve members, not to make a profit. Any surplus revenue is reinvested in running the business.

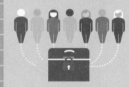

Owned by members
Shareholders elect a board of directors to run the business. Each member has one vote.

Community orientated
Members share a common link such as employment, religion, or the area where they live.

Personalized service
Staff are committed to helping members improve their financial situation.

Financially inclusive
Customers are often from financially disadvantaged groups who fail to qualify for mainstream financial products.

Credit Union

57,000
number of credit unions in 105 countries around the world

For-profit
The goal is to make money and maximize profit for owners and shareholders. The organization's own goals and interest are put before those of its customers.

Owned by private companies/shareholders
Banks are run by highly paid directors, and voting rights depend on the amount of stock owned.

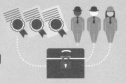

Business orientated
Banks develop and sell money-making products to return a profit to shareholders.

More online services
Run partly or completely online, banks offer little face-to-face or personalized service.

Focus on creditworthy customers
Customers who don't meet the bank's preferred credit profile are routinely rejected.

Bank

CREDIT UNION PRODUCTS

❯ **Loans** There are no hidden charges, and loans can often be repaid early without a penalty charge. Some loans include life insurance.

❯ **Savings** Deposits are made available to members who need to borrow money. Returns can be low and will be paid either by interest or by annual dividend. Some credit unions have maximum savings limits.

❯ **Current accounts** No credit checks are required, there is no monthly fee for the account, and no overdraft is available. Some accounts offer budgeting facilities and advice.

⚠ WARNING

❯ **Loan rates and terms** may be attractive compared to loans, but rates and terms can get high for those with below-average credit.

❯ **Maximum loan amounts** are comparatively low. Approval is often conditional on having saved with the credit union.

❯ **As nonprofit organizations**, credit unions often have limited capital to install ATMs in convenient locations or to invest in technology such as websites or online account access.

Credit cards

Issued by lenders such as banks or credit unions, wallet-sized plastic credit cards function as flexible borrowing facilities that allow their holders to purchase goods or services on credit.

A credit card account allows an individual to make purchases on credit up to an agreed maximum limit. Users can spend as much as they want up to that limit without being charged—as long as they pay off the balance (accrued debt) in full by an agreed date each month. Interest is charged on any outstanding balance beyond this point, but users are obliged to meet only a minimum repayment (see below). The minimum amount may vary, but generally users pay a percentage of the remaining balance or a fixed minimum amount, whichever of the two is higher, plus the interest and any default charges.

There is not usually a deadline by which a credit card debt must be repaid in full—it is up to the users to make repayments as they see fit—but repaying only the credit card's minimum payment each month is one of the most expensive ways to manage credit card bills, as interest will build up on the unpaid amount.

Minimum repayments

Unlike loan and mortgage borrowers, credit card users can choose how much over and above the prescribed minimum repayment they repay each month. The minimum repayment is the lowest amount users must repay each month in order to avoid a fine. If they pay only the minimum amount each month, however, the remaining unpaid balance will continue to accrue interest, and the amount they owe will increase. This means that their debt will last for longer than it would if they were to repay a larger, fixed amount each month, or if they paid off the monthly balance in full.

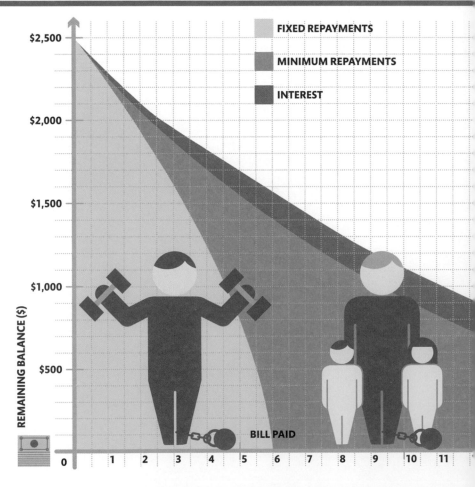

✓ NEED TO KNOW

> **Balance transfer** Using a balance transfer credit card that has a 0% APR intro rate is one strategy to get out of debt.

> **Cash advance** The use of a credit card to withdraw cash from an ATM. A credit card company normally charges more interest and additional fees when cards are used in this way.

> **Revolving credit** A line of credit that allows customers to use funds when they are needed. However, the interest starts right away, and may be a poor choice when you need cash.

> **Credit limit** The maximum amount an individual can borrow at any one time.

REVOLVING CREDIT

A credit card is a form of revolving credit. This is an arrangement that allows for a loan amount to be withdrawn, repaid, and then redrawn again any number of times. The borrower can withdraw funds up to a set limit.

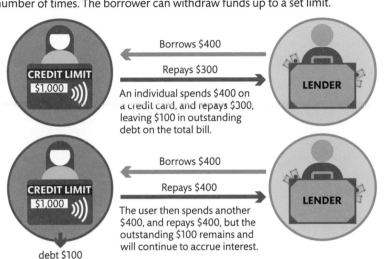

Borrows $400

Repays $300

An individual spends $400 on a credit card, and repays $300, leaving $100 in outstanding debt on the total bill.

Borrows $400

Repays $400

The user then spends another $400, and repays $400, but the outstanding $100 remains and will continue to accrue interest.

CREDIT LIMIT $1,000

CREDIT LIMIT $1,000

LENDER

LENDER

debt $100 accrues interest

⚠ WARNING

Credit card fraud involves using a credit card as a fraudulent source of funds in a transaction.

In the simplest form of the crime, the fraudster obtains an individual's credit card details and uses them over the phone or on the internet to make purchases in the cardholder's name.

At the other extreme, the fraudster may use the cardholder's details to assume his or her identity and fraudulently open bank accounts, obtain credit cards, or take out loans and other lines of credit in the cardholder's name.

It's a good idea to check online credit card accounts a few times a week to look for fraudulent purchases.

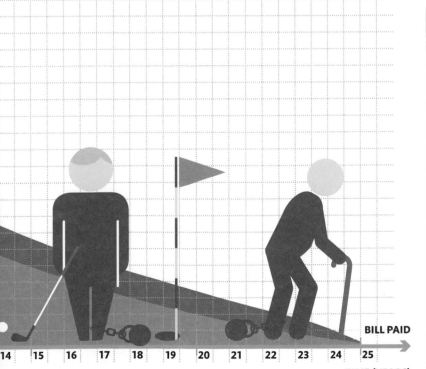

BILL PAID

| 14 | 15 | 16 | 17 | 18 | 19 | 20 | 21 | 22 | 23 | 24 | 25 |

TIME (YEARS)

Money in the digital age

In the same way that the internet revolutionized communication and made globalization possible, digital money, also known as cryptocurrency, promises to change the way people pay for goods and services. Digital money offers a single international "currency" that is not under the control of any financial institution. Instead of notes and coins being printed and minted by individual national banks, computers are used to generate units of digital money.

Breaking free

The money of the future, cryptocurrency, is a medium of financial exchange produced digitally by teams of experts known as "miners." The miners use specialized hardware to process secure transactions by solving the complex mathematical puzzles that encrypt the electronic currency. Cryptocurrencies can be traded between individuals, and bought and sold through online exchanges. Cryptocurrency can also be used for new methods of exchange such as peer-to-peer lending and crowdfunding.

26%
of Millennials
are expected to be using digital currencies by 2020

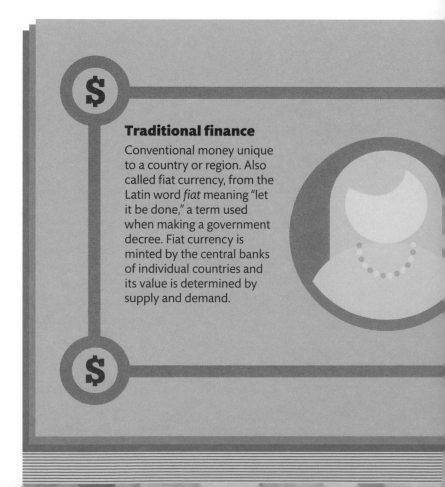

Traditional finance
Conventional money unique to a country or region. Also called fiat currency, from the Latin word *fiat* meaning "let it be done," a term used when making a government decree. Fiat currency is minted by the central banks of individual countries and its value is determined by supply and demand.

TIMELINE OF DIGITAL MONEY

Since the technology for digital money was perfected, many cryptocurrencies have been released—although Bitcoin remains the largest. Now even central banks have begun investigating the potential of digital money.

TIME (YEARS)

Bitcoin introduced	First Bitcoin transaction	Ripple launched	Highest value of Bitcoin to date	Mazacoin introduced	Eretheum released	Bank of England announces RSCoin
October 2008	May 2010	September 2013	November 29, 2013	February 2014	August 2015	March 2016

Digital currency

Money that can be traded on exchanges directly between individuals using a computer or mobile device that is connected to the internet. Digital currency can also be bought and sold using conventional currencies. *See pp.222–225*

Crowdfunding

A way for individuals and groups to raise donations from donors via the internet, bypassing banks, charitable organizations, or government institutions. It is managed via on online intermediary who takes a percentage as a fee. *See pp.226–227*

Peer-to-peer lending

Loans arranged by online marketplaces who match would-be borrowers with lenders. Peer-to-peer lending is usually subject to fewer regulations than with conventional lending. Borrowers are screened for risk, which is reflected in the interest rate they pay. *See pp.228–229*

Cryptocurrency

A form of encrypted digital currency, a cryptocurrency is created, regulated, and kept secure by a network of computers. Bitcoin was the first example of a cryptocurrency, but there are now several thousand types.

How it works

There are two main features of a cryptocurrency. The first is that it exists only in the form of virtual "coins." Instead of being generated by a national central bank, it is created digitally by teams of specialists known as "miners," who use dedicated computer hardware. Encrypted in constantly changing digital codes to reduce the risk of counterfeiting, cryptocurrency can be transferred online between individuals independently of financial or government institutions.

The second feature is that the total amount of a cryptocurrency is capped. Each "coin" created by a "miner" is listed on a virtual public ledger called a "blockchain." Every coin spent is registered on the same ledger, so unlike currencies generated by central banks, once this cap is reached no more coins can be created. As a result, cryptocurrencies are considered less prone to the pressures of inflation and deflation resulting from political and economic changes that affect conventional currency.

Conventional currency and cryptocurrency

The appeal of a cryptocurrency is that it can be used to make direct financial transactions anywhere without requiring a bank account. Transactions are virtually anonymous, there is no central control from banks or governments, and fees are minimal. Cryptocurrencies differ from national currencies in every way, such as how they are valued, generated, and controlled, to their storage and transfer.

! WARNING

> **Cryptocurrency balance is stored on a computer** If the currency holder's computer crashes and there is no back-up of the transactions, there is no proof of cryptocurrency funds held by that person.

> **Not many retailers accept cryptocurrency** In general, the more retailers that accept it, the better, but some cryptocurrencies have specialty uses.

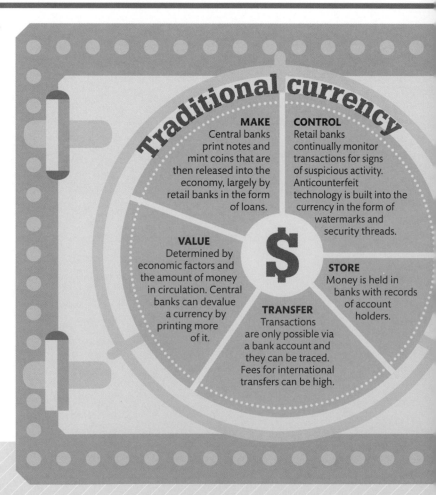

Traditional currency

MAKE
Central banks print notes and mint coins that are then released into the economy, largely by retail banks in the form of loans.

CONTROL
Retail banks continually monitor transactions for signs of suspicious activity. Anticounterfeit technology is built into the currency in the form of watermarks and security threads.

VALUE
Determined by economic factors and the amount of money in circulation. Central banks can devalue a currency by printing more of it.

STORE
Money is held in banks with records of account holders.

TRANSFER
Transactions are only possible via a bank account and they can be traced. Fees for international transfers can be high.

700+
number of cryptocurrencies available for trading

HOW TO VALUE CRYPTOCURRENCY

Look at market capitalization and daily trading volume

A high market capitalization can indicate a high value per "coin," or it can simply mean that there are a lot of coins in circulation. The daily trading volume is an indicator of the number of coins that change hands in a day. It is best to review the two statistics together. A cryptocurrency that has a substantial trading volume as well as a high market capitalization is likely to have a high value.

Find out how transfers are verified

Different cryptocurrencies have varying ways of verifying and securing transactions. The systems rely on complex mathematical problems, and their effectiveness is based on the time a transaction takes and its vulnerability to attack. Most currencies use one of two systems, Proof of Work (bitcoin) or Proof of Stake, or a combination of both, to ensure the best network security.

Cryptocurrency

MAKE
"Miners" create virtual "coins" using special hardware. The coins are then registered on an online public ledger.

CONTROL
Secure encryption is built in to the code of each virtual coin. Continually changing complex mathematical puzzles reduces counterfeiting.

VALUE
Cryptocurrencies become more valuable when they are easier to use, transaction time is faster and more secure, and the number of retailers using them rises.

STORE
Cryptocurrencies are held in the digital wallets of individuals. Records are kept on a virtual public ledger.

TRANSFER
Anyone with online access can make transfers. Such transfers are virtually anonymous and fees low or negligible.

Bitcoin

Bitcoin and other cryptocurrencies are generated online. They can be transferred directly from one person to another across the internet, or bought with and sold for conventional currency.

How it works

Launched in 2009, Bitcoin was the first ever cryptocurrency and is still the most widely used. Unlike conventional currency, which is backed by the state, a bitcoin is based on cryptography, a system that creates mathematical codes to provide high levels of security. This makes it almost impossible for anyone to spend funds from another user's digital wallet, or to corrupt transactions, as each transaction needs to be verified by other users. This is done by users transforming it into a piece of unique digital code using open source software. Users who verify transactions are rewarded with bitcoins. Coins can be traded on digital exchanges or by individuals.

A bitcoin transaction

Bitcoin users first set up a virtual "wallet," downloaded from various online providers. This acts like a highly secure online bank account for sending, receiving, and storing bitcoins. When bitcoins are moved from one wallet to another, individuals in the Bitcoin network, called "miners," compete with one another to be the first to verify the transactions. Once verified, the funds will appear in the recipient's Bitcoin wallet. Transactions are sometimes free but usually buyers pay a small fee of about one percent, which is distributed among the miners.

2. Mining for bitcoins

To prove that the transactions contained in the block are legitimate, and do not contain coins that have already been spent elsewhere, bitcoin miners use computer programs to solve the complex mathematical puzzles protecting the block. The first miner to do so is rewarded with new bitcoin—this is how currency is issued—and the block joins the blockchain.

1. Buyer pays seller for item

A buyer pays a seller in bitcoins using an online transaction form, stating the wallet of the recipient and the amount to send. The transaction becomes visible to the buyer, and to everyone on Bitcoin's network. It contains a secret code called a private key, showing which wallet it is from. It is grouped with other transactions from a set period into an encoded list called a "block."

MINERS

BITCOIN TRANSACTION

Buyer

3. Blockchains

The blockchain is a bit like a public ledger that can be viewed online. Each verified block is added to the previous one. As the "hash" or signature of each file is generated using part of the previous block's signature, it timestamps each transaction. This makes them very difficult to tamper with.

VALUE OF BITCOINS

The number of bitcoins that can ever be produced is limited to 21 million. This is intended to prevent a devaluation of the currency due to oversupply. In addition, as the number of bitcoin in circulation increases, the program will make verification more difficult, meaning the mining process will take longer, fewer coins will be produced, and the limited supply will ensure the value of the currency remains high.

Seller

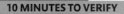

10 MINUTES TO VERIFY

MINERS

4. Bitcoins arrive for use

Once bitcoins arrive in the seller's account, they can be used to make purchases through a retailer, or sold through an exchange or directly to an online buyer. Using websites such as LocalBitcoins.com and Meetup.com, users can make face-to-face transactions, bringing their digital wallets (on a mobile device) to make the trade.

WHY BITCOIN IS SO SECURE

As all transactions must be verified, it is difficult for individuals to tamper with the system. If an attacker does attempt to interfere with a transaction in the blockchain, it will change the resulting hash and invalidate all following blocks. In addition, as users are only known by a public key, transactions can be kept anonymous.

Crowdfunding

Unlike conventional fundraising, crowdfunding allows anyone to raise money directly from potential donors—often online via social media. It works on the principle of asking many people to make a small contribution.

How it works

Most fundraising focuses either on charitable causes or on investment in a worthwhile or potentially lucrative venture. In the days before social networking, fundraising was typically organized through a third party such as a bank or a charity, through a subscription plan, or by asking family and friends for financial help. Crowdfunding is an evolution of these that mostly takes place online instead of face-to-face.

Crowd advantage

Crowdfunding differs from conventional fundraising in that it cuts out the "middleman," ensuring that more of the donated money goes to the cause. It also enables anyone, regardless of their venture, to petition online for money, and it can reach a much wider audience than, say, enticing potential investors via a subscription plan.

Screening process

Crowdfunding platforms screen applicants before they launch a campaign. As with banks, some platforms have stricter criteria than others.

Choice of platform

Usually crowdfunding platforms offer templates, donation tallies, and automatic reminders. Some specialize in charity cases, others in investment projects.

Creating a pitch

The pitch, designed to appeal to as many potential donors as possible, sets out the project or charitable cause to be funded, and usually stipulates a financial target.

Launching online

Digital marketing techniques help target those who are most likely to contribute. Reward incentives offering pledgers a return for their investment can help maximize donations.

$2.6 billion

plus - the amount pledged on Kickstarter since its launch in April 2009

Online pledges

Most donations are made in the early part of a launch, but it is important to keep the campaign "live" with reminders, updates, and new posts.

FEES

Fees for crowdfunding platforms vary, but are typically around five percent excluding any design charges or fees for payment processing, which can be 3–5%. Some platforms offer an "all or nothing" structure, where the funds donated are returned to donors if the money raised falls short of the target.

Follow-up

When the campaign closes, the funds go to the host or are returned to the donors, depending on the agreement. The host might then prepare donors for the next venture.

Peer-to-peer lending

Also known as crowdlending, peer-to-peer lending is a way to match savers looking for a return on their cash with borrowers or companies that require investment. A relatively new form of lending, it can offer good returns on savings.

How it works

Like a virtual dating agency for borrowers and lenders, peer-to-peer lending bypasses banks and other financial institutions by using a dedicated crowdlending broker to vet potential borrowers and match them up with investors who are prepared to loan their spare cash.

The appeal for investor-lenders is higher rates of return than they would receive from banks—typically twice the rate. Borrowers, on the other hand, may benefit from lower rates on their loans (unless they are considered high risk due to a low credit score.) The broker runs credit checks on borrowers and offers some protection by holding funds in trust to cover any bad debts. It also usually charges a fee to both borrower and lender. While P2P lending has exploded since the 2008 crash, it is relatively untested and unregulated, meaning that there are potential risks for lenders.

Using peer-to-peer lending

Any individual or business can register with a peer-to-peer lending company. Loan terms are usually between one and five years, and interest rates and fees vary. This is a typical scenario.

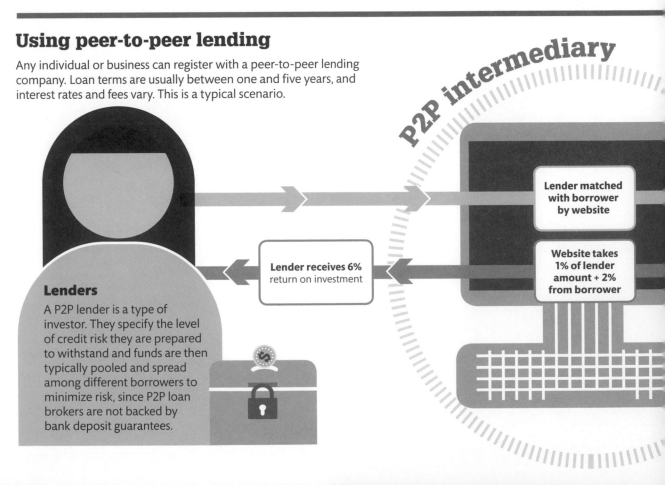

P2P intermediary

Lenders
A P2P lender is a type of investor. They specify the level of credit risk they are prepared to withstand and funds are then typically pooled and spread among different borrowers to minimize risk, since P2P loan brokers are not backed by bank deposit guarantees.

Lender receives 6% return on investment

Lender matched with borrower by website

Website takes 1% of lender amount + 2% from borrower

SPREADING YOUR RISK

Some lenders reduce their risk by actively managing their loans, providing a portion of what they are willing to lend to one borrower, and leaving other lenders to provide the rest.

Lenders to borrower The amount loaned to an individual borrower is pooled from the funds of several lenders.

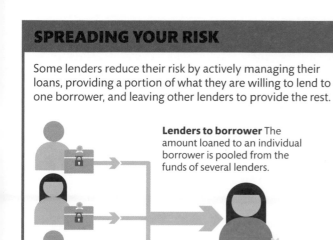

LENDERS

BORROWER

Lenders to borrowers Lenders spread the amount they are willing to lend among several borrowers, reducing their risk.

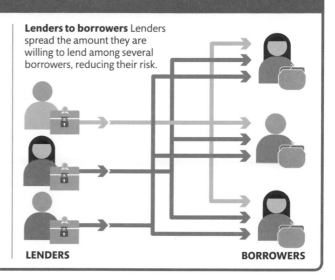

LENDERS

BORROWERS

$1 trillion

the forecasted value of global P2P lending by 2025

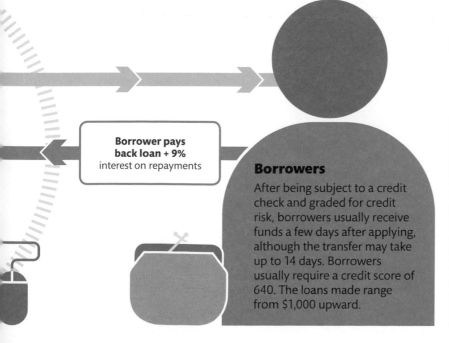

Borrower pays back loan + 9%
interest on repayments

Borrowers

After being subject to a credit check and graded for credit risk, borrowers usually receive funds a few days after applying, although the transfer may take up to 14 days. Borrowers usually require a credit score of 640. The loans made range from $1,000 upward.

⚠ WARNING

> **Defaults** A P2P lender risks not being repaid if the borrower defaults on their loan.

> **Intermediary only** P2P firms do not have large cash reserves.

> **Protection** Savings are not FDIC-insured.

> **Liability** If a P2P firm goes bust, lenders are then liable for collecting the loans themselves.

> **Untested** As P2P is a relatively new form of lending, it has not yet been tested in a tough climate such as a recession.

MONEY
IN THE **US**

Stock exchanges

Stock exchanges enable companies to raise money, increase their profiles, and obtain market valuation. The main exchanges in the US are the New York Stock Exchange, NASDAQ, and NYSE MKT and NYSE Amex Options.

New York Stock Exchange

The center of the US financial world is the New York Stock Exchange (NYSE) on Wall Street in New York City. It is the world's largest stock exchange in terms of market capitalization, which is the market value of the company shares traded on the exchange.

The market capitalization of the NYSE was listed at $19.3 trillion as of June 2016. The average daily trading value in 2013 was $169 trillion. The NYSE, called "the Big Board," lists close to 1,900 companies, of which about 400 are outside the US. It is owned by Intercontinental Exchange, a US holding company.

The NYSE is an auction market where brokers buy and sell securities on behalf of investors. The goal is to match the highest bidding price to the lowest selling price. In addition, the NYSE sells securities such as options, mutual funds, bonds, derivatives, exchange-traded funds (ETFs), warrants, commodities, and US Treasury bonds.

There are two major markets to consider: the primary market and the secondary market.

Primary market

In the primary market, companies sell new issues of common and preferred stocks, also called an Initial Public Offering (IPO), as well as notes, government bonds, corporate bonds, and bills. This facilitates funding for business expansions and is usually done through investment banks (or securities dealers), which set the price for the IPO and administer the sale. Trading then takes place on the secondary market.

Secondary market

Most sales occur on the secondary market, which is so named because it's where investors buy and sell securities they already own. The sale is the second transaction the security has gone through.

Secondary markets operate as marketplaces that compete with each other. Each secondary market has its own requirements for listing on the exchange. A company can appear on more than one exchange.

NYSE To be listed on the NYSE, a company must meet certain standards. The application includes details such as articles of incorporation, bylaws, confirmation that shareholder requirements are met, and information about key executives. A security underwriter confirms that the company meets the standards for listing.

In addition, a company must have a combined pretax income for the last three years of at least $10 million and earned at least $2 million in the previous two years. (Or have earned $12 million in pretax dollars in the past three years with at least $5 million in the most recent year and $2 million in the year before that.)

At least 400 shareholders need to own more than 100 shares of stock each. There must be 1.1 million publicly held shares and a market value of the public shares must be at least $40 million (with stock trading for at least $4 per share).

Nasdaq Unlike the NYSE, the Nasdaq (National Association of Securities Dealers Automated Quotation System) has a virtual presence only. It operates via a telecommunications network for listing and trading securities. The NYSE operates on an auction system, but the Nasdaq utilizes dealers or "market makers."

The Nasdaq is known for attracting firms in the high-tech industry. An estimated 3,100 companies are listed on the exchange. About 2 billion shares are traded daily and, among the US exchanges, it handles the most IPOs.

To apply to be on the list, a company must have a minimum of 1,250,000 publicly traded shares and the bid price of at least $4 per share. Other requirements include a minimum of 2,200 total shareholders, or 550 total shareholders with 1.1 million average trading volume over the past year.

The pretax earnings requirement is a combined $11 million for the past three years, with $2.2 million in earnings for the prior two years. Over the last 12 months, the average market capitalization must be $550 million, with at least 1.1 million in trading volume. There cannot be a net loss in the previous three years, and aggregate cash flow, revenues, and operating income standards must be met.

NYSE MKT and NYSE Amex Options Formerly known as the American Stock Exchange (AMEX), the NYSE united with AMEX in 2008. Both the NYSE MKT and NYSE Amex Options are owned by Intercontinental Exchange.

The AMEX market was renamed NYSE MKT in 2012. It was created with young, high-growth companies in mind. Companies listed on the NYSE MKT benefit from using the NYSE's fully integrated platform. This union enhanced the NYSE's role in exchange traded funds (ETFs), cash equities, options, and more.

Other exchanges Other exchanges include the Philadelphia Stock Exchange (PHLX), Chicago Stock Exchange (CHX), International Securities Exchange (ISE), National Stock Exchange (NSX), and the Boston Stock Exchange (BSE).

In Canada

The Toronto Stock Exchange (TSX) is the largest exchange market in Canada. It is overseen by the Ontario Securities Commission. There is also the Canadian Securities Exchange (CSE) as well as stock markets in Vancouver and Montreal.

VALUATION AND REGULATION

Stock indexes attempt to measure the value of a section of the stock market. Indexes are tools used by financial managers and investors.

Nasdaq Composite

The Nasdaq Composite is an index of the securities listed on the exchange.

Standard & Poor's 500 (S&P)

The S&P is comprised of the top 500 companies that are listed on either the NYSE or the Nasdaq. They are the largest companies, based on market capitalization.

Dow Jones Industrial Average (DJIA)

The DJIA includes the 30 largest (and most influential) companies in the US. The companies are considered to have "blue chip" stocks. They are very large corporations with good reputations.. With only 30 companies included in the index, the DJIA isn't considered an indicator for the entire market. But the companies are considered stable and offer the possibility of dividends as well as less risk for an investor.

The Securities and Exchange Commission (SEC)

The SEC is designed to protect investors and to maintain orderly and efficient markets. Public companies are required to disclose financial information to the public. The goal is to give investors accurate data so they have what they need to make investment decisions.

The SEC oversees the securities exchanges, brokers, dealers, funds, and investment advisors to push transparency for the public. The SEC is authorized to bring action to companies (and individuals) who break the laws. For example, insider trading, deceptive information about securities, and accounting fraud.

Banking regulations

Some complaints don't involve securities, so the Federal Reserve System (the Fed) responds to problems with banks and other types of financial institutions. Other federal regulatory agencies include the OCC, FDIC, and the FASB.

The Fed and CFPB

The Fed investigates claims made by individuals who have been treated unfairly. Complaints can be filed on the Fed's website or by phone, mail, or fax.

The Consumer Financial Protection Bureau (CFPB), is an independent agency funded by the US Federal Reserve. The CFPB was created to protect consumers from deceptive and unfair treatment practiced by financial institutions, including banks, payday lenders, credit unions, mortgage lenders, and debt collectors.

OCC

The Office of the Comptroller of the Currency (OCC) is an independent bureau that operates within the US Department of Treasury. The OCC has the ability to charter, supervise, and regulate national banks and federal savings associations (and branches and agencies of foreign banks). The mission of the OCC is to make sure that banks treat all customers fairly and that they comply with applicable laws and regulations.

Individual state regulators

Each state has a government agency that regulates state-chartered banks, trust companies, and credit unions. These agencies often also monitor and regulate state business by insurance companies, bail bond agents, mortgage bankers, and more.

FDIC

The Federal Deposit Insurance Corporation (FDIC) encourages public confidence in the US financial system by insuring some bank deposits up to $250,000. The FDIC insures a variety of savings accounts, including certain retirement accounts, joint accounts, employee benefit plan accounts, and revocable (and irrevocable) trust accounts. Consumers with FDIC-insured banks are protected in case of a bank failure.

FASB

The Financial Accounting Standards Board (FASB) establishes the standards for financial reporting in the US. FASB standards are known as "generally accepted accounting principles," or GAAP.

These standards are created to ensure accurate and acceptable accounting practices by corporations, which provide transparent information for investors. The standards help prevent accounting fraud.

In Canada

OSFI The Office of the Superintendent of Financial Institutions (OSFI) is an independent agency that reports to Parliament via the Minister of Finance. The OSFI regulates financial institutions and private pensions subject to federal oversight.

FRAS The Financial Reporting & Assurance Standards (FRAS) is the Canadian version of the US's Financial Accounting Standards Board. As in the US, the organization's purpose is to establish standards on accounting and auditing to protect the public interest

OCA The Office of Consumer Affairs (OCA) protects the interests of Canadian consumers and provides valuable information to help educate consumers about credit cards, debt, credit scores, collection agencies, and more.

Companies

A company doing business in the US must register its business name to comply with the law.

Types of companies

The filing procedure to register a business name varies by state, although forms are usually filed with a state's Secretary of State. Businesses can register as a corporation, LLC or other partnership, S corporation, or sole proprietorship.

If a business is under the owner's name, registering a trade name is not required, but is advisable. Some sole proprietors set up an LLC, corporation, or partnership due to the legal protections these offer.

All businesses must get an IRS Federal Employee Identification Number (FEIN). The EIN is used for financial purposes, such as filing tax returns and applying for business licenses.

The accounting year

The IRS has an accounting and tax filing calendar for businesses and the self-employed. Estimated taxes are filed quarterly. International businesses that operate under the Foreign Account Tax Compliance Act (FACTA) must also meet IRS tax requirements.

Most businesses use the calendar year for accounting and tax purposes. The year runs from January 1 through December 31. Businesses using a year-end date that isn't December 31 follow a "fiscal year." To use a fiscal year, the business needs IRS approval.

Large corporations have flexibility when choosing their calendar year, and the taxes required on income differ by the type of corporation. For instance, an S corporation doesn't pay corporate income tax. The income and expenses are passed through to the shareholders as dividends, which are taxable.

A "short tax year" is another accounting year. It applies to businesses operating for less than a year.

CALENDAR AND RESOURCES

Corporate tax rates

The US federal corporate tax rate is 35%, but there's an additional state and municipal corporate tax rate that varies by state and that pushes up the rate to about 39%. Branch profits tax adds an additional 30% tax on foreign corporations engaged in US business or trade.

Federal due dates for estimated corporate taxes

Date	Action
March 15	File Form 1120 and pay taxes due
April 18	Deposit first installment of estimated income tax for the year
June 15	Deposit 2nd installment of estimated income tax for the year
September 15	Deposit 3rd installment of estimated income tax for the year
December 15th	Deposit 4th installment of estimated income tax for the year

Due dates, timing, and required forms differ, depending on the type of business entity. These also vary for fiscal year taxpayers. Forms required for each type of business entity can be found on the IRS website: *www.irs.gov*.

Find filing requirements and rules of regulation by state on the Small Business Associations website: *www.sba.gov*.

The US tax system

Money the government receives in federal income taxes comes from three main sources: individual income taxes, payroll taxes, and corporate taxes. Other revenue sources include estate tax, excise taxes, and other fees and taxes.

Revenue from US taxes

In 2015, the federal government spent $37 trillion on services for the public. These services included Medicare and Medicaid programs, infrastructure improvements, and social security benefits.

According to the Office of Management and Budget, 47 percent of the 2015 revenue came from individual income tax. Payroll tax was next, at 33 percent, and corporate income tax came in at 11 percent. The remaining revenue, 9 percent, was from excise and other taxes. Other revenue sources are profits on assets that are held by the Federal Reserve, regulatory fees, and custom duties.

Policies used to deal with the Great Recession of 2008 are one reason the share of revenue from individual income taxes and payroll taxes is so high.

Payroll tax

Payroll taxes are paid by corporations and by individuals. They are calculated based on a percentage of an employee's income. Employers collect several types of taxes.

Federal taxes are collected by employers from employees' paychecks. Employees must also pay part of their income for social security taxes and Medicare. For 2016, the social security tax rate was 6.2 percent each for the employer and employee (12.4 percent total). This tax is capped once the employee's wages reach $118,500. The Medicare tax rate is 1.45 percent for both employer and employee (2.9 percent total).

Self-employed individuals must pay a self-employment tax (a Social Security/Medicare tax for the self-employed) as well as income tax. Self-employed individuals must file annual returns, but also pay estimated quarterly taxes.

Excise tax

The US does not impose a Value Added Tax (VAT), but does levy excise tax on some products. Excise taxes are paid when purchases are made.

Revenue from highway-related excise tax made up 38 percent of excise tax revenue in 2014. Revenue from gasoline and diesel taxes make up 90 percent of the Highway Trust Fund revenue.

The second-largest amount of excise revenue comes from tobacco taxes—$15.6 billion in 2014. Tobacco tax is collected by the the US Treasury Department. The tax for other goods is collected by the Internal Revenue Service (IRS). Aviation, alcohol, and health care (the Affordable Care Act, or ACA) also have excise taxes.

Capital gains tax

A capital gain is realized when an asset is sold for more than an individual or a corporation paid for it. This type of profit is common with investments and property. There are two types of captial gains.

Short-term capital gains are from assets held for a year or less, and are taxed at the same rate as income. Long-term capital gains are from assets that were held longer than a year. The tax rate on a net capital gain (the gain minus capital losses) depends on income. The maximum tax rate is usually 20 percent. However, for high-income taxpayers and for certain types of net capital gains, the tax can be up to 28 percent.

State taxes

Some states levy tax on income and impose other taxes, such as sales tax. As of 2016, 43 states collected income tax; seven did not. Forty-one states tax wage and salary income. Two tax dividend and interest income only.

Individual income tax is one of the biggest sources of revenue for most states. Tax rates vary widely among states. Florida has no income tax, but California has a 13.3 percent income tax rate.

Differences exist in other taxes, such as sales taxes, that are collected by states. Five states do not impose any statewide sales tax: Alaska, Delaware, Montana, New Hampshire, and Oregon. However, Montana and Alaska do let sales tax be charged at the local level.

Forty-five states collect statewide sales taxes and 38 states impose only local sales taxes. The five states with the highest average combined state-local sales tax rates are Tennessee (9.45 percent), Arkansas (9.26 percent), Alabama (8.91 percent), Louisiana (8.91 percent), and Washington (8.89 percent).

It is essential to understand how the tax system works in the state where a person lives. Differences occur not only in what type of tax is collected, but also at what level (state versus local) the tax is levied.

State governments use the tax collected to meet the needs of that state. The 50 states (and the District of Columbia) spent $1.1 trillion in state revenues in fiscal year 2013, according to the most recent survey by the National Association of State Budget Officers (NASBO).

For most states, the largest area for spending is education (K-12 education), Medicaid, and children's health programs. Other areas include higher education, transportation, corrections, and public assistance.

In Canada

The Canada Revenue Agency is the Canadian version of the IRS. Taxes are levied at the federal, provincial, and municipal levels. Common taxes include sales tax, property tax, business tax, and income tax.

The federal income tax rates for Canadians in 2016 was 15 percent on the first $45,282 of taxable income and up to 33 percent of taxable income over $200,000. Some indirect taxes paid by Canadians include the goods and services tax (GST), the harmonized sales tax (HST) systems, and provincial sales taxes (PSTs).

GOVERNMENT SPENDING

How revenue is spent

- Non-security international 1%
- All other 3%
- Defense 16%
- Science and medical research 2%
- Education 3%
- Infrastructure 2%
- Benefits for federal retirees and veterans 8%
- Interest on debt 6%
- Safety net programs 10%
- Medicare, Medicaid, CHIP, etc. 25%
- Social Security 24%

Revenue received by the government through taxation funds public spending. Most revenue goes to meeting social security obligations, social welfare programs, and public sector pensions. Defense spending makes up 16 percent of the budget. The charts above and below reflect data from the Office of Management and Budget.

Sources of excise tax revenue in 2014:

Highway	38%
Tobacco	17%
Aviation	14%
ACA	14%
Alcohol	11%
Other	6%

The government debt market

When a country spends more money than it takes in, the result is a budget deficit, which creates national debt. Sometimes, the US national debt is referred to as "the deficit," although debt and deficit are not the same thing.

The national debt

The national debt is the result of the US government borrowing money to cover years of operating with a budget deficit. When there is a deficit, the US has to borrow the money by selling Treasury securities to the public. For instance, selling savings bonds and Treasury bills. All of this becomes part of the debt.

The national debt in early October 2016 was over $19.5 trillion. The debt grows larger every second due to the interest owed. The interest paid on the debt in 2015 was $402 billion.

Handling a budget this way is similar to a consumer charging items to a credit card, and when the bill comes due borrowing to pay part of the balance. Now, they have a balance and loan accruing interest.

The national debt does impact consumers. It increases the cost of living and slows the economy. Issuing Treasury securities is one way to produce a revenue stream that can be used to fund budget deficits, specific projects, unemployment benefits, or whatever is needed at the time.

Government securities

A government security is a bond that is issued by the government. There is a promise of repayment when the bond matures. Examples of other securities are Treasury Bills, Treasury Bonds, and savings bonds.

US Savings bonds are appealing to some because they have a fixed (but low) interest rate for a period of time. But they must also be held for a minimum of 12 months. Savings bonds can be redeemed (return of the investor's principal in a fixed-income security) after the 12-month period. However, redeeming the bond during the first five years results in a three-month interest penalty.

There are two different types of savings bonds: Series EE and Series I bonds. The Series EE bonds pay a fixed rate. The Series I bonds earn interest from a combination of a semiannual inflation rate and a fixed rate.

Rates for savings bonds are set on May 1 and November 1 each year. As of May 2, 2016, Series EE bonds earn an annual fixed rate of 0.10 percent. The Series I bond earns a composite rate of 0.26 percent (a portion is indexed to inflation every six months). Both types have an interest-bearing life of 30 years.

Clearly, no one gets wealthy by investing in savings bonds, but they used to be a popular gift. This is one way the government borrows money from the public.

The government also issues many other types of securities including Treasury Bonds (T-bonds), Treasury Bills (T-bills), and Treasury Notes (T-notes). T-bonds mature in 10 to 30 years. T-notes are called intermediate-term bonds because they mature between one year and 10 years but not more than 10 years from the issue date. T-bills have maturities of less than a year. Treasury bonds and notes pay a fixed rate of interest semiannually.

Floating Rate Notes (FRNs) and TIPS

A Treasury FRN has a price that is determined by auction. They have a term of two years and they can be bought in multiples of $100.

An FRN has an interest rate that "floats" over the life of the security. The rate is the sum of an index rate and a spread. FRNs are indexed to the highest accepted discount margin of the most recent 13-week Treasury Bill. The spread will stay the same until maturity. Interest rate is applied to the par amount of the FNR every day. Interest is paid quarterly.

Treasury Inflation-Protected Securities (TIPS) are slightly different securities. The principal amount is adjusted by the changes in Consumer Price Index. TIPS do pay interest at a fixed rate, but the amount of the interest payment will vary from month to month.

If inflation is involved, the investor gets a bigger interest payment. But if the opposite happens—deflation—the investor's interest payment goes down.

The interest rate is set by an auction and TIPS are issued at five, 10, and 30 years. It's possible to bid for TIPS via a TreasuryDirect account.

There are two types of bids: noncompetitive and competitive. With a noncompetitive bid, the investor must accept the rate that's determined at auction. With a competitive bid, the investor is the one who decides what the yield must be. A competitive bid requires the use of a bank or broker.

Municipal bonds

There are investment opportunities at the state government level, too. Municipal bonds (called "munis") are debt securities issued by state governments and local governments, such as cities and counties that need to sell bonds for funds.

A benefit for the investor who buys munis is that the interest is exempt from federal income tax. The bondholder is repaid the principal amount of the bond plus interest covering a specified number of years.

Two types of munis are commonly bought: General obligation bonds and Revenue bonds.

General obligation bonds are not secured by assets. The investor relies on the reputation and credibility (referred to as "full faith and credit") of the issuer to repay the debt. These bonds are issued by states, cities, and counties. The issuer has the power to impose a tax, if necessary, to pay back the public.

Revenue bonds are backed by the revenues that come from a specific project or source, such as a local stadium, highway tolls, or even a hospital. Revenue bonds are riskier so interest rates are higher.

PUBLIC FINANCE RESOURCES

Internal Revenue Service (IRS)

Filing income taxes to the IRS can be done online, by mail, by using commercial tax software, or by a tax preparing service: www.irs.gov

The IRS website has current information about excise taxes and what forms to file: www.irs.gov/businesses/small-businesses-self-employed/excise-tax

State Taxes

For information about state income taxes and filing options by state, visit the Federation of Tax Administrators (FTA): www.taxadmin.org/state-tax-forms

National Debt

The Office of Management and Budget (OMB) assists the president in meeting budget, policy, and regulatory objectives: www.whitehouse.gov/omb

To track the US debt, visit www.usdebtclock.org

To bid for TIPS via a TreasuryDirect account: https://www.treasurydirect.gov/indiv/myaccount/myaccount_treasurydirect.htm

The Federal Reserve Bank

The Fed's goal is to keep the economy of the US stable and secure. It also offers valuable information for consumers to help them understand personal finance: www.federalreserve.gov

Spending and interest on federal debt in 2015

Discretionary spending	$1.1 trillion	29.34%
Interest on the debt	$229.15 billion	6.03%
Mandatory spending	$2.45 trillion	64.63%

Federal reserve

The Federal Reserve System was established as the US Central Bank by Congress on December 13, 1913. Signed into law by President Woodrow Wilson, the Federal Reserve Act was the response to a period of financial instability and panic.

The Fed and the US economy

The Federal Reserve Act produced a decentralized bank that could also handle the competing interests of popular sentiment and financial institutions and banks.

The Federal Reserve Bank (the Fed) uses policy to subtly impact economic conditions. In 1929, the market crashed and the US plunged into what would be known as the Great Depression. During the next few years, 10,000 banks failed. The Fed was criticized for not taking action to avert the crash.

This event led to Congress passing the Glass-Steagall Act in 1933. This law requires a separation of commercial banks and investment banks. It also required that government securities would be used as collateral for Federal Reserve notes. The Glass-Steagall Act also created the Federal Deposit Insurance Corporation (FDIC), which insures bank deposits up to a certain amount. In 2016, that amount is $250,000 per single account. For joint accounts, it's $250,000 for each owner.

Another major piece of legislation is the Full Employment and Balanced Growth Act, which is often referred to as the Humphrey-Hawkins Full Employment Act. It was signed by President Jimmy Carter on October 27, 1978. Part of this legislation mandates that the Fed must pursue a monetary policy that encourages long-term growth and controls inflation. If this is done well, it promotes maximum employment and stable prices.

Role of the Fed

The Fed has four primary roles: regulating banks and financial institutions, using monetary policy to prevent an unstable economy and unstable financial markets, using policy to influence the credit environment, employment numbers, and price and money, and providing the US government with certain financial services.

Interest rates

The Fed also has another important role. It sets what's called the federal funds rate and the discount rate. The federal funds rate is the rate in which banks can lend money to each other overnight. The Fed can affect this rate by lowering the the discount rate, or the interest rate charged by the Fed, below the federal funds rate. This makes banks want to borrow from the Fed as opposed to other banks due to the lower rate. Thus, it puts pressure on banks to lower their overnight rates.

The law requires banks to also have a reserve amount at all times. Since the banks don't earn interest on their own reserves, they like to lend the money to other banks and earn some interest.

The current interest rate set by the Fed for banks to borrow money from each other is 0.50 percent. If the Fed decides to increase the rate, it's passed on to consumers and it makes borrowing money more expensive. If the Fed lowers the rate, it makes borrowing less expensive and so more consumers borrow money.

The prime rate, which is of interest to consumers, is published by *The Wall Street Journal* every day. This rate is the index used by credit card companies, for instance, to set APRs for their credit card products. It's also the benchmark for loan companies, lines of credit, home equity loans, and more. Changes in the federal funds rate impact the prime rate.

The current prime rate is 3.50. A credit card issuer will use 3.5 percent as the base rate and add a range to that. The APR might be 3.5 percent + 10.5 percent, or 14 percent. If the prime rate goes up (prodded by the increase in the federal funds rate), then the 14 percent APR will increase by the same amount.

The money supply

The US Treasury is responsible for the actual printing of money, but it's the Fed that is in charge of the money supply. To increase the money supply, the Fed might change the reserve amount that banks must have on hand. If the reserve amount is lowered, banks can lend out more money.

The Fed can also change interest rates. If the discount rate is lowered, then it lowers the cost of borrowing and increases economic activity. But this move could also lead to inflation, so it is done carefully and with great thought.

Another way to increase the money supply in the economy is to conduct open market operations. This action impacts the federal funds rate. Simply put, to increase the money supply, the Fed buys government bonds.

The Fed might want to decrease the money supply. If so, then it does the opposite of what's required to increase the supply. One way for the Fed to decrease the money supply is to change the reserve amount that banks must have on hand. If the reserve amount is increased, banks are forced to decrease lending. Again, the Fed could also change interest rates. If the discount rate is raised, then it decreases the money supply and dampens economic activity.

FED ACTIVITIES

Quantitative easing

Sometimes, a policy called Quantitative Easing (QE) is used to influence interest rates. The Fed buys government securities (a bond-buying program) from the market to try and lower interest rates and increase the money supply. This, in turn, can lead to a more robust economy as consumers find credit cheaper and start borrowing again.

This action is considered unconventional and it's used when more conventional methods haven't stimulated the economy. Since the 2008 recession, the Fed has used a QE policy more frequently than in the past.

After 9-11

On September 11, 2001, terrorists attacked New York City, Washington, D.C., and Pennsylvania, killing many Americans. This tragic event also disrupted the financial markets. The Fed took action to contain the damage and prevent further market instability during a difficult time in American history. Some of the actions included lowering interest rates and loaning billions to financial institutions. Within a few weeks, the US economy had stabilized from the attacks. The Fed played a big role in helping America maintain an even footing during a frightening and unpredictable time.

Mortgages

The United States has one of the most diverse and innovative mortgage markets in the world, offering a wider range of products and lenders than are available in most countries.

Mortgages

There are many different types of mortgage lenders in the US, from banks to credit unions to nonbank lenders, such as Quicken Loans. Competition is fierce, which helps to stabilize rates for consumers.

Although a vast number of lenders operate in the US, a few dominate the industry. During the fourth quarter of 2015, Wells Fargo originated twice as many mortgages as Chase, according to *Mortgage Daily*, an industry publication. Wells Fargo totaled $47 billion in originations and Chase originated $23 billion.

As of June 30, 2016, the total mortgage balances on consumer credit reports was $8.36 trillion, according to the Federal Reserve Bank of New York's *Household Debt and Credit Report*.

Several types of mortgages are available in the US. Deciding between a fixed- and adjustable-rate mortgage is one of the first decisions a borrower has to make. With a fixed rate, which is the most common choice, the interest stays the same for the entire repayment of the loan. Most fixed mortgages are either for 30 or 15 years. Many borrowers opt for the 30-year fixed mortgage to secure a lower monthly payment.

An adjustable rate mortgage (ARM) has an interest rate that "adjusts" over the period of the loan. With a hybrid ARM, the rate is usually fixed for a certain number of years and then it is subject to change.

There are also government-insured loans such as FHA loans, VA loans, and USDA/RHS loans, which are programs for income-eligible buyers in rural areas.

Mortgage eligibility

Lenders consider many factors when determining the eligibility of buyers. One of the requirements for a mortgage is an acceptable credit score. The credit score required for approval of a mortgage varies among lenders. With a FICO score that is 720 or higher, the buyer gets the most favorable rates and terms. But according to the Federal Deposit Insurance Corporation (FDIC), if the score is below 660 (or down to 620 if the economy is good), the buyer is considered a subprime customer. Subprime borrowers can still get mortgages, but the rates and fees are higher.

But a borrower also needs a favorable loan-to-value ratio (LTV), which shows how much the property is worth compared to the amount you need to borrow. The more favorable the ratio, the better.

It is also best to have the down payment, preferably around 20 percent, on hand before applying for a mortgage. Knowing the down payment helps buyers determine how expensive a house they can afford.

Once the mortgage shopping has begun, preapprovals are necessary. This is when the lender will look at the borrower's credit report and check the credit score. While this does result in a hard inquiry on the credit report, the good news is that the FICO score, the score used most often by lenders, recognizes inquiries that are the result of mortgage rate shopping and treats multiple rate inquiries as only one inquiry that impacts the score.

Another test for eligibility is the debt-to-income ratio. Mortgage lenders like to see a debt-to-income ratio of less than 36 percent of the buyer's gross monthly income. Mortgage payments will be higher though when taxes and property insurance are added.

Lenders also take into account the employment history of borrowers. A stable history is considered to be positive. Those who are self-employed may need to provide tax returns or bank statements to show they have a stable financial situation.

Mortgage Trends

The housing market has improved to the point where new home sales have hit their highest levels since April, 2008. In 2008, the housing market as well as the US economy went into a downward spiral. In the mid-2000s, many subprime mortgages had been approved and this contributed to the mortgage crisis.

The housing market is now rebounding and this encourages home sales. The best selling time is in the spring and summer because it allows families to get settled into a new home before the start of the school year.

Currently, down payments range from zero (unlikely, but not impossible) to about 20 percent. Most lenders require at least 3 percent and FHA loans require at least 3.5 percent.

Long-term mortgage rates were around 3.42 percent at the end of 2016, according to the big mortgage lender, Freddie Mac. The 15-year mortgage, which is popular with refinancers, was at 2.81 percent.

MORTGAGE ASSISTANCE

Government programs for mortgage assistance

Several programs designed to help homeowners are available. Here's an overview, and for more details, go to the Making Home Affordable website: www.makinghomeaffordable.gov

HOME AFFORDABLE MODIFICATION PROGRAM (HAMP)
Helps those who need lower monthly payments so they continue to pay their mortgage in the long-term.

HOME AFFORDABLE REFINANCE PROGRAM (HARP)
Assists those who are current on their mortgages, but have had difficulty refinancing the loan.

HOME AFFORDABLE FORECLOSURE ALTERNATIVES PROGRAM (HAFA)
Advises homeowners who need to exit their homes and be relieved of their remaining mortgage debt either via a short sale or a deed-in-lieu of foreclosure (DIL). HAFA provides $10,000 for relocation expenses.

HOME AFFORDABLE UNEMPLOYMENT PROGRAM (UP)
This program reduces or even suspends monthly mortgage payments for job hunters.

FEDERAL HOUSING ADMINISTRATION SHORT REFINANCE FOR BORROWERS WITH NEGATIVE EQUITY (FHA SHORT REFINANCE)
For those who are up-to-date on payments, but owe more than their home is worth (called an underwater mortgage).

HARDEST HIT FUND PROGRAMS (HHF)
These programs in 18 states and the District of Columbia were designed to help homeowners who have issues such as unemployment, inability to pay mortgages, and finding a new affordable home to move to. Program details vary by state.

Credit cards

The US has a highly developed credit card market, with more than a billion credits cards in use. The credit card market has, however, gone through major changes in recent years.

Credit debt

In 2000, there were 1.4 billion credit cards in circulation. Fast forward 12 years to 2012 and there were 1.17 billion credit cards in circulation, according to data from the US Census Bureau. The number of credit cards decreased during the recession years, which occurred around 2008 to 2010. Today, issuers are pickier about who they approve for a card, and many young adults are postponing the use of credit.

The average credit card debt per household is $9,600. In 2009, during the recession, 44 percent of Americans were carrying a balance. In 2014, the proportion of Americans carrying a balance was down to 34 percent. Those who carry a balance pay interest on their balances. This compound interest can increase the debt on the card quickly.

Calculating interest

Interest on accounts that are not paid in full can be calculated in a few different ways. The most commonly used methods are "average daily balance" and "daily balance." With average daily balance, the interest charged depends on whether the credit card company adds in new purchases or excludes them. With daily balance, the company charges interest for each day's balance and then adds it together to get the total finance charge.

Credit card companies don't start charging interest on credit cards as soon as a purchase is made unless the card is already carrying a balance. There's an interest-free grace period of between 21 and 25 days, which is the time between the purchase date and the payment due date. This offers consumers an interest-free period. But this is only applicable if the balance of each payment cycle starts at zero.

Credit CARD Act

The Credit CARD Act of 2009 offered significant new consumer protections. Credit card issuers were no longer permitted to do many activities, including the following: suddenly raise annual percentage rates (APRs) without a 45-day notification, inflict retroactive rate increases on an outstanding balance (except under certain circumstances), charge special fees on subprime cards, and give away "freebies" on college campuses.

The CARD Act helps to protect college students by prohibiting issuers from giving credit cards to anyone under 21 unless they have the income to pay back any debt. Issuers are no longer allowed to set up tents on campuses and give away incentives to get students to sign up for cards.

The Act also made the terms and conditions for credit cards more transparent. Consumers receive clearer due dates than before, explanations for changes to the terms, and the right to have highest-interest balances paid first.

Retirement

Preparing for the golden years can be complex. Most Americans find that they need their own retirement funds to supplement the amount they receive in Social Security benefits.

Social Security

Americans pay a special tax on their income under the Federal Insurance Contributions Act (FICA). Also referred to as the Social Security tax, it is used to fund US social programs. Included is a hospital insurance tax, which is also known as the Medicare tax.

There's a limit on the amount of earnings subject to FICA taxes. In 2016, the limit is $118,500. So income exceeding that amount is not subject to FICA. So for the year 2016, the Social Security tax rate was 6.2 percent on the first $118,500 of earned income. The Medicare tax rate is 1.45 percent on the first $200,000 and 2.35 percent above $200,000.

Social Security benefits are based on the total of your past earnings. The exact amount you'll get every month when you're eligible is calculated based on a formula that uses the Average Indexed Monthly Earnings (AIME). The formula favors people with lower incomes.

The Social Security system also calculates your benefit based on the age you start receiving money from the system. The longer you work, the more likely you are to have a higher monthly benefit. Benefits are also adjusted for inflation.

A divorced spouse might qualify for survivor benefits if the marriage lasted at least 10 years. But there are other conditions that must be met. For example, the surviving spouse must be unmarried and be 60 years old for survivor benefits and at least 62 for spousal benefits.

It's possible to track your Social Security benefits online. Having access to the amount of your benefit can help you plan how much income will be needed from additional sources when you're older.

IRA and Roth IRA

Some people set up an Individual Retirement Account (IRA). An IRA is an excellent investment in the future. There are two major types of IRAs: Traditional IRAs and Roth IRAs.

Contributions to traditional IRAs are taxed when you withdraw the funds, ideally after retirement. If money is withdrawn before the age of 59½, there might be an additional 10 percent tax to pay.

The point is that your future earnings will be lower than they were when you were in the prime of life and working many hours. So earnings will be taxed at a lower rate in the future. There are limitations to the amount of contributions that can be made each year.

Contributions to a Roth IRA are made after taxes are paid. But once your contributions are in the fund, the interest or investment earnings are tax-free when you retire. To set up a Roth IRA, your income must not exceed the amount that is set by the IRS. This limit depends on how you're filing as well as other factors. For more details, go to www.rothira.com/roth-ira-eligibility.

401(K)

Another type of retirement plan is a 401(K). Taxes on contributions are not paid until its later withdrawn. These plans are sponsored by employers, who sometimes match the employee's contribution as a company benefit. With a 401K, the employee controls how the money is invested.

There are limits to what you can contribute. In 2016, for those under 50, the maximum contribution to the 401K was $18,000. For those over 50, an additional $6,000 (up to $24,000) was allowed.

Taxes and investments

Any US resident who earns interest on a savings account or investments in other financial products is subject to tax on income received from these activities. With some retirement accounts, such as IRAs, the interest is tax-deferred.

Taxing savings and investments

Savings accounts, in general, have low returns right now, but the amount is still taxable. This requires submitting a 1099-INT form to the IRS. Interest income is taxed at marginal rates, which means your interest income is taxed at your personal income tax rate.

Examples of interest taxed as ordinary income include: interest on deposit accounts (such as checking and savings accounts), the value of gifts received for opening an account, dividends on deposit or share accounts in cooperative banks, credit unions, and other banking associations, interest on certificates of deposit (CDs), and interest on insurance dividends.

Different rules apply to dependents' accounts. Federal filing is required in the following cases: The dependent had unearned income of more than $1,000, or had earned income of more than $6,200. Gross income total is also a factor. If the dependent's gross income total was more than $1,000 or the dependent had earned income up to $5,850 plus $350.

Parents can give a child up to a $14,000 gift before taxes must be paid. The gift tax is complex and might need to be discussed with an attorney if there are several children involved as well as ex-spouses and remarried spouses. Likewise, trust funds have many rules, depending on the specific type of trust.

Tax breaks on investments

Income earned from certain types of investments are treated differently than ordinary income in terms of taxation. There is exempt interest income as well as deferred interest income.

Examples of exempt interest income include: exempt-interest dividends from a mutual fund, municipal bond interest (depending on the state, it might also be exempt from state tax), and private activity bonds. Private activity bonds might be taxable as an alternative minimum tax (AMT) so seek expert advice about this type of bond.

Examples of deferred interest income include some US savings bonds, interest earned on tax-deferred accounts, such as 401(K)s and traditional IRAs (until earnings are withdrawn), and interest income on fixed-income instruments, which must be reported when paid upon maturity.

College savings

College education in the US has become expensive and one way to save for this is to start a 529 Plan, which is a savings plan operated by a state or educational institution. The goal is to set aside funds to pay for college expenses. It's advisable to start as early as possible so the amount can grow.

The earnings in a 529 Plan are tax-free and it will not be taxed when the money is withdrawn to pay for college. Note that the money from the plan must be used for college to be tax-free. Check with the state to find out details regarding funding, tax implications, and the specific type (either prepaid tuition plans or savings plans) of the 529 Plan that's available. It's also possible to choose a plan from a state where you don't reside.

It's common for close relatives and friends to set up an account for a child. Grandparents often do this to help contribute to their grandchild's college education.

Property tax

Property tax is payable on property owned in the US. The tax is set by and levied by the governing authority of the jurisdiction where the property is located.

According to RealtyTrac's US Property Tax Rates Report for 2014, the average effective property tax rate for single family homes was 1.29 percent in 2014. The report showed that owners of high-end homes and owners of low-end homes tend to pay the most property tax rates.

Of course, rates also vary by geographic location. States with the highest average property taxes were New York ($15,625), New Jersey ($8,108), New Hampshire ($5,795), Connecticut ($5,646), and Hawaii ($5,024).

The lowest were Alabama ($618), West Virginia ($931), New Mexico ($1,096), Tennessee ($1,116), and Indiana ($1,418).

Tax on digital currency

Digital currency is money exchanged via the internet. An example is Bitcoin. A digital asset, it isn't printed like paper currency. Bitcoin uses a peer-to-peer payment network.

The community of digital currency users is growing. As of August 2013, the value of bitcoins in circulation exceeded $1.5 billion. Millions of dollars worth of bitcoins are exchanged daily via the payment network.

For federal tax purposes, the IRS treats bitcoin as property. The general tax principles that apply to property transactions also apply to virtual currency transactions.

INHERITANCE AND ESTATE TAX

Inheritance tax

In the US, inheritance tax is levied by the state. It applies when you inherit money or property from a deceased person. The beneficiary is the one who is deemed responsible for paying the tax. As of 2015, however, only eight states imposed this tax.

There are some exemptions to the inheritance tax rule. Some states exempt the surviving spouse from paying the tax. Children and other dependents may also qualify as exempt, depending on the state.

Estate tax

A similar tax is the estate tax. This differs from inheritance tax in a significant way. Estate tax is paid by the estate of the deceased instead of by the beneficiary. There are also thresholds that must be reached before tax is imposed.. With estate tax, the heir isn't responsible. The estate pays the tax, which is a flat 40 percent.

Every American has a federal tax exemption amount, which in 2016, was $5.45 million. The 40 percent tax rate is applied to the amount that exceeds the threshold. The good news is that each spouse gets that threshold amount. So a couple has an exemption of $10.9 million.

State taxes might also be due, but it depends on the state and whether there's an estate tax levied there. Most Americans are not affected by estate tax because the threshold values are so high.

Index

D

R

raw materials, cost of 132, 133
real profit 28
real rate 121
real values 133
real-estate cycle, 18-year 179
real-time trading 77
recession 146, 215
  and depression **94–5**
  and money supply **92–3**
regulation
  banks 82, 83, 92, 234, 240
  credit cards 244
  insurance industry 79
  mortgage products 215
  peer-to-peer lending 221
  stock exchange 233
remortgage 213
rental income 154, 158, 159, 163, **170–71**,
  174, 186
repairs, property 170, 171
repayment mortgages 212
representative currency 87
reserve currency 139
reserve rates 100–103
reserve ratio 90, 98, 102
reserves, banking **90–91**, 124–5
residential property 178
retirement 156, 157, **196–203**
  age of 161, 196
  managing state pensions 140–41
  planning for financial independence
    150–51
  United States **245**
  see also pensions; state pensions
returns
  on assets 88, 113, 188, 189, 198
  credit unions 217
  crowdfunding 227
  government 130, 131
  on investment 40, 47, 51, 79, 81, 130, 131,
    141, 154, 161, 162, 174, 186, 198
  managed funds 168, 169, 185
  optimal portfolios 194–5
  peer-to-peer lending 228
  pensions 201, 203
  on property 176, 177, 178
  savings and deposit accounts 159, 162, 163
  snowball effect 208
  standard deviation of 191
  vs risk 166, 187, 192–3, 194
  see also yield
revenue
  analysis 62

government 96, 115
  and net income 28
  and taxation 106, 236
Revenue bonds 239
reverse annuity mortgages 212
revolving credit 204, 219
Ricardo, David 21
Riksbank (Sweden) 103
Ripple 221
risk
  balancing with rewards 187, 189, 194–5
  control 46
  gearing ratio and 40–41
  insurance 78–9
  investments 47, 162–3, 186
  and managed funds 168, 169
  peer-to-peer lending 229
  risk tolerance 187, **192–3**
rogue traders 55, **66–7**
Roosevelt, Franklin D. 95
Roth IRAs 245
Royal Mint 19
royalty payments 159
RSCoin 221
Russian financial crisis 65

S

safeguarding 228
salaries and wages 13, 31, 36, 117, 154, 156, 158
  cost of 132, 133
sales predictions 38
sales revenue 36
sales tax 37, 237
Sargent, Thomas 145
savings
  credit unions 216, 217
  earning income from 162, 163, **166–7**
  from income 150, 154, 155
  interest rates 121, 123
  and investing for a pension **198–201**
  regular savings plans 185
  savings accounts 72, 73, 159, 162–3, 246
  savings bonds 50, 51, 238
  savings rates 72
  tax on 246
  and wealth 154, 155, 156, 157, 160, 161
scalping 69
scandals
  accounting 35
  Libor 67
scientific research 128, 131
secondary markets 60, **61**, 68, 102, 232
secured loans 121, 204, 210
securities 51, 60, 76, 80, 101

government 238, 239
Securities and Exchange Commission (SEC)
  233
seed capital 43
self-employment tax 236
Shanghai Stock Exchange (SSE) 55
shareholders
  payments to 36, 48, 49
  say in running of companies 182
shares
  arbitrage 64–5
  as assets 155
  brokerage 76–7
  buying 54
  day trading 68–9
  dividends from **164–5**
  earnings per share 28
  as financial instruments 46, **48–9**
  and gearing ratio 40
  guarantees 75
  high risk investment 163
  how to buy 182–3
  investment in **182–3**, 186
  issuing 42
  liquid 68–9, 76
  manipulating prices 66–7
  predicting market changes 62–3
  primary and secondary markets 60–61
  repurchases 36
  stock exchange 54–5
  unsold 61
  and wealth-building 175
  why share prices matter 183
sharesave plans 182
Shenzhen Stock Exchange (SZSE) 55
shopping 157
short selling 66
short-term liabilities 152
Simmel, Georg 17
single asset funds 168
SIPPs (Self-Invested Personal Pension) 198
slump 34
Smith, Adam 14, 20–21
smoothing earnings 26, **34–5**
social housing 131
Social Security **245**
  taxes 236
soft drinks, tax on 126–7
specialty lenders 83
speculation 52, 53
spending
  government 96, 97, 115, **128–9**, 135, **237**, 239
  increasing/cutting 119
  personal 156–7
  vs cuts 128
  and wealth 156, 160

Acknowledgments

Dorling Kindersley would like to thank Alexandra Beeden for proofreading, Emma Wicks for design assistance, Phil Gamble for icon design, and Helen Peters for indexing.

Credits

Jacket: blogs.spectator.co.uk/2016/09/paper-5-polymer-origins-banknote/; en.wikipedia.org/wiki/List_of_circulating_currencies; www.worldbank.org/en/topic/poverty/overview; en.wikipedia.org/wiki/Crowdfunding; en.wikipedia.org/wiki/1891; money.howstuffworks.com/currency6.htm; en.wikipedia.org/wiki/European_debt_crisis; www.bbc.co.uk/news/business-18944097; en.wikipedia.org/wiki/Rai_stones; www.worldbank.org/en/news/press-release/2015/04/15/massive-drop-in-number-of-unbanked-says-new-report; manchesterinvestments.com/portfolio-compass-january-20-2016/; www.imf.org/external/pubs/ft/fandd/2014/09/kose.htm **p.13:** money.visualcapitalist.com/; **p.19:** blockchain.info/charts/total-bitcoins; **p.27:** www.moodys.com/research/Moodys-US-non-financial-corporates-cash-pile-increases-to-168--PR_349330; **p.29:** www.apple.com/uk/pr/library/2016/01/26Apple-Reports-Record-First-Quarter-Results.html; **p.33:** www.theaa.com/motoring_advice/car-buyers-guide/cbg_depreciation.html; **p.39:** www.modestmoney.com/cash-flow-problems-small-business-startups-tackle/9820; **p.41:** www.tutor2u.net/business/reference/gearing-ratio; p.47: www.cnbc.com/2015/07/17/googles-one-day-rally-is-the-biggest-in-history.html; **p.49:** en.wikipedia.org/wiki/New_York_Stock_Exchange; **p.51:** https://www.ft.com/content/ed4dbdb2-23c2-11e5-9c4e-a775d2b173ca; **p.53:** en.wikipedia.org/wiki/2012_JPMorgan_Chase_trading_loss; **p.59:** www.wsj.com/articles/pound-drops-to-31-year-low-against-dollar-on-brexit-concerns-1475566159; **p.60:** www.nyxdata.com/nysedata/asp/factbook/viewer_edition.asp?mode=table&key=3003&category=3; **p.65:** www.dbresearch.com/PROD/DBR_INTERNET_EN-PROD/

PROD0000000000406105/High-frequency_trading%3A_Reaching_the_limits.pdf; **p.71:** www.investopedia.com/articles/economics/09/lehman-brothers-collapse.asp#ixzz4M7KQIMTg; **p.72:** www.federalreserve.gov/monetarypolicy/reservereq.htm; **p.76:** www.tdameritrade.com/about-us.page; **p.81:** www.morganstanley.com/im/emailers/media/pdf/liq_sol_updt_012013_rule_2a-7.pdf; **p.83:** www.ey.com/Publication/vwLUAssets/ey-global-consumer-banking-survey/$FILE/ey-global-consumer-banking-survey.pdf; **p.88:** www.newyorkfed.org/aboutthefed/fedpoint/fed01.html; **p.93:** www.statista.com/statistics/188165/annual-gdp-growth-of-the-united-states-since-1990/; **p.95:** www.nber.org/chapters/c2258.pdf; **p.97:** www.usgovernmentspending.com/; **p.100:** www.ecb.europa.eu/home/html/index.en.html; **p.103:** www.riksbank.se/en/The-Riksbank/History/Important-date/1590-1668/; **p.105:** www.worldbank.org/en/country/libya/overview; **p.107:** www.forbes.com/sites/frederickallen/2012/07/23/super-rich-hide-21-trillion-offshore-study-says/#386b08de73d3; **p.110:** www.nationaldebtclocks.org/debtclock/unitedstates; **p.115:** fred.stlouisfed.org/series/MKTGNIJPA646NWDB; **p.117:** www.bls.gov/k12/history_timeline.htm; **p.123:** www.tradingeconomics.com/argentina/inflation-cpi; **p.125:** www.aei.org/publication/since-2009-feds-qe-purchases-transferred-almost-half-trillion-dollars-treasury-isnt-gigantic-wealth-transfer/; **p.127:** www.economist.com/news/finance-and-economics/21623742-getting-greeks-pay-more-tax-not-just-hard-risky-treasures; **p.128:** federal-budget.insidegov.com/l/120/2017-Estimate; **p.135:** www.federalreserve.gov/faqs/economy_14400.htm; **p.139:** www.dailyfx.com/forex/education/trading_tips/daily_trading_lesson/2014; **p.143:** *This Time It's Different: Eight Centuries of Financial Folly* – Preface Reinhart, Carmen and Rogoff, Kenneth University of Maryland, College Park, Department of Economics, Harvard University 2009; **p.145:** www.globalfinancialdata.com/gfdblog/?p=2382; **p.147:** en.wikipedia.org/wiki/European_debt_crisis; **p.151:** www.forbes.com/sites/jamiehopkins/2014/08/28/not-enough-people-

have-financial-advisers-and-new-research-shows-they-should/#4e7ad5fd7648; **p.153:** en.wikipedia.org/wiki/Ultra_high-net-worth_individual; **p.157:** www.forbes.com/sites/afontevecchia/2014/10/02/the-new-forbes-400-self-made-score-from-silver-spooners-to-boostrappers/#2cf326c97d40; **p.161:** time.com/money/3925308/rich-families-lose-wealth/; **p.164:** www.investopedia.com/articles/markets/071616/history-sp-500-dividend-yield.asp; **p.167:** www.cnbc.com/2016/06/21/66-million-americans-have-no-emergency-savings.html; **p.175:** usatoday30.usatoday.com/money/perfi/stocks/2011-06-08-stocks-long-term-investing_n.htm; **p.176:** en.wikipedia.org/wiki/Subprime_mortgage_crisis; **p.179:** www.reuters.com/article/us-property-poll-usa-idUSKCN0VX1L1; **p.180:** www.mybudget360.com/negative-equity-nation-for-1-out-of-5-homeowners-the-psychology-of-the-10-million-american-homeowners-with-zero-equity/; **p.183:** money.cnn.com/2016/04/29/investing/stocks-2nd-longest-bull-market-ever/; **p.187:** en.wikipedia.org/wiki/Closing_milestones_of_the_S%26P_500; **p.194:** en.wikipedia.org/wiki/Efficient_frontier; **p.199:** www.moneysavingexpert.com/savings/discount-pensions; **p.201:** www.un.org/en/development/desa/population/publications/pdf/ageing/WPA2015_Report.pdf; **p.203:** www.irs.gov/retirement-plans/retirement-plans-faqs-regarding-iras-distributions-withdrawals; **p.205:** www.nerdwallet.com/blog/credit-card-data/average-credit-card-debt-household/; **p.207:** libertystreeteconomics.newyorkfed.org/2016/08/just-released-recent-developments-in-consumer-credit-card-borrowing.html; **p.210:** www.theguardian.com/business/2014/dec/16/wonga-cuts-cost-borrowing-interest-rate; **p.213:** eyeonhousing.org/2013/01/latest-study-shows-average-buyer-expected-to-stay-in-a-home-13-years/; **p.215:** news.bbc.co.uk/1/hi/business/7073131.stm; **p.217:** www.woccu.org/; **p.220:** thefinancialbrand.com/45284/banking-mobile-payments-bitcoin-research/; **p.223:** en.wikipedia.org/wiki/List_of_cryptocurrencies; **p.227:** www.kickstarter.com/about; **p.229:** www.statista.com/statistics/325902/global-p2p-lending/